Backyard Harvest

Jo Whittingham

LONDON, NEW YORK, MUNICH, MELBOURNE, DELHI

Project Editor Chauney Dunford
Editor Ann Baggaley
Senior Art Editor Alison Shackleton
Designers Vanessa Hamilton, Lucy Parissi
Jacket Designer Mark Cavanagh
Production Editor Joanna Byrne
Picture Researcher Sarah Hopper
DK Picture Library Jenny Baskaya

Managing Editor Esther Ripley
Managing Art Editor Alison Donovan
Associate Publisher Liz Wheeler
Art Director Peter Luff
Publisher Jonathan Metcalf

US Consultant Fern Marshall Bradley
US Editors Rebecca Warren, Jill Hamilton

First American Edition, 2011

Published in the United States by
DK Publishing, 375 Hudson Street, New York, New York 10014

11 12 13 14 15   10 9 8 7 6 5 4 3 2
003 – 272489 – Feb/2011

Published in Great Britain by Dorling Kindersley Limited.

A catalog record for this book is available from the Library of Congress
ISBN 978-0-7566-7163-1

DK books are available at special discounts when purchased in bulk for sales promotions, premiums, fund-raising, or educational use. For details, contact: DK Publishing Special Markets, 375 Hudson Street, New York, New York 10014 or SpecialSales@dk.com.

Colour reproduction by Colourscan, Singapore
Printed and bound by Star Standard, Singapore

Discover more at
www.dk.com

Jo Whittingham is a gardener and writer with a postgraduate degree in horticulture from the University of Reading and a passion for growing fruit and vegetables. Awarded the Garden Writers' Guild News Journalist of the Year 2004, she writes a monthly column for *The Scotsman* newspaper, as well as features for many leading gardening magazines. She authored DK's bestselling *Simple Steps to Success: Vegetables in a Small Garden*, and was consultant on *Grow Vegetables*, *Kitchen Garden*, and *Grow Fruit*.

Contents

Introduction

More and more people are discovering that the advantages of growing your own fruit and vegetables go far beyond being able to go outside and pick something to eat.

Home-grown produce tastes better than grocery store produce because it's freshly picked and perfectly ripe, which shines through even when cooked or preserved.

Grow fresh

For those who look for local, seasonal produce, what could be better than a perfect summer strawberry or handsome winter cabbage, picked at their prime, mere steps from the kitchen? Fruit and vegetables from your garden can also be produced organically if you choose, and it's amazing how trivial the odd chewed leaf and misshapen apple become when they've been raised under your own watchful gaze.

Whether you are starting out or a seasoned gardener, growing your own fruit and vegetables is enormously satisfying, even if the yields are small at first. It doesn't matter if you have just a few patio pots, some spare space in a border, or a community garden, you can grow your own, and it's much easier than you might think.

Something every day

Eating something every day of the year that you have grown yourself might sound like an impossible dream, achievable only for those with a gigantic yard and a team of gardeners. But with careful planning, and the most basic food preservation and storage methods, anyone with growing space can enjoy home-grown produce, fresh or stored, throughout the year.

(right) **Preserve** surplus summer crops to enjoy during the colder, leaner months.

(far right) **Community gardens** are a great place for city dwellers to find space to plant.

(below) **Small beds** are all you need for many crops. Make use of every inch of space.

The aim here is not full self-sufficiency, rather the pleasure in knowing that you and your family will be able to enjoy something tasty and nutritious, every day, grown on your own yard. Come summer, that could well be a feast of fresh crisp salad leaves, juicy fruit, and wholesome beans, while fall brings a bounty of tree fruits and hearty root crops. You won't go hungry winter to spring either if you take advantage of stored produce, not just dried beans or bagged potatoes, which are good anyway, but also rich chutneys, sweet jam, and indulgent homemade wines.

Even if you only grow a few radishes in a pot, they're yours, and you'll never taste fresher.

How to use this book

This month-by-month guide takes you through all the stages of growing, picking, storing, and preserving your own fruit and vegetables. Each chapter opens with a summary of what you might be eating, and tells you what to do each month. You may need to adjust the timing of tasks to suit the climate in your local area.

Ready to eat calendars
These guides highlight crops to enjoy now, picked fresh or taken from your stores. There's something every day.

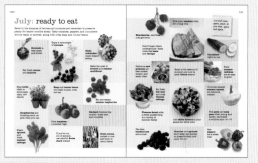

What to sow/plant
These pages offer clear advice on what to sow and plant, taking into account weather and climate. The central bar shows the final produce.

What to do
Use these pages as a calendar of tasks that will keep your crops growing and healthy. The central bar illustrates the developing crops.

What to harvest
Pick your crops when they are at their best, especially if you plan to store them. These pages help you identify when they are ripe and explain the best techniques.

Your growing space

You might imagine that you would need ample space to make growing your own fruit and vegetables worthwhile, when in fact even the tiniest sunny corner or windowsill is enough to get a good start. With a little imagination, time, and effort, you can transform almost any space, however small, into a productive plot.

Where to grow

The happy truth is that you can grow fruit and vegetables anywhere with reasonable soil, as long as it's not in deep shade all day long. If you're lucky enough to have a large yard, you might consider setting up a separate vegetable garden, several fruit trees, and even a cage to protect soft fruit bushes from marauding birds.

Having a smaller garden need not restrict the range of crops you grow, you just need to be more creative in how you use space to fit them in. For instance, you might try filling the vertical space on walls and fences with trained fruit trees and bushes, or plant climbing crops, like peas, beans, and cucumbers. Productive plants can also make attractive additions to your flower borders—don't be afraid to plug summer gaps with fast-growing lettuces, add height to your planting with tall, leafy corn, or give a neatly pruned redcurrant center stage.

Containers are another way of turning almost any outside space into a burgeoning edible garden.

It is possible to grow almost any fruit and vegetables in pots on sunny patios, roof terraces, and balconies, as long as they are protected from strong winds; and you can keep them well watered and fed. Even small windowboxes and hanging baskets can provide good crops of salads, herbs, and cherry tomatoes, if well cared for.

Try experimenting with crops in pots, from pears to potatoes, lettuce to lemons, and be sure to try special dwarf varieties that have been specifically bred to suit cultivation in containers.

(above) **Vertical spaces** allow you to grow more crops in a smaller space. Fruit trees, such as apples, pears and figs, can be trained against walls.

(left) **Crops in containers** are the ideal solution if you have limited growing space. Any good-size container with adequate drainage is suitable.

(above) **Sunny windowsills** are warm and bright, and provide a convenient spot to raise young plants for extra early crops.

(right) **Community gardens** offer welcome growing spaces; and are a great way to meet like-minded people to share advice and produce. Ask your library about local gardens in your area.

Alternative spaces

If your own yard doesn't have enough space to fulfill your ambitions, consider renting a plot in a local community garden, or ask a neighbor if you can share garden space. These can be great places to learn, with more experienced gardeners who are usually generous with their time and advice. They may even organize practical workshops for novice growers.

With the increased popularity of growing your own, there is often considerable demand for a patch to cultivate, so be patient, and be prepared to join a waiting list if necessary.

Where outdoor garden space is limited, don't overlook growing indoors on windowsills, and in glassed-in porches and sunrooms. The light and warmth found here is ideal for raising seedlings and for growing heat-loving plants, such as tomatoes, sweet peppers, chiles, and eggplant, which may struggle outside in a cooler regions. Choose smaller varieties though, so the mature plants don't block out too much daylight when fully grown.

Many herbs thrive on windowsills, where they are convenient for picking. Seeds can also be sprouted on the kitchen countertop at any time of year.

Plan your plot

Whether you have a generous plot or a tiny postage stamp in which to grow, it is important to plan how you use the space, both to maximize productivity and to facilitate maintenance.

First consider the location of permanent structures—work out if the greenhouse will get enough sunlight, the paths are wide enough, and the compost bins sited in a convenient place.

Once you have decided a layout, think about where you will plant trees, fruit bushes, and perennial vegetables like rhubarb. It's important to put these in the right place first time because they take a few years to establish and start producing, and will be set back if you have to move them. The great thing about the rest of your vegetable crops is that you grow them fresh each year. You can be bold, because any errors won't be with you for long.

Well-planned spaces make growing fruit and vegetables easier and more productive. Take time to plan where permanent features, such as paths and greenhouses, should go.

Using space

Constructing raised beds (see page 33) is one of the best ways of creating growing space where there was none before. As long as the beds themselves are well drained, they can be built on very poor or badly drained soil, or on a patio, then filled with plenty of good topsoil and compost to give good results.

If you have, or are planning, a dedicated kitchen garden, you can make the most of your space by using a bed system, setting up

(right) **Raised beds create instant** growing space on any surface; filled with good-quality soil and compost they can be very productive. Keep them small for easy access and maintenance.

a series of narrow beds separated by access paths (see page 16). With this system you don't need to allow room for walking on the soil between rows, so you can pack your plants more closely in the growing area for a higher yield.

Flowers, fruit, and veg

Using flower beds to grow crops is a more attractive idea than it might sound. Many vegetables have appealing foliage and flowers, while fruit bushes and trees bear blossoms and bright berries that merit a place in any garden. Just be aware that crop plants are more demanding than flowering plants; dig in plenty of manure or compost before planting, and give them ample light and space. Perennial herbs and edible flowers are particularly suitable as border plants, but colorful salads, kales, and Swiss chard can be highly effective, too, especially if you use every scrap of space by intercropping them between ornamentals (see pages 124–125). Train climbing beans or squashes up decorative supports with spectacular results.

(above left) **An old metal tub** makes an interesting container for this crop of garlic. Make sure recycled containers have adequate drainage.

(left) **Make the most of your growing** area, whether it is large or small, by planting your crops as closely as practicable in evenly spaced rows.

Crops in pots

Containers are an obvious way to make the best use of space; and can instantly imbue your plot with its own style. Sleek metal, rustic terracotta, or quirky reclaimed containers, such as old sinks, and tin buckets and baths, can all look great. However, plants will be just as happy in functional plastic pots or growing bags, as long as they have good drainage.

Fill your containers with good-quality potting mix, with water-retaining granules to help prevent them from drying out. Since containers make plants mobile, you can move smaller planters into the sun, away from the wind, and under cover during winter, when necessary.

(above) **Even a tiny patio** has room for a few container-grown crops. They look attractive and can be moved around as required.

(above left) **Make a vegetable plot** on a windowsill. Small plants such as herbs will love the sun.

(left) **Hanging baskets** don't encroach on your growing space and look wonderful crammed with trailing tomatoes or edible flowers.

Be realistic

Hopes are invariably high when sowing starts in spring but, sadly, disappointment sometimes follows. To keep your enthusiasm going for years to come, it is vital to be realistic about what you are likely to achieve in the space and time you have available. Don't make the mistake of initially clearing a huge plot if you have only limited time to spend on it. Nothing is more disheartening than watching the weeds regain the upper hand after you have recently spent hours digging them out. It is better to start out small, and then expand as your knowledge and experience increase. Success will soon build up confidence.

There is no escaping the fact that whichever methods you use to grow fruit and vegetables, time and effort invested at every stage of the process are what bring good returns. Think carefully about how much you can plant without giving yourself an impossible amount of work later on.

Crop care

Planting directly into the soil involves early preparation, but once young plants are well established they usually grow happily without much input, except periodic weeding, watering during dry spells, and routine checks for pests and diseases.

Getting plants started in containers is initially less effort than planting in beds, but then you will have to spend time watering them, possibly twice daily in a hot summer, for as long as you want them to produce.

Keep it simple

If you have never grown your own before, keep it simple. Start with crops that are easy to cultivate and almost guaranteed to harvest. Buy transplants, so not everything has to be raised from seed.

Radishes, salads, potatoes, and beans are all reliable, and zucchini and tomatoes fruit all summer, paying back your investment in purchasing transplants. Leave challenging melons, cauliflowers, and grapes until you're confident with other crops.

(top) **Cut-and-come-again** salad greens will produce several crops from just one sowing. They can be grown all year round.

(above) **If you want freshly picked greens** in midwinter, then try growing kale, one of the most resilient of all brassicas.

(left) **Asparagus** needs time and plenty of room to grow. It has a short season, but an established bed will crop for many years.

What to grow

It seems obvious, but use your space to grow what you like to eat. Although it's tempting to try weird and wonderful crops seen in catalogs, or to plant a glut of the latest superfood, what you really want is everyday produce that tastes fabulous. Even in a large garden there won't be time or space for everything, and to grow something to eat every day, you need to consider a few points.

The most important point to consider is the return that each crop will give for the amount of space it takes. Asparagus, for example, needs a large dedicated bed to produce a decent crop over a couple of months. On the other hand, a few rows of cut-and-come-again lettuce can supply daily salads all year round. Many winter crops, such as parsnips and sprouting broccoli, need to be in the ground for months before they are ready for harvesting; so you either need to squeeze fast-growing crops between them or limit their numbers in small spaces.

Locally grown

You should also take into account which crops grow well locally. If you are not sure, find out by visiting nearby gardens, talking to your neighbors, or asking the growers at your local farmers' market. Use your common sense, too, when it comes to selecting crops that will do well on your plot. If you live in an area where the summers are cool and wet, then heat-loving crops such as eggplant and tomatoes will produce well only in a greenhouse. Gardeners in hot, dry climates may struggle to keep leafy salads and brassicas going during the height of summer.

It makes sense to put your effort into growing things that are either expensive or impossible to buy in the stores. What these crops might be depends on your local suppliers, but soft fruits, such as currants and berries, are often pricey, as are herbs, runner beans, and good salad varieties. Globe artichokes, kohlrabi, and the full range of winter squashes are often unavailable in the stores, so if you like them, why not grow your own?

If you have never harvested food fresh from the garden before then you might not know how incredibly different it can taste,

even compared to produce bought straight from the farmers' market. When there are just minutes between picking and eating, none of the precious sugars have been turned to starch and the cells are still plump with water, so you get sweetness and crispness that simply cannot be bought. Some crops, including peas, beans, corn, tomatoes, and new potatoes, lose this freshness faster than others, making them worth growing just because their flavor can't be matched by produce in the stores.

Smaller plots

Where space is at a premium, grow high-yielding fruit and vegetables that get the most out of every scrap of soil by cropping quickly or consistently over a long period. Watch for dwarf and bush varieties, bred to take up less room and often to grow well in containers. Use pots and grow bags and fill them with attractive varieties for a colorful display.

(right) **Raspberries** often produce heavy crops that give you enough fruit to freeze or make into preserves, as well as to enjoy straight from the bush.

(below) **Freshly lifted new potatoes** have an incomparable flavor. You could grow a small crop in containers if you don't have room for a vegetable plot.

- **Bush tomatoes** – Great in hanging baskets, these can produce sweet cherry fruit for most of the summer.

- **Bush beans** – Many types of beans are available as bush varieties that yield heavily in a tiny space.

- **Herbs** – Both perennials and annuals deserve space for their long picking seasons and good looks.

- **Salad greens** – Cut-and-come-again salads, like arugula and mizuna, will regrow three times in summer.

- **Blueberries** – These compact bushes thrive in pots; their berries ripen gradually for picking right through late summer.

- **Strawberries** – They look pretty in pots or at the edge of a border. Plant both Junebearers and everbearers to extend the harvest.

- **Summer radishes** – Ready to eat 6 weeks after sowing, peppery radish is perfect for filling a gap in your crops.

- **Beets** – The striking red-veined leaves look beautiful and are as good to eat as the earthy baby roots.

- **Swiss chard** – Neon-colored stems make this leafy crop a must.

- **Zucchini** – A single bush can provide more than 20 fruits, along with glorious yellow flowers.

Growing under cover

This isn't some kind of covert gardening, but the practice of protecting plants from the worst weather, to extend the growing season. It is particularly useful if you live in a cold area where spring comes late and fall arrives early, but almost all gardeners looking to produce crops year-round will benefit from growing crops under cover.

(above) **Greenhouses** come in a range of materials and styles to suit all plots. They can be expensive, so consider buying a second-hand one locally.

(left) **Ideal growing conditions** are the main advantage of greenhouses and hoophouses, and they also provide somewhere to work in bad weather.

Grow indoors

Greenhouses and hoophouses offer exciting possibilities for extending the season for tender crops such as tomatoes, peppers, eggplant, and more. Even unheated, these structures provide enough protection to grow extra Junebearing strawberries in spring, to raise winter crops such as radishes and cut-and-come-again salads, and give many crops a head start.

Greenhouses are expensive to buy new, so make sure the shape and size you choose suits your garden and growing ambitions. Also ensure that there is adequate ventilation to keep air flowing around your plants; aim for one roof- and one side-vent for every 6 ft (2 m) of length.

Hoophouses are cheaper to construct, but not as attractive as a stylish greenhouse. The plastic that covers them has a limited lifespan, as does the plastic used in some greenhouses, and they are more difficult to ventilate, but they still provide a great growing space.

Whichever structure you choose, position it on a bright, level site, away from the shade of buildings and trees, and sheltered from strong winds. Be sure to provide good access, and try to find space outside for a rain barrel and also a tool shed.

Simple cover

Small-scale covers, such as cloches and cold frames, are invaluable for warming the soil to allow seeds to be sown early. They can also be used to harden off plants raised indoors, keep out damaging winds and hungry pests, and protect overwintering crops.

Cloches, whether made of glass, plastic, or row cover, are relatively cheap and have the advantage that they can be moved where needed, although they must be securely pinned to the soil. Use cut-off plastic bottles to cover individual plants, or low, wire-framed tunnels to protect whole rows.

Cold frames usually have a soil base and a sloping, glazed lid. Although lighter frames can be moved where required, many are permanently positioned against south-facing walls, to give maximum light and heat, and extra frost protection. They are ideal for raising early-sown seeds, hardening off young plants, or growing heat-loving crops like cucumbers and melons.

Plastic mini-greenhouses perform many of the same functions as a cold frame. Taller models are ideal for protecting growing bags planted with tomatoes, although they must be anchored securely and have a sheltered, sunny site.

Even sunny windowsills are perfect for raising tender plants from seed. To stop seedlings from bending toward the light, grow them in a simple light box made by cutting the front away from a small cardboard box, and lining the back with reflective silver foil.

(far left) **Cloches** provide enough warmth and protection to give crops a useful head start.

(left) **Mini-greenhouses** are ideal for tender crops, like tomatoes, if you have limited space. They can be easily packed away when not in use.

(below) **Cold frames** can be made from recycled materials to a size and shape to suit your plot. They can be permanent or temporary.

A perfect spot for crops

You will want your vegetable and fruit plants to deliver large, healthy crops over the longest period possible. To help them achieve this, offer them the best possible conditions for growth. Provide your plants with light, water, good airflow, and well-drained, fertile soil – in other words, give them a perfect spot for crops.

Ideal conditions

A long-neglected corner where nothing much ever seems to grow is not the right place to start a vegetable garden. Provide an open site for your crops, with plenty of sunshine during the day to warm the soil and give the plants energy for rapid growth. A position away from the shade and competing roots of shrubs or large trees is essential. If your site isn't ideal, try to improve it as best you can. This will not only ensure better harvests, but also make growing much simpler.

Let in as much light as possible by cutting back overhanging growth, and create raised beds to lift crops above competing roots.

Good exposure

Open ground gets the full benefit of any rainfall, so that you are less likely to have to water the plants yourself. However, an open site can leave your crops at the mercy of the weather, particularly damage from strong winds.

In exposed gardens, you should put up windbreaks to reduce the force of gusts as much far as possible. Don't build a solid wall, because air pressure creates turbulence on the leeward side of the barrier that can be worse than the unimpeded wind. Choose a

(left) **For healthy plants** and maximum productivity, choose the site of your vegetable plot with care, taking account of light, temperature, and soil quality.

(below) **Frost may not harm** a hardy brassica such as this, but can cause severe damage to less robust crops that have been planted in a frost pocket.

Lattice makes an effective and attractive windbreak for the vegetable plot, and can be used to support crop plants or ornamental climbers.

permeable barrier, such as a fence or a hedge, that will break the force of the wind without creating unpredictable eddies. Also watch out for gaps between buildings and walls that could funnel wind.

Frost pockets

Temperature is another important consideration when it comes to choosing a site for your crops. Some gardens have frost pockets, which are low-lying areas, where cold air gets trapped on still winter nights, increasing the likelihood of frosts. Check your garden after a hard frost to see if there's a patch that is still white when everywhere else has thawed. Planting in such a cold spot will lead to frost damage and slow growth, and should be avoided.

Know your soil

Soil is a vital source of nutrients and water for plants. Knowing what type of soil you have and how it can be improved is key to growing success. To establish the soil type of the spot you plan to plant, take a small handful, wet it slightly and squeeze it lightly in your palm. If the soil sticks together into a smooth, shiny ball you have a heavy, clay soil. If it feels gritty and doesn't clump together, your soil is light and sandy. Often soils are a combination of these two types, and contain fine silt particles as well, which gives good garden soil known as a loam.

Soil types have different characteristics that influence not only the way plants grow but also how you should treat them.

Sandy soil feels gritty in the hand and does not clump together when you squeeze it. This soil does not retain moisture or nutrients well.

Clay soil holds together when squeezed and feels heavy and sticky when wet. It holds nutrients well but is prone to waterlogging.

Kits for testing soil pH are inexpensive and usually reliable. Most involve the simple process of checking a soil solution against a color scale.

Clay soils retain nutrients well but can easily become waterlogged, while sandy soils drain freely but quickly lose nutrients and dry out. If drainage is very poor and water pools on the surface, the cause could be deeper. Dig down and check for a compacted "hard pan" layer that will need to be broken up to allow water through.

Soil pH level

The pH (acidity) of your soil determines which crops will grow well on your plot, so check it before planting. Simple-to-use kits to measure pH are widely available; just follow the instructions given.

Soil is considered neutral at pH 7.0; acid below this figure; and alkaline above it. A slightly acid pH of 6.5 is ideal for most fruit and vegetables, although in general they tolerate all but the extremes. If you intend to grow brassicas on acid soil, try applying lime the fall before planting to raise the pH level, which will help prevent clubroot disease (see p.241).

Improving soil

Digging and preparing beds may seem like a chore, but once you see the difference it makes to fruit and vegetable yields it's easier to motivate yourself. If you do only one thing, add as much well-rotted manure or compost to the soil as you can. Mix it with sand on heavy clay soil in the fall to improve drainage and reduce stickiness. Work manure into light sandy soil in spring to improve water-retention and add nutrients. Unless the ground is very compacted, single digging to one spade's depth, adding the organic matter, and backfilling, is enough. Avoid standing on the soil whenever possible, and use a plank to work from if it is wet.

Defining the beds with paths in between improves access. Mulch the paths with a weed-suppressing material and concentrate on improving the soil in the beds.

Rotate your crops

Separate beds facilitate crop rotation, where related crops are grown in different areas every seasonto prevent soil-borne pests and diseases from building up. Some plant groups have their own nutrient requirements, and can deplete the soil of these, if grown repeatedly. Plan a three-year rotation where the hungry cabbage family (brassicas) follow nitrogen-fixing peas and beans, which follow potatoes and the root vegetables.

(above) **Worth all the hard work**, this flourishing plot, supporting a variety of healthy crops, begins with soil improvement and preparation.

(below) **Dividing your growing areas** with mulched paths reduces the need to walk on the soil to reach the plants. Defining beds also makes it easier to organize your crop rotation schedule.

Keeping plants well fed and watered

If you expect your plants to grow rapidly they must have adequate nourishment and water. Their roots take up water, as well as three main nutrients (nitrogen, phosphorus, and potassium) from the soil, along with a range of trace elements such as manganese, copper, and iron. It makes sense to improve the soil every year, to ensure that these needs can be met without having to give your plants continual extra help. As long as the soil isn't excessively acid or alkaline, it is likely that most nutrients will be made available to plants from the soil's own mineral content or from the breakdown of organic matter into humus by microorganisms. This is another reason to keep digging in plenty of well-rotted manure and compost.

Big eaters

Although many plants in good soil may not need feeding, "hungry" crops, like tomatoes and brassicas, benefit from additional fertilizers, as do container-grown crops.

Concentrated fertilizers like organic blood, fish, and bone, or blended fertilizers, often come in powder or granular forms that are easy to apply to open soil. Liquid fertilizers just need diluting and are ideal for feeding container plants.

Watering is not as simple as it seems. A plant that is wilting in dry soil will benefit quickly from a good soaking, but plants can also look sickly growing in waterlogged soil, so check first.

Plants under cover and in containers need regular watering, every day in the height of summer. Those growing in open soil are less dependent on you, unless they are newly planted or there is a drought. Here it is better to water thoroughly, soaking the soil to a good depth occasionally, rather than wetting the surface every day. Check by digging down after watering if you are unsure how much water is needed.

(far right) **Sprinkle a top-dressing of fertilizer** around the base of your plants to deliver nutrients close to the roots.

(right) **Soaker hoses** are an efficient way of irrigating rows of crops without wasting water.

(below) **Regularly digging** in mature, homemade compost is the best way to improve the structure and fertility of your soil.

(left) **Hoverflies**, like many beneficial insects, not only pollinate flowers but also prey on crop-damaging pests.

(below) **Spray chemical pesticides** carefully. Check the label to ensure they are safe to treat food crops and only spray late in the evening.

Organic or not?

Many people grow their own to ensure that their crops are produced organically, but every gardener has to decide whether to use synthetic chemicals or not.

Organic gardening relies upon establishing a balance, where plants grow strongly thanks to the addition of organic matter to the soil (ideally homemade garden compost), and pest numbers are controlled by beneficial wildlife. It takes time to achieve this balance, and there will be occasions when pests and diseases win the day, but there are easy steps you can take to swing the odds in your favor.

Planting fruit and vegetables with ornamental plants is a great way to maximize productivity and color in smaller gardens, but it also helps protect them from pests. While a large patch of cabbages or carrots is an obvious target, the same plants scattered through a flower border will be harder for pests to spot. In a similar way, planting strongly scented flowers, such as French marigolds, among vegetables helps distract insect pests and attracts their predators; a practice known as "companion planting."

Planting flowers alongside your fruits and vegetables also attracts pollinating insects that will visit the crops, improving their yield.

If pests do get the upper hand, biological control, which involves introducing an organism to kill your chosen pest, can be effective if used properly. The conditions must be right however, and at those rare times when your crops are under severe attack you may choose to save your crop by applying a selective insecticide to target a heavy infestation.

When using sprays on or near food plants, always check the label carefully to see that it is safe to use. It will also say how soon your crops will be safe to harvest. Also, only spray insecticides late in the evening, after beneficial insects have stopped flying, so you kill the target pests, not allies like bees and hoverflies (see pages 104–105 on organic pest control).

Natural allies such as birds, toads, and beneficial insects play a vital role in keeping pest numbers under control. Try to attract them into your garden by providing cover and water.

Tools and equipment

A small range of good-quality tools makes gardening a pleasure, and it's worth investing in the best you can afford, and looking after them so they last. Exactly which tools you will need depends on the space to be cultivated. If you grow only in pots, you can do without the large tools required to cultivate open soil, but otherwise their needs will be much the same as someone with a generous plot.

Wherever you grow, find yourself a sturdy trowel for planting and an ergonomic hand fork for weeding in tight spots. Clippers are essential for fruit pruning, but will also save your kitchen scissors being blunted on many other occasions when things need to be cut or chopped.

A good watering can, with detachable fine and coarse roses, is indispensable, particularly if you grow crops from seed.

Choose tools the right size and weight for your stature and strength to make heavy work as manageable as possible. In a larger garden a wheelbarrow is also useful.

You'll find that you collect seed trays and pots, all sorts of plant supports, and possibly a shed, as you go along, but don't forget that it's useful to have sundries like potting mix, labels, and string, before the season starts.

(clockwise from left)
Fork—Ideal tool to use when incorporating organic matter into the soil, and for lifting crops and plants.

Rake—Used to clear stones and debris from the soil surface, and to create a fine tilth for sowing seeds.

Spade—Can be used in place of a fork on light, sandy soils. Also useful for moving dry materials, like compost.

Trowel—An essential hand tool for planting out and removing weeds.

Hoe—Used for killing annual weeds among crops, severing them at the roots so they wither.

To sow or buy?

Raising plants from seed is by far the cheapest way to fill your plot, and allows you to choose from an enormous range of varieties. But seed is not the only option.

Potatoes and onions are grown easily from tubers and bulbs, and an impressive range of vegetables, fruit trees, and bushes are available to buy as young plants.

Seed selection

You can buy seeds from garden centers, mail order from seed catalogs (see pp.246–247), or collect your own from previous year's crops (see pp.172–173).

Select varieties that suit your particular needs. For instance, consider dwarf or trailing cultivars if you garden in small beds or containers; pick those that mature early if you live in a colder area; and select varieties bred for good disease resistance if you garden organically.

When buying seeds, some are labeled "F1 hybrid" or have "F1" in their name. These are modern varieties, specially selected to be uniform, vigorous, and often more disease resistant than standard varieties. They are more costly, and won't come true-to-type if you save your own seeds. Some cheaper varieties are described as "F2" or "open pollinated."

Plants grown from this seed will be more variable but are perfectly good for most gardeners.

Order only as much seed as you need for the coming season. If you have any left over, keep it cool and dry; most (except parsnip and carrot) will still germinate after several years in storage. You will find information on sowing seed both indoors and out on pages 42-43, and specific advice on crops within the monthly chapters.

(far left) **Seeds are an** economical way of raising vegetables, such as this sturdy young corn.

(left) **Seed sown directly** outdoors in the right conditions often produces gratifyingly quick results.

(below) **You can start things** off earlier with seeds; all you need is a seed-starting kit or a warm windowsill.

(above) **Buying a few trays** of seedlings is the quickest and easiest way to start a vegetable garden, although probably not the cheapest. Reputable garden centers and nurseries only offer healthy plants.

(left) **Young container-grown fruit trees** can be bought and planted from spring through fall. Make sure they look well tended when you buy them.

Young plants

Tubers for crops such as potatoes and Jerusalem artichokes, and the small bulbs, known as sets, from which onions and shallots are cultivated, are available from late winter into spring. Ensure that you buy disease-free stock from a reputable nursery, garden center, or mail order supplier.

You can also buy young plants from the same sources. Buying plants is more expensive than growing from seed, and you don't get the same choice of varieties, but for those with limited time or outdoor space for sowing seed, this is a good option. Look for sturdy, dark green plants and acclimatize them gradually to outdoor conditions before planting out. Beware of buying tender plants, such as tomatoes and zucchini, too early if you have nowhere frost-free to grow them on. Plants delivered by mail should be opened immediately, watered, and potted up as soon as possible. (For details on planting individual crops, see the planting pages that follow for each month.)

Fruit bushes and trees

In mild climatess, container-grown bushes and trees are available all year round, and they can be planted at any time of year—although high summer is best avoided. Don't buy old stock, which may be pot-bound and often goes unpruned in garden centers, and steer clear of bulging, weedy pots and poorly shaped plants, even if they are offered at reduced prices.

Bare-root plants, lifted from nursery fields when dormant, are normally available in the spring. Specialty fruit nurseries stock the widest range, offering many different varieties and rootstocks, often by mail-order. Look for "maidens," which are one-year-old trees that establish quickly, can be pruned as you wish, and cost less than larger specimens.

Once out of the ground, the exposed roots must not be allowed to dry out, and planting should be done as soon as possible. See pages 202–203 for information on choosing and planting fruit trees.

Month-by-month guide

Growing year-round crops needs a bit of planning, so use this calendar guide to track all your sowing, planting, growing, and harvesting, month-by-month. Remember that climates vary, even from one garden to the next, so keep an eye on the weather, and treat sowing and planting dates as approximate. For a summary of each crop, see the planners on pages 230–235.

January: ready to eat

Enjoy freshly dug parsnips, celeriac, and Jerusalem artichokes in soups and stews, along with potatoes, carrots, and rutabagas from your storage. Cut the first spears of sprouting broccoli this month.

Dig up some **Jerusalem artichokes**

Brussels sprouts are sweet and nutty

The first tender spears of **purple sprouting broccoli** are ready now

Dried **herbs** from last year's crop are still full of flavor

Cut **endive** grown under cover for winter

Raid your stores of **onions**, **shallots**, and **garlic**

Use **stored vegetables** to make **soup** *pages 226–227* and freeze any left over for later

Pick tasty young leaves of **chard (spinach beet)**

Enjoy the unusual taste of newly lifted **salsify**

Use frozen **beans** and **peas** from last summer *pages 148–149*

Winter cabbage should be doing well—use some for pickling *pages 176–179*

Leeks will taste good for some weeks yet

Braise some stored **celery** or add it to casseroles

Use dried or frozen **chiles** in spicy dishes

Kale is a good winter standby

*If you planted late **potatoes** for winter, eat any that are left*

There may be greenhouse **citrus fruit** *pages 222–223* to pick—if you're lucky

Cut-and-come-again greens will supply fresh new leaves

Pick bright heads of **radicchio**, grown under cover, for winter salads

Make pies and crumbles using **frozen soft fruit** *pages 150–151*

Grate **winter radishes** into your salads

Eat **pickles** prepared last fall *pages 176–179*

Bring **winter squashes** out of storage for a splash of color

Try **sprouting seeds** *pages 36–37* on your kitchen work top
- alfalfa
- beansprouts
- broccoli
- fenugreek

Boost your fruit intake with crunchy **stored apples** *pages 194–195*

Lift overwintering **celeriac** or take it from your stores *pages 210–211*

It's harvest time in January with the first of the forced **Belgian endive**

Parsnips should be keeping well in the ground

Use stored **root crops** *pages 210–211* for winter meals
- rutabaga
- potatoes
- carrots
- beets

Pull up pungent **green onions** overwintering under cloches

Toast the New Year with a glass of **homemade wine** *pages 180–181*

January: what to sow

EARLY-SEASON LEEKS

Early varieties of leeks, such as 'King Richard' (p.225) and 'Jolant', are best sown in January. They need a soil temperature of at least 46° F (8° C) in order to germinate, so a heated propagator in a greenhouse, or a cool room indoors, is essential for success. Sow seed thinly, about ½ in (1 cm) deep, into flats or pots filled with seed-starting mix, and grow them on indoors. The young plants will be ready to harden off and plant out later in spring.

HARVEST: **SEPT–APR**

TASTY SUMMER ONIONS

Maincrop onions need an early start, especially in colder areas where spring growth can be slow. Sow them indoors this month in a heated propagator at a temperature between about 50–59° F (10–15° C) and get them off to a flying start. Sow seed thinly, ½ in (1 cm) deep, in trays and prick them out as they grow. Alternatively, sow about five seeds per cell and grow them on as little space-saving clusters of mature bulbs.

HARVEST: **JUL–OCT**

SOW

LEEKS

ONIONS

BROAD BEANS

LETTUCE

BROAD APPEAL

For early crops of broad beans, sow seed 2 in (5 cm) deep in large peat pots. Keep them under cover in a greenhouse or cold frame and they will be ready to plant out in early spring. Sow your beans outside only in mild-winter areas, with a temperature of at least 41° F (5° C), and give them some protection, such as row cover.

HARVEST: **MAY–AUG**

LETTUCE BEGIN

In mild areas, lettuces sown now under frames or cloches can be planted out in early spring for a really early supply of tender greens. Sow thinly, ½ in (1 cm) deep, either in modules or in drills, 4 in (10 cm) apart. Look for early cos, butterhead, and loose-leaf salad-bowl varieties (p.81).

HARVEST: **APR–OCT**

CUT AND COME AGAIN

If you crave some fresh baby salad leaves, then try sowing a variety of cut-and-come-again crops under cover, either in the greenhouse or cold frame in beds, or in compost-filled boxes or seed trays. The best to try at this time of year are cress, arugula, endive, or winter mixes, such as 'Oriental Saladini'. Scatter the seeds thinly apart, ½ in (1 cm), and cover with about ¼ in (½ cm) of soil before watering well. The leaves will be ready to harvest in a matter of 5–6 weeks.

HARVEST: **ALL YEAR**

SALAD RADISH

Sow small-leaved radish, such as 'Saxa', in your greenhouse borders or in large containers this month. Growth will be slow, but harvestable roots will form. Provide extra protection with row covers or cloches on cold nights. Sow thinly, ½ in (1 cm) deep, in drills, 4 in (10 cm) apart. Thin the seedlings to ¾ in (2 cm) apart.

HARVEST: **APR–NOV**

SALADS

RADISHES

PEAS

See SOWING INSIDE
page 42

DON'T FORGET

Windowsills are ideal for raising seedlings but they can become cold at night. To keep your plants safe, bring them into the room on frosty nights, then return them to their sills in the morning.

EARLY PEAS—THE EASY WAY

HARVEST: **JUN–OCT**

Peas, which you can sow indoors this month, hate root disturbance, so sow them in peat pots or a length of plastic gutter to make transplanting easier.

1 PREPARE THE GUTTER
Cut plastic gutter into lengths that match the peas' final spacing. Block both ends, then fill them with growing mix.

2 SOW THE SEED
Choose dwarf early varieties and sow the seed ¾ in (2 cm) deep, 2 in (5 cm) apart. Standard gutter will accommodate two rows.

3 PLANT WHEN READY
When the seedlings are ready and hardened off, dig a gutter-sized trench and gently ease the entire length into position.

Cut-and-come-again salads

Baby salad leaves are tasty, nutritious, and one of the quickest crops you can grow. The great thing is that they regrow after being cut, not just once, but two or three times, giving a bumper harvest from a small space. They are ideal for small plots and containers, and can be grown under cover for salad throughout winter.

Winter leaves

Anyone with a greenhouse, cold frame, or even a bright windowsill in a cool room can successfully grow cut-and-come-again salads, to harvest right through the lean winter and early-spring months. Not all leafy crops grow well when daylight is short and conditions are cool. If you are sowing under cover from mid- to late winter, choose peppery arugula and oriental mustards, mild mizuna, colorful loose-leaf lettuces, and crisp endive and bok choy, for a range of interesting textures and flavors. At this time of year it usually takes 5–6 weeks to grow baby leaves that are ready to cut, whereas in summer they can reach a good size in 3–4 weeks. For a crop ready to harvest earlier in winter, sow the same selection of seeds under cover from early- to mid-fall.

Summer crops

From early spring, you can sow cut-and-come-again salads directly outdoors, in rich, well-weeded soil, or into patio containers or windowboxes. Most of the winter crops listed above will now grow well outdoors. Increase the variety by adding baby spinach and kale, if you like their taste. Normally, mid- to late spring is not a good time to sow salad crops if you want mature plants, because they bolt—rapidly run to seed—as the weather turns hot weather. Since the plants suggested here will be cut as baby leaves, there is no need to worry about them going to seed. For a continuous supply of salads, keep sowing successionally every 3–4 weeks until mid- to late summer, and cut batches of baby leaves regularly so that more regrow to take their place.

How to harvest

Exactly when to harvest your cut-and-come-again salads is a matter of personal taste. Cut them small, and you'll find them sweet and tender; leave them to grow a little longer, and they'll develop a stronger flavor and a tougher texture. Whenever you decide to cut them though, the technique is the same. Take scissors or a sharp knife and slice through the plants just above the lowest leaves, from where they will regrow. This may appear brutal, and the bare stems won't look promising, but keep them well watered, and new shoots will soon start to appear. After a few harvests, your plants will be past their best, and can be composted. Grow on new sowings.

1 Upland cress has a peppery taste that is delicious in salads and can be used instead of watercress. It is ready for harvesting 6–8 weeks after sowing. It grows well under cover during winter.

2 Corn salad is also known as mache or lamb's lettuce, and produces a steady supply of small leaves, even during winter. Wash well before use to remove grit that can build up between stems.

3 Wild arugula has a stronger taste than normal garden arugula. Its serrated leaves also look more attractive and make a better garnish. Peppery in taste, it gives a welcome kick to salads.

4 Oriental mustards are usually cooked when fully grown, but can also be eaten raw when harvested as baby leaves. The plants grow well, even in the coldest areas, and also look quite decorative.

5 Mizuna has a mild mustard flavor, and makes an attractive and tasty addition to salads when picked as baby leaves. Let summer crops grow a little longer for larger leaves to stir-fry.

6 Bok choy is more commonly grown in summer as a mature crop, although the baby leaves can be picked when just a few weeks old in spring. It has a mild flavor and a good crisp texture.

7 Mibuna is similar in taste to mizuna. Its narrow, spear-shaped leaves grow in clumps, but are slow to appear in spring, so it is best grown as a summer crop. Try adding the leaves to soups.

8 Baby lettuce leaves are loose-leaf varieties cropped at an earlier stage. Sow a large batch in spring, using some as cut-and-come-again crops and letting some mature for summer salads.

Other varieties to try:
Endive (p.51)
Arugula (p.50)
Tatsoi (p.50)

CUT-AND-COME-AGAIN SALADS

January: what to do

STOCK UP

When bad weather keeps you indoors, spend some time comparing the catalogs of mail order seed suppliers. These offer a huge range of varieties to choose from, and you can shop around for competitive prices. Also take the opportunity to stock up on spring essentials such as pots, potting mix, flats, labels, stakes, and twine.

SOIL MAKEOVER

Double digging and incorporating manure is the best way to improve your soil before planting. It can be done in fall (p.204) or now, providing the soil isn't frozen.

1 DIG TRENCH ONE
Mark out the area being dug, dig out a trench two spades deep, and put the soil to one side.

2 DIG TRENCH TWO
Dig a second trench next to the first, turning the upper layer of soil into the base of the first trench.

3 ADD MANURE AND MIX
Add manure to the part-filled first trench, then the rest of the soil from trench two. Repeat.

TEND

GARDEN ESSENTIALS

DOUBLE DIGGING

FORCED FRUIT

BRASSICAS

EARLY WARMING

To encourage some of your plants, such as strawberries, to produce earlier than normal, in May instead of June, cover them now with cloches. The extra heat will allow them to flower and fruit earlier. This is also the time to place a rhubarb forcer over your plants to promote earlier stems that are sweeter and more tender. Remove the forcer in March and allow the plants to recover. Only force established plants.

STAY NEAT

As winter progresses, most hardy brassicas, including winter cabbages, sprouting broccoli, cauliflowers, and kales, tend to drop their more mature lower leaves. These can accumulate around the base, harboring pests and diseases, and can also start to smell. Pick up and compost fallen leaves regularly.

BAD APPLES

One bad apple can spoil all the rest, so check through your stored fruit (pp.194–195) for signs of brown rot fungus, damage from mice and other pests, or problems caused by fluctuating temperatures. Discard any diseased or spoiled produce, even if damage is minimal. Make sure your storage area is well ventilated and insulated.

NEW FRUIT TREES

Most tree and bush fruits planted in late fall need pruning as soon as they are in the ground (pp.206–207). Cut blackcurrants right back so that all shoots have one bud above soil level. Redcurrant and gooseberry stems should be cut back by half, and raspberry and blackberry canes cut to 12 in (30 cm). On young, feathered maiden apple and pear trees, cut back the leading shoot and select lateral shoots to form the first branches. Don't prune cherries, plums, peaches, and apricots until spring (p.86).

STORED FRUIT

FRUIT PRUNING

WINTER PRUNING

PRUNE FRUIT TREES

Free-standing mature apple and pear trees need some winter pruning now to keep them fruiting well and to maintain an open, balanced shape. Your aim should be to remove any weak, congested, or damaged branches that are likely to be unproductive.

1 PRUNE TO SIDE BRANCH
To prune back to a side branch, undercut with a saw to about halfway through the stem. Make the final cut from above, to meet the undercut.

2 SHORTEN THIN BRANCHES
To encourage the formation of flowers in spring, cut back long spindly growth to a short branch, using sharp pruners.

3 REMOVE WEAK GROWTH
If you have pruned your tree in previous years, check the old pruning sites and remove any weak stems growing around the cut areas.

4 PREVENT CONGESTION
Take out branches that are crossing over others, or growing toward the center of the tree. This prevents congestion and disease.

See PRUNING FRUIT IN FALL pages 206–207

Preparing a seedbed

Plants are at their most vulnerable as seeds and tiny seedlings. At this stage they need as near-perfect conditions as possible in which to germinate and grow quickly. Providing your seedlings with well-drained, weed-free soil that has been worked to a fine texture will get them off to a good start. Time and effort spent on your seedbeds now will be well rewarded later with strong, healthy young plants.

Creating a tilth

Although seedlings do not need the most fertile soil, they are unlikely to thrive unless their environment has been prepared carefully beforehand. Creating what gardeners call a "fine tilth", where the soil surface is raked into fine crumbs, is important for successful germination, but this is easier on some soils than others. All soil types will benefit from the addition of a good organic compost. On heavy clay soils, working in a layer of sand helps reduce stickiness and improve structure and drainage.

1 CLEAR WEEDS
Thoroughly weed the seedbed, taking care to remove whole perennial roots, like those of dandelions, which will regrow if left in the soil. Remove any large stones, too.

2 IMPROVE THE SOIL
Add a layer of well-rotted compost, as well as sand, to help drainage if you are working heavy clay. Dig the soil over lightly with a fork to break up the surface and work in the compost.

Jo's tips

If you want to create a nursery seedbed in which to raise young plants, such as brassicas, for transplanting, then choose a good open site rather than a neglected corner at the back of the garden.

Seedlings require sunshine, plenty of rain, and a soil that holds some moisture. Keep them away from the shade, shelter, and competing roots of tall trees and hedges as much as possible.

3 RAKE TO A TILTH
Firm the soil gently with the back of your rake, then move the rake backward and forward across the bed, removing stones, until you have a good, even, crumbly tilth.

4 MARK OUT A FURROW
Once you are happy with the soil texture, you can start sowing. Draw the pointed edge of a hoe through the soil to make a tidy furrow at the correct depth for your chosen seeds.

Making a raised bed

Raised beds offer a low-maintenance way to grow your own crops, and suit busy lives and small spaces. They can be made from a range of materials, to heights and sizes to suit any plot. Because the beds can be constructed where there is no soil, or where the soil is poor, any bright spot can become a miniature garden. They can provide temporary growing spaces, and be dismantled easily if you need the space.

Benefits

Raised beds make life easier: you only have to dig, weed, and cultivate the area used for growing, not the paths between them, and they can be filled with quality purchased soil or compost, which reduces how much routine soil preparation you need to do. Where drainage is a problem, raised beds help keep roots out of cold, wet earth. They also allow the soil to warm up more quickly in spring so that seeds can be sown sooner, giving your crops a useful head start.

Easy access

Avoid having to stand on your raised bed, compacting the soil with your feet, by making sure they are not too wide. Unless you are very tall, build your beds no more than 4 ft (1.2 m) across, so you can reach to the center without over-stretching. Of course, beds can be narrower if you choose, and they can be whatever length and height you like. Taller beds are ideal for those who need plants in easy reach.

To provide a sound footing to work from when tending your bed, leave a wide path all the way around, preferably covered with weed-suppressing mulch.

OLD LANDSCAPE TIMBERS
Landscape timbers make an excellent material for raised beds because you can build them up layer by layer to suit your needs. They are very heavy, so get help when moving them.

BRICKS
You can make beds any size and shape using bricks. They are also durable and maintenance-free. Brick beds must have drainage channels to prevent waterlogging.

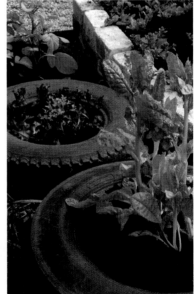

RECYCLED MATERIALS
Many different materials can be used for beds, including wooden pallets, old water tanks, or even old tires. Whatever you use, make sure it can support the weight of the soil safely.

January: what to harvest

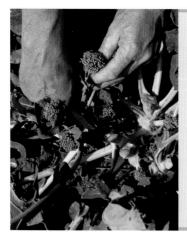

TENDER BUDS

Early varieties of sprouting broccoli, such as 'Rudolph', sown last May, should start sending forth tender stems, topped with tight purple or white buds, this month. Be sure to cut or snap off shoots before they get too long and the flowers open, and each plant could keep cropping for up to 8 weeks. Sprouting broccoli is delicious lightly steamed or stir-fried, and has a sweet flavor. The shoots must be cut before the flowers open, so freeze any that you can't eat within 2–3 days because they soon go past their best (pp.148–

GRATE RADISH

Try to bite into one of these large hardy winter radishes in the same way that you would a summer salad variety, and you may be disappointed with their rather tough texture. Instead, these unusual vegetables are a treat when grated into salads, or cooked in hearty winter stews. Sown in July, they keep their flavor best when left in the ground, but if winter conditions turn too harsh, lift and store them in sand, like carrots (pp.210–211).

HARVEST

SPROUTING BROCCOLI

WINTER RADISH

CELERIAC

APPLES

TWO CROPS IN ONE

This gnarled root vegetable, first sown in spring, will survive in the soil through most winters, and can be pulled when required. You can also cook and eat the leaves, which have a potent celery flavor. Try them added to soups or mixed with cabbage. To protect the roots in cold regions with regular hard frosts, cover the roots with shredded leaves or straw.

IN STORE NOW

Not all apples will keep past Christmas, but in ideal storage conditions (pp.194–195) some dessert varieties, such as 'Fuji', and late culinary varieties, like 'Melrose' and 'Suncrisp', will still be good to eat. Don't forget the sliced and stewed supplies squirreled away in the freezer.

COUNT YOUR CHICONS

About 3–4 weeks after being plunged into darkness (p.216) tasty, pale chicons, the forced new shoots of Belgian endive, should be ready to harvest. Cut them about 1 in (2.5 cm) above the root with a sharp knife and eat the crisp, slightly bitter leaves raw in salads or braised. Chicons will keep in the refrigerator, but wrap them to exclude light and prevent them from turning green. The cut root may resprout, giving a second crop, so don't forget to put it back in the dark. If it doesn't, discard the old root and

SPRING GREENS

Cut-and-come salads can be sown throughout the year (pp.28–29), and will crop through winter under cover, especially if you grow hardier varieties, such as corn salad. Pick regularly but sparingly, and try to alternate the plants you pick from, so they have time to re-grow. Only harvest healthy growth and discard any leaves damaged by frost.

BELGIAN ENDIVE

CUT-AND-COME-AGAIN SALAD

GARLIC

CHECK YOUR STORED GARLIC

Planted in fall or early spring and lifted the following summer, stored garlic bulbs start to sprout as spring approaches. Check your bulbs and roast them before they show green shoots.

SIGNS OF GROWTH
Discard any soft bulbs. Once one bulb shows signs of green shoots, the rest will quickly follow. Roast the bulbs to store for longer.

ROAST WHOLE
Remove any green shoots, drizzle olive oil over the bulbs and roast them in the oven at 350° F (180° C/ Gas 4) for about 30 minutes.

BACK IN STORAGE
Allow the garlic to cool before you store in jars under olive oil. Use the sweet-tasting cloves to flavor soups and stews.

DON'T FORGET

Keep a close eye on your stored crops, especially if they're still outside or in the garage or shed. Mice, birds, and many insects will be active in warmer spells, looking for something to eat.

Try also MAKING SOUP pages 226–227

HARVESTING IDEAS

Growing sprouting seeds

Packed with protein, vitamins, and minerals, sprouting seeds add a healthy fresh crunch to salads, sandwiches, and stir-fries all year round. They are incredibly quick and easy to grow—just add water—and in only a few days your crop will be ready to eat. All you need are some recommended seeds and a large jar with a perforated lid.

1 **Wash the jar well**, add the seeds and rinse them thoroughly with cold water. Only fill the jar about a third full to allow room for the seeds to grow. Fill with water and leave seeds to soak for 6–12 hours.

2 **Drain the jar thoroughly** and put it in a well-ventilated place out of direct sunlight. Rinse the seeds with cold water and drain completely twice daily. This keeps them fresh and will prevent them from drying out.

3 **After 2–4 days** for peas and beans, or 4–6 days for other seeds, the crop should be ready to eat. Try the sprouts at various stages to see which you prefer. Allow them to dry for a few hours before storing in the refrigerator.

4 **Make your own** sprouting jars by stretching muslin over the neck of a jar with an elastic band. Tiered trays are ideal for sprouting several types of seeds simultaneously. Sprouting bags are perfect for larger beans or peas.

Jo's TIPS

Only white mung beansprouts need to be kept in the dark. All other seeds will sprout in daylight, out of direct sun, and are less likely to go moldy in a well-ventilated spot than in a stuffy cabinet.

TRY THESE

Use only seeds sold specifically for sprouting to make sure they are suitable and that they have not been treated with chemicals such as synthetic fertilizers.

Aduki beans—Slightly sweet, these red-skinned beans produce short white sprouts. Ready to eat in 2–4 days.

Alfalfa—Always a favorite with its mild, nutty flavor and crisp shoots, this small seed sprouts in 4–6 days.

Broccoli—High in antioxidants, with a bold brassica taste. Best sprouted in seed mixes that take 3–6 days to crop.

Mung beans—Sprout in the dark for traditional Chinese beansprouts, or enjoy shorter shoots in 2–4 days.

GROWING SPROUTING SEEDS

February: ready to eat

There are plenty of treats this month. Think of luscious roast garlic in oil, or stored berries and apples made into winter pies and crumbles. If it's cold, brussels sprouts will be at their sweetest and best.

Raid the cabinet for the last pots of summer **jam**
pages 128–129

Leeks should be lasting well, so make the most of them

Green onion bulbs are swelling nicely under cover

Make some hearty **parsnip** soup

Hardy **winter cabbage** is usually reliable

There may be a few **apples** left in storage

Brussels sprouts taste best after frost

Stored **winter squashes** give a glow to gloomy days

Use up stored **winter radishes** while they're good to eat

Purple sprouting broccoli is getting into its stride—freeze some for later on

Make pies and crumbles using frozen **soft fruit**

Cook **Swiss chard** in the same way as spinach

Uncover stored **rutabagas** and use them in soups and stews

Keep cutting **radicchio**

Kale tastes delicious
boiled or used
in stir-fries

Use **salsify** as soon as you lift
it—this root dries out quickly

No need for a supermarket
trip if your stored **root
vegetables** are still good

Always
something
green with
**cut-and-
come again
salads**

Harvest **winter
cauliflower** when the
curds reach a good size

Never a dull meal—if
you use last fall's
pickles *pages 176–179*

Don't forget any **Jerusalem
artichokes** still in the ground

Sprouting seeds
pages 36–37 make a
crunchy salad topping

Endive
should still
be in good
shape under
cover

Shrubby **herbs**, such
as bay, sage, and
rosemary, can still be
clipped sparingly

Newly lifted **celeriac**
makes a good alternative
to mashed potato

*Use the
homemade
pesto put in
the freezer last
year page 147*

Enjoy roast **garlic**,
stored in oil in
January *page 35*

Use up
stored
onions
and
shallots

February: what to sow

CRUNCHY CELERY
Celery and celeriac need a long growing season, so should be sown indoors at 50–59° F (10–15° C). Sow celeriac, ½ in (1 cm) deep in cell packs or flats, to crop fall to spring. Sow celery on the surface of damp soilless mix, to enjoy from summer to winter. Grow both on indoors, to harden off and plant out later in spring.

HARVEST: **VARIOUS**

CHILE START
These heat-loving plants need a long, hot season to ripen well, and benefit from being sown early. Sow the seed indoors, ½ in (1 cm) deep, into pots or flats standing on a heating mat, or on a warm windowsill. Keep them moist and warm, at around 70° F (21° C).

HARVEST: **JUL–OCT**

SOW

CELERY & CELERIAC

CHILE PEPPERS

BROAD BEANS & PEAS

GLOBE ARTICHOKES

SOW PEAS AND BEANS
HARVEST: **VARIOUS**

If your soil isn't frozen or sodden, sow early broad bean outdoors, such as 'Windsor', to pick in May, plus early peas, like 'Early Frosty', for a June crop.

1 SOWING BEANS
Sow broad beans in drills, to bury them 2 in (5 cm) deep, and at 10 in (25 cm) apart, using a dibber at 8–10 in (20–25 cm) intervals.

2 SOWING PEAS
Peas prefer warm soil and germinate better if cloched. Sow 1½ in (4 cm) deep, 3–4 in (8–10 cm) apart, in 8 in (20 cm) wide drills.

3 STILL TOO COLD?
If outdoor conditions aren't suitable for sowing, start beans off in peat pots, and sow peas in gutters (p.27), under cover.

GOURMET VEG
Globe artichokes are gourmet vegetables that are expensive to buy, so it makes sense to grow your own. If you have space, and want plenty of these statuesque plants, the most economical way is to grow them from seed. Sow them ½ in (1 cm) deep in cell packs or flats in a propagator, or on a windowsill. Seed-raised plants can be variable, so only grow on the strongest seedlings.

HARVEST: **JUN–SEPT**

GROW BRASSICAS

Sow brussels sprouts and kohlrabi (p.208) ½ in (1 cm) deep in cell packs or trays in a heated propagator, or on a bright windowsill, to give them an early start. Choose early varieties of brussels sprouts to sow now, for a tasty crop from winter to spring. Kohlrabi, sown in a propagator this month to crop in early summer, need planting out before the plants are 2 in (5 cm) tall to reduce the risk of bolting. This fast-growing vegetable can also be sown successionally outdoors from early spring to late summer.

HARVEST: **VARIOUS**

SPEEDY SPINACH

Spinach is a fast-growing crop that can be prone to bolting when sown early. To help prevent this, sow the seed under cloches or in cold frames this month and next, using special bolting-resistent varieties, such as 'Tyee'. Sow the seed ½ in (1 cm) deep, in rows spaced about 12 in (30 cm) apart, thinning the seedlings 4–6 in (10–15 cm) apart.

HARVEST: **APR–NOV**

PARSNIPS

BRUSSELS SPROUTS & KOHLRABI

SPRING SPINACH

EARLY PARSNIPS

HARVEST: **NOV–APR**

If you live in a mild area, sow parsnips early for a long growing season, warming the soil with cloches or plastic to help improve germination.

1 MARKING OUT
Rake the seedbed to a fine tilth, removing any large stones. Make rows with a hoe, ¾ in (2 cm) deep and 12 in (30 cm) apart.

2 SPACE THE SEED
Sow three seeds per hole, spaced 4 in (10 cm) apart. Cover the seed and water well. Parsnips are slow to germinate.

3 GROW THEM ON
Cover early sowings with cloches for best results, and thin seedlings to one per space. Protect plants from carrot fly.

DON'T FORGET

If you live in a colder region, this may be your first opportunity to sow leeks, lettuce, onions (all p.26), cut-and-come-again salad, radish, peas (all p.27).
Indoors, grow sprouting seeds (pp.36–37).

See SOWING INSIDE page 42

SOWING FEATURE

Sowing inside

Even if you are new to vegetable growing, you will probably want to sow some crops indoors, and the advantages are undeniable. Sowing early, and providing additional warmth and shelter, gives tender plants a useful head start, allowing them to produce sooner and for longer. Seedlings raised under cover also often show stronger growth than those sown directly outside—and give better harvests.

A protected environment

There is nothing complicated about sowing seeds indoors, and it is not necessary to have a greenhouse. You simply need to give your plants a protected environment, whether you sow them in flats, or individual pots, or cell packs. The protection you provide could consist of a cold frame, a cloche, or just a sunny windowsill indoors.

Seedling plants under cover can be highly susceptible to diseases. You should constantly monitor their condition to ensure that warmth and humidity are maintained at the correct levels.

1 PREPARE SEED FLATS
Fill seed flats to about ½ in (1 cm) from the top with a high-quality seedstarting mix. Firm lightly, using the base of another flat or your fingers. Water well and allow to drain.

2 SOW SEEDS
Sow small seeds thinly over the surface, shaking them carefully from the packet or your hand. Plant larger seeds deeper, using a dibble or pencil to make a hole for each seed.

3 ADD TOP LAYER
Use a sieve to distribute a fine layer of mix or peat moss over the seeds. You may need to push soil over larger seeds with a dibble. If the seeds are vry small, try not to disturb them.

4 WATER GENTLY
Damp down the mix, using a watering can with a fine rose and taking care not to overwater. You should maintain this level of watering throughout germination.

5 COVER THE FLAT
To create a warm, moist atmosphere for germination, use a specially designed seed-starting kit. Alternatively, you can set the flat on a heating mat.

Pricking out seedlings

As soon as your seeds have germinated, remove them from the heating mator remove the lid from the flat, to help prevent fungal diseases. When the seedlings are large enough to handle, prick them out to grow on in individual pots.

6 LIFT SEEDLINGS
Holding each seedling very lightly by either of its first leaves, use a dibble or pencil to ease the plant out of the moist mix. Take care not to pull on the fragile roots.

7 PLANT INDIVIDUALLY
Fill individual pots or multi-celled seed flats with new mix and transfer the seedlings one at a time. Grow them on until they are sturdy enough to be planted out.

Sowing outside

Sowing directly into the soil is the simplest and cheapest way to raise vegetables. Preparing your seedbed well, sowing at the right depth, and getting the timing right can make the difference between a lush row of healthy plants and a frustratingly patchy harvest.

Good preparations

It is much easier to distinguish germinating vegetables from weed seedlings if they come up in a straight line. To achieve this, mark out your row by running string between pegs pushed into the ground at either end.

Sow larger seeds deeper than smaller ones. As a rule, make your row three times as deep as the seed. When you have sown your seeds (as illustrated below), carefully pull soil across the row to cover them, using a hoe or rake, or your hands.

Label the row clearly before removing the string line, because it is all too easy to forget what you have sown and where. Water the seeds in thoroughly, using a can fitted with a fine rose to avoid washing them away.

Jo's tips

Never sow into cold, wet soil because seeds may rot, or if they do come up, they're likely to bolt. Delay sowing until the weather improves or cloche the soil to warm it. Always protect seedbeds from mice, birds, and cats.

1 SOWING IN A ROW
To make a row, run the point of a hoe, or a bamboo cane, along the string line at a consistent depth. Pour seeds into the palm of your hand, take a pinch and sprinkle them thinly.

2 SPOT-SOWING
To reduce the need for thinning out, try "spot-sowing." Mark the row and use a dibble to create holes at the right depth and spacings for your crop. Sow three seeds in each hole.

February: what to plant

DON'T FORGET

Even hardy crops planted out now can be damaged by severe frosts, so always check the forecasts. Clear any snow from greenhouses, tunnels, and cold frames to prevent its weight from damaging them.

CHOOSE RHUBARB

HARVEST: **MAR–JUL**

Although rhubarb is best planted in fall when newly dormant (p.198), you can also plant now when the new stems are about to sprout.

'CHAMPAGNE'
This variety produces long, vibrant red stems with a sharp, sweet taste. It is good for cooking.

'TIMPERLEY EARLY'
Is an early variety, ideal for forcing in spring, that giving a heavy crop of long, thick, juicy stems.

'VICTORIA'
A late variety, suitable for colder areas where early growth could be damaged by spring frost.

PLANT

RHUBARB

JERUSALEM ARTICHOKES

SPRING GARLIC

TASTY ARTICHOKES

Before planting these knobbly tubers, bear in mind that they grow up to 3m (10ft) tall. The plant tolerates all but the worst soil and some shade, and can be planted in under-used corners. Artichokes also make a good screen because of their height. Plant the tubers 10cm (4in) deep, about 30cm (12in) apart, and leave 90cm (36in) between rows for maximum harvests. These plants can be invasive.

HARVEST: **NOV–MAR**

LATE GARLIC

If you have heavy soil and find that over-wintered garlic rots in the ground, prechill the bulbs and plant them in spring. Split the cloves and push them into the soil, flat end down, tops covered. Cloves planted in fall under cover (p.184) should be planted out now. Position 4 in (10 cm) apart, in rows with 10 in (25 cm) between them.

HARVEST: **JUL–AUG**

SHALLOTS AND LOTS OF ONIONS

HARVEST: **JUL–OCT**

Sets are small bulbs to plant now for an earlier crop than from seed-raised plants. Plant into well-prepared soil ¾ in (2 cm) deep.

Space onions 4 in (10 cm) apart, shallots 6 in (15 cm) apart, in rows spaced 12 in (30 cm). Buy virus-free stock if possible.

'RED BARON'
A productive onion with firm, dark red bulbs. Like all red varieties, it is mild enough to be eaten raw.

'STURON'
This is a storage onion, producing large, fleshy, brown-skinned bulbs. It has good resistance to bolting.

'LONGOR'
Described as a 'banana' shallot due to its elongated shape, this variety is easy to chop when cooking.

'RED SUN'
This is a red shallot, with white flesh and a mild flavor that can be eaten raw. It is good for pickling.

SHRUBBY HERBS

FRUIT TREES

ONIONS & SHALLOTS

HERBS IN POTS

HARVEST: **ALL YEAR**

Plant shrubby and evergreen herbs, such as bay, sage, and thyme in pots now to establish before summer.

1 PICK A POT
Choose a large enough container, make sure it has plenty of drainage holes, and part-fill with soil-based potting mix.

2 POSITION THE PLANT
Position the plant at the same depth as in its own pot, 2 in (5 cm) below the rim of the container. Fill with more mix and water well.

FRUIT TREES

This is a good time to plant bare-root fruit bushes and trees (pp.202–203), while they are still dormant. Before planting, improve the soil, digging in well-rotted manure or compost. Dig a hole deep and wide enough so the roots can be spread out fully. Drive in a stake for trees. Plant to the same level as the soil line on the stem. Backfill the hole, firm in well, and water thoroughly.

HARVEST: **VARIOUS**

Try COLD & HOT PICKLING pages 176–179

February: what to do

PROTECT BLOSSOM

Apricot and peach blossoms open so early in spring that they're highly vulnerable to damage from even relatively minor frosts. Damaged flowers will not set fruit. To protect your crop, cover the flowers with row cover draped over the branches. Protect wall-trained trees with a covered frame. Remove the cover on warmer days to allow insects in for pollination — see below.

WALL-TRAINED FIGS

In cool regions, fig trees crop once a year, forming embryonic fruit near the tips of their summer shoots. These are carried through winter to ripen the following summer. Prune trees now to encourage new fruit-bearing growth on fan-trained trees in spring, cutting back half the shoots that carried fruit last summer to one bud. Tie the unpruned fruit-bearing shoots to the horizontal wires, filling in spaces in the framework.

TEND

APRICOTS

FIGS

FRUIT CANES

PEACHES

PRUNE CANE FRUIT

Fall raspberries will fruit on canes produced this year, so cut all the canes back to the base now, before new growth appears. Summer raspberries and blackberries crop on last year's canes; these can be battered by harsh winter weather. Check your plants and cut any damaged tips back to a healthy bud. Secure any loose canes to their supports.

BE A BEE

Peaches and apricots come into flower this month, and must be pollinated if they're to produce fruit later in the year. If the weather remains cold, there will be few insects around to do the job. To ensure a crop, use a small, soft paintbrush to transfer pollen between flowers. Don't forget any trees covered against frost.

WINTER PRUNING

This is a good time to prune your currant and gooseberry bushes while they are still dormant. Prune up to a third of the older shoots at the base from your blackcurrant bushes. Also trim back by half the leading shoots of gooseberries; red- and whitecurrants, cut back sideshoots to two buds, and remove dead or overcrowded wood to open up the center of the bush. You can also prune hazelnuts now by shortening long sideshoots, which you may have "brutted" last summer (p.157), to three or four buds.

TURN COMPOST

This is a quiet month in the garden so take the opportunity to turn your compost heap. All heaps need to be turned at least once. Using a fork, break up any matted lumps, and move drier, uncomposted material from the top and edges of the heap, to the center. If the contents are mostly composted, empty the heap now and start again (pp.190–191).

FRUITS & NUTS

COMPOST

EARLY POTATOES

PRESPROUT POTATOES

To give your early potatoes a head start and produce a better crop, start the tubers indoors— presprouting. This isn't necessary with late varieties.

1 CHECK TUBERS
To plant out in 6 weeks' time, check through your seed potatoes now and discard any that are shriveled or diseased.

2 STAND IN BOXES
Take each tuber and find the end with the most buds or eyes. Stand it, this end up, in a box in a cool, light, frost-free place.

3 PLANT OUT
Stocky shoots should develop from each eye. When these are about 1 in (2.5 cm) long the tubers are ready for planting out.

DON'T FORGET

Take care when clearing fallen leaves and other debris, or turning the compost heap because at this time of year they may be sheltering beneficial animals, such as frogs, toads, and snakes (pp.104–105).

See START A COMPOST HEAP pages 190–191

Potatoes

Potatoes are easy to grow, and a good choice for new gardens because they tolerate and help break up recently cultivated soils. Many varieties have large, leafy tops and sprawling roots, and require lots of room for a family-size crop. If space is limited, get a decent harvest of new potatoes by growing them in containers or bags.

Early or late?

Choosing from the enormous range of varieties available is a hard task, even for experienced growers, but understanding the terminology is the first step to finding the right potato for you. Varieties are grouped as "early," "mid-season," and "late," according to the amount of time it takes them to mature. As you might expect, early varieties grow fastest and are ready in about 90 days, while late varieties can take up to 150 days before they are ready to harvest. Many gardeners choose to grow early varieties because they can be planted closer together, and produce a crop of baby new potatoes by early summer. They do give lower yields than late varieties, which are also a better choice if you want tubers to lift and store.

Eating qualities

When deciding between varieties, you'll also want to consider the texture, flavor, and even the color of varieties, before you select what to plant. Perhaps the most important factor is whether the flesh has a waxy or mealy texture. Waxy potatoes stay firm when cooked and are ideal for boiling, which makes them a good choice for salad potatoes. Varieties with a drier, mealy texture have an annoying habit of disintegrating when boiled, but are wonderful baked, roasted, or fried. Flavor is subjective, but there's no doubt that some varieties have a distinct nutty taste, while others are extremely mild. The color of both the skin and flesh can also influence your choice. Red-skinned varieties are irresistible baked, while yellow-fleshed types make appetizing salad potatoes.

Disease resistance

Like other crops, potatoes are susceptible to a number of pests and diseases, which rarely destroy the plants, but can often adversely affect the quantity and quality of tubers. Although not immune to them, early varieties tend to be less seriously affected by diseases, such as blight (p.242), and pests such as root-knot nematodes (p.238), simply because they are not in the ground as long as late varieties. If you are aware of a particular problem in your garden or area, then choose varieties that have some built-in resistance to the pest or disease. Blight-resistant potatoes include 'Elba', 'Kennebec', 'Sebago', and 'Rosa'.

TAKE YOUR PICK

1

4

7

EARLIES

1 'Foremost' is a tasty variety with firm white, waxy flesh that holds together well when boiled. It gives a good yield, stores well, and resists common scab.

2 'Red Duke of York' is a red-skinned variety with mealy flesh that is good eaten boiled, baked, roasted, or fried. This is a highly rated all-rounder.

3 'Accent' is a heavy-cropping variety, producing white-skinned potatoes with firm waxy flesh—best boiled. It has good resistance to nematodes and scab.

MID-SEASON

4 'Charlotte' matures later than most mid-season types, and has firm yellow, waxy flesh, with a good flavor. It also has some blight and scab resistance.

5 'Belle de Fontenay' is an early, white-skinned, waxy variety, often grown for salad potatoes. It has a good flavor; later tubers store well.

LATER VARIETIES

6 'Yukon Gold' produces large tubers, with golden skin and flesh. It has a good flavor, and is best baked, roasted, or fried. It keeps its attractive, buttery color after cooking.

7 'Pink Fir Apple' is a waxy, red-skinned potato, with long nobbly tubers. It crops in October and stores well. Best boiled, but can be fried.

8 'LaRatte' is usually grown as a salad potato. With a waxy texture and a delicious nutty flavor, it is highly versatile in the kitchen.

Other varieties to try:
'All-Blue'—late
'Caribe'—early
'Carola'—mid-season
'Chieftain'—early
'German Butterball'—late
'Kennebec'—mid-season

POTATOES

February: what to harvest

HEEL IN PARSNIPS
These large roots take up a lot of space, which is needed now for new seedbeds. To make room for spring planting, lift your remaining parsnips and store them in another part of the garden. Using a fork, carefully ease out the parsnips, taking care not to damage the roots, and heel them in elsewhere. Heeling-in simply involves digging a shallow-angled trench, where the roots can be laid close together and covered with soil. They will take up far less space and can be unearthed as required.

LAST CHANCE FOR SWEDES
If you left part of your swede crop to overwinter in the ground, now is the time to dig up any remaining roots. Even if they survive for longer without rotting or pest damage, they will become increasingly woody and inedible. This is your last chance to make use of the crop, and a good moment to clear ground that will soon be needed for new plantings. It's also worthwhile checking swedes in storage for pest damage or decay.

HARVEST

WINTER SALAD

PARSNIPS

SWEDES

WINTER CUT-AND-COME-AGAIN
Winter salads needn't be dull. Many leafy crops can be grown under cover as cut-and-come-again salad (pp.28–29) at this time of year.

Once the leaves are the size you prefer, cut them with scissors ¾in (2cm) above the soil and a new crop should regrow in a few weeks.

CHERVIL
This is commonly grown as an herb, and has a mild, parsleylike flavor. It can also be harvested as young leaves to spice up your salads.

TATSOI
With a mild, mustard flavor and a crisp texture, this salad leaf can be eaten raw or cooked. The plants are very hardy, ideal for cold areas.

ARUGULA
A few leaves of arugula can transform a salad. Cut the leaves when they are new and fresh because they turn bitter when older.

PERPETUAL SPINACH
The tender new leaves are delicious either in salads or cooked. Cut them from alternate plants to leave room for new growth along the row.

INDOOR HERBS

It's a real treat to have fresh herbs to pick throughout winter. Container-grown herbs, such as marjoram, mint, thyme, and parsley, will continue to thrive on the windowsill or in the conservatory with minimal attention. As long as you ensure that the plants are warm and watered, they should keep new growth coming until it's time for them to go back outdoors in spring. Use scissors to snip off the fresh tips when required.

LIFT ARTICHOKES

Jerusalem artichokes don't store well, so it's best to dig them up as required. Unearth the tubers with a fork, being careful not to spear any. Remove even unusable small ones because they will regrow in spring if left in the soil. Scrub the tubers with a brush, peel them, and use quickly for soups and side dishes before they discolor.

HERBS

JERUSALEM ARTICHOKES

LEEKS

ENDIVE

LATE LEEKS

Late-season leek varieties are very hardy and will stand in the ground until spring without spoiling their texture or flavor. Lift them as required with a fork. Their roots can hold on tightly, so loosen the soil to a good depth, to allow the leek to pull away without breaking. To avoid carrying a lot of soil into the kitchen, cut off the roots and drop them on the compost heap.

CUT ENDIVE

Endives growing under cover should resprout after cutting, so never uproot a plant when harvesting. Instead, cut the base of a mature endive head with a sharp knife and trim off any damaged leaves. Endives will keep for several days somewhere cool, as long as they are not stored damp.

March: ready to eat

As the days begin to lengthen, pick new leaves from windowsill herbs and cloched leafy crops, such as Swiss chard. Sprouting broccoli will be cropping profusely; freeze extra spears for later.

Keep picking your **sprouting broccoli**

Eat **sprouting seeds**
- alfalfa
- beansprouts
- broccoli
- fenugreek
pages 36–37

Windowsillherbs are starting to grow

This month, dig the last **Jerusalem artichokes**

Make hot desserts from **frozen fruit** *pages 150–151*

Brussels sprouts are finishing, freeze some for later *pages 148–149*

Eat stored **onions** and **shallots**

Pick fresh **cut-and-come-again** greens

Use cubes of frozen **herbs** and **pesto** *page 147*

Winter cabbage will soon be over—keep harvesting

Use stored **beets**, **potatoes**, **carrots**, and **rutabagas**

Unearth the last fresh **celeriac** roots now

Covered crops of **Swiss chard** and **spinach** will see you through until spring

New season **forced rhubarb** is deliciously sweet and tender

Use up fruit jams, made last year, ready for your new crops

Chutneys and **pickles** taste better as they mature

Kale is still cropping

Forced endive— end of season

This is your last chance to lift or use stored **winter radishes**

Lift more **leeks**

Cut **winter cauliflowers** while the heads are tightly closed

Drink **homemade wine**, made in summer
pages 180–181

Covered crops of **endive** finish this month—enjoy them in salads

Use the last **radicchio**, grown under cover

Salsify, freshly lifted, is a real culinary treat

Eat **roasted garlic** prepared in January
page 35

Cut undercover **green onions**

Dig sweet **parsnips** while you still can

Eat up late **frozen vegetables** to make space for new harvests

March: what to sow

TWO ROOTS
To keep them from bolting, sow summer beets and turnips in soil warmed under cold frames or cloches or in a greenhouse. Try bolt-resistant 'Red Ace' beet or 'Purple Top White Globe' turnip . In rows 8 in (20 cm) apart, sow seed ½ in (1 cm) deep. Thin beets to 3 in (8 cm) apart, and leave 4 in (10 cm) between turnips.

HARVEST: **VARIOUS**

EASY BROCCOLI
Unlike other brassica crops, broccoli does not transplant well from seedbeds. So, either sow directly outside at its final spacing of 12 in (30 cm) each way, or sow into cell packs outdoors or in a cold frame. You can then plant the seedlings out at the same spacing.

HARVEST: **JUN–OCT**

SOW

BRASSICAS

BEETS & TURNIPS

GREEN ONIONS

BROCCOLI

BRASSICA BASICS
Sow summer cabbage and cauliflowers now to harvest in summer and fall. Sprouting broccoli sown this month will produce spears in winter and early spring. Sow them in ½ in (1cm) deep rows in a seedbed, and transplant to their final spacing 5–6 weeks later. Net the young plants to keep birds off.

HARVEST: **VARIOUS**

NONSTOP ONIONS
For a constant supply of full-flavored salad onions throughout the year, start sowing outdoors now, and continue making further successional sowings every 2–3 weeks all summer. Weed the bed thoroughly first and make narrow rows about 4 in (10 cm) apart. Sow the seed very thinly, about one seed every ¾ in (2 cm), to reduce the need for thinning out later on.

HARVEST: **ALL YEAR**

EGGPLANT – BLACK MAGIC

HARVEST: **AUG–OCT**

Sow seeds ½ in (1 cm) deep, prick out, and pot them on once the seedlings reach 2 in (5 cm). Keep the seeds at a minimum temperature of 68° F (20° C).

'MONEYMAKER'
This is a reliable, early variety that produces large, deep purple fruit. Suitable for growing indoors or out, and also in patio containers.

'CALLIOPE'
Almost free of spines, this compact variety produces an abundance of small, 4 in (10 cm) long fruit. Pick often to ensure a sustained crop.

'BLACK ENORMA'
As its name suggests, this variety produces exceptionally large pure black fruit. Just two or three plants should keep you going.

STILL TIME TO SOW

In warm areas, sow outside: broad beans, onions, leeks (p.26), peas (p.27), arugula (p.29), parsnips and spinach (both p.41). Inside sow: radish, lettuce (both p.27) celeriac, celery, globe artichoke (all p.40), brussels sprouts and kohlrabi (p.41).

TOMATOES, PEPPERS & CHILES — CARROTS — EGGPLANTS

CROPS FOR SALSA

For indoor crops of tomatoes and chiles, sow now at about 68° F (20° C), in a heating mat or on a warm windowsill. Sow about ¾ in (2 cm) deep in cell packs or flats, and make sure seedlings get plenty of light to keep them from getting tall and leggy. Prompt pricking out and potting on will give plants plenty of space and ensure strong specimens. For outdoor crops, only sow when frosts are less severe, so the plants won't be ready too early to plant out.

HARVEST: **JUL–OCT**

COZY CARROTS

Carrots won't germinate in cold soil, so sow them now under cloches, and remove them as the weather warms. Choose early varieties like 'Early Nantes' and 'Parmex'. Rake the seedbed to a fine tilth and sow thinly in rows ½ in (1 cm) deep, 6 in (15 cm) apart. Early crops usually miss the worst carrot fly attacks.

HARVEST: **MAY–DEC**

TAKE YOUR PICK

Peppers

Heat-loving peppers are easy to grow in raised beds or on a sunny patio. Sow now, or buy young plants later in spring to give them a long season to grow and mature.

1 'Gypsy' is an early variety, maturing from greenish yellow to orange or red 2 weeks sooner than standard crops. The thin-skinned fruits reach up to 4 in (10 cm) long and are ideal in salads.

2 'Marconi' produces 6 in (15 cm) long, attractive, thick-walled fruits that are delicious eaten cooked or raw. Peppers can be harvested when green or left to sweeten as they turn red.

3 'California Wonder' produces 5 in (12 cm) long, bell-shaped fruits, that mature from green to deep red, and are perfect for stuffing. It is high-yielding and is ideal for growing in containers.

4 'Gourmet' is an early-ripening variety that produces a large crop of bright orange fruits, which are excellent cooked or eaten raw. It is compact and ideal for growing in containers.

5 'Tasty Grill' produces tapered red or yellow fruits up to 10 in (25 cm) in length, which, as the name suggests, are perfect for grilling. This is a sturdy plant, and very early bearing.

6 'Ingrid' is an unusual variety that matures dark brown, and is a change from familiar-looking peppers. The thick-skinned fruit have a mild flavor and ripen best in warmer areas.

Other varieties to try:
'Bell Boy'
'Jingle Bells'
'Lady Bell'
'New Ace'
'Red Knight'

Chile peppers

Compact and colorful, chiles are perfect for hot-summer areas or containers. The crop from just a few plants will spice up your cooking for a whole year.

1 'Aji Amarillo' is native to, and incredibly popular in, South America. It produces long, thin fruits that are medium-hot and especially useful for making sauces and salsas.

2 'Padron' produces 2 in (5 cm) long fruits, which can be eaten when young, green, and relatively mild, or left to heat up as the skin turns fiery red.

3 'Prairie Fire' produces masses of fast-growing, extremely fiery-tasting chile peppers. Fruits are only 1¼ in (3 cm) in length, and mature from cream to yellow and finally to a rich, bright red.

4 'Cherry Bomb' produces high yields of round, thick-walled fruits that ripen from green to red. Chiles are medium-hot and good for salsas or salads.

5 'Alma Paprika' fruits grow to around 2 in (5 cm) long, maturing from cream color through to red. They have a warm, sweet flavor and are perfect for grinding for use as paprika or eaten raw.

6 'Apache' is a compact plant, growing to 18 in (45 cm) high, so is ideal for growing in a container. Fruits are medium-hot and 1½ in (4 cm) in length.

Other varieties to try:
'Anaheim'—mild
'Caribbean Red'—hot
'Habanero'—hot
'Hungarian Hot Wax'—mild

PEPPERS AND CHILE PEPPERS

Beets

A breeze to grow in good soils, try successional sowings of white, yellow, striped, and red varieties, for a summer and fall of technicolor salads.

1 'Red Ace' is high-yielding and produces round to oval roots that are dark red in color. It is tolerant of a variety of soils, and also keeps well.

2 'Chioggia Pink' is rich dark pink on the outside with a striking pattern of pink and white circles inside. It is sweet and tender, and the young leaves can be used in salads or cooked like spinach.

3 'Pablo' produces high yields of round, smooth, dark red roots that are sweet and tasty, and can be grown as baby beets. The young leaves can be cooked like spinach or used in salads.

4 'Bulls Blood' is often grown as an ornamental, or as a cut-and-come-again salad crop, but its roots are a striking rich color and tender when young.

5 'Forono' produces 7 in (18 cm) long, cylindrical, red-purple roots, which are full of flavor. They have dark red flesh, and are particularly good for pickling, or for eating young in salads.

6 'Boltardy' is a popular choice, with globe-shaped, sweet, red roots. Both the leaves and the roots can be cooked or eaten raw in salads. It is high-yielding and very resistant to bolting.

Other varieties to try:
'Albina Vereduna'
'Burpee's Golden'
'Cylindra'
'Detroit Globe'
'Pronto'

Broccoli

For summer and fall crops, sow broccoli from now into summer. Sow thin-stemmed sprouting broccoli in summer to overwinter for a spring harvest.

1 'Bordeaux' is a heavy cropping sprouting variety with an usually long harvesting season. It produces very tender, tasty spears and is ideal to grow as an early crop.

2 'White Star' produces attractive creamy white spears in April and May. It can be cooked or eaten raw because it has a delicious, sweet flavor.

3 'Fiesta' is a variety that produces large, domed heads. Once the main head is harvested the plant will produce sideshoots, which can also be eaten.

4 'Romanesco' is excellent eaten raw or cooked because it has an exceptional, nutty flavor and a good firm texture. Worth growing for its attractive heads formed of distinctive, vivid green spirals.

5 'Late Purple Sprouting' is an unusual variety that produces an abundance of hardy, tender spears. Heads are packed with flavor and turn bright green when cooked.

6 'Claret' is a vigorous plant that produces large yields of thick, succulent, vividly colored spears. It is sown in late summer for a spring harvest.

Other varieties to try:
'Belstar'
'Blue Wind'
'DiCicco'
'Green Magic'
'Gypsy'

BEETS AND BROCCOLI

TAKE YOUR PICK

Tomatoes

Home-grown tomatoes taste so superior plucked ripe from the plant that it's hard to go back to grocery store ones when the harvest ends. They are easy to grow outside in a warm spot and, depending on variety, will also flourish in containers and on sunny windowsills. In cooler areas tomatoes may be more reliable grown in a greenhouse.

Right plant, right place

Before you buy tomato seed or young plants, consider where they will be growing. If you want a bumper crop from your greenhouse, you'll probably want to train tall plants to the roof apex to maximize your space. If you plan to grow them on windowsills or in hanging baskets, miniature bushy plants will be more suitable. Beefsteak tomatoes or special heirloom varieties ripen reliably planted in raised beds or beds covered with black plastic mulch. There is a variety to suit every gardener's needs, but you have to know what you're looking for to find what's right for you.

Vining or bush?

Tomatoes are only divided into two main growth habits, but are confusing because more than one name is commonly used for each. Tall "vining" or "indeterminate" varieties have a main stem that will grow to more than 6 ft (2 m) long in ideal conditions. In greenhouses, they are usually trained up supports, and their growing tip needs to be pinched out when they reach the desired height (p.103). Any sideshoots between the leaves and main stem are also removed to redirect the plant's energy from leaves to fruit production. When grown outdoors, vining tomatoes do well with more moderate pruning. In contrast "bush" or "determinate" varieties need no pinching out, because it is their sideshoots that develop and spread out over the soil carrying the fruit. These varieties often mature earlier and also perfect for growing under cloches, or in patio containers.

Choose your favorite fruit

By now, every tomato-lover knows that tomatoes aren't just red and round—some varieties ripen to orange, yellow, purple, or pink, and they can be found in an extraordinary array of shapes and sizes. Cherry tomatoes are small, often sweetly flavored types that are the easiest to grow and ripen outdoors in cooler climates. Standard, round salad tomatoes are good greenhouse performers, and will also do well outdoors in warmer areas. Boxy plum tomatoes are fleshy and solid, good for canning as whole tomatoes or tomato sauce. Large, ribbed beefsteak and marmande-types are well known for their meaty flesh and excellent flavor, but they need a long, hot growing season in order to do well.

BUSH TOMATOES

1 'Tumbler' has a trailing habit, making it ideal for baskets and containers. Keep basket-grown plants very well watered and fed for a good crop.

2 'Tumbling Tom Yellow' is a trailing variety that produces long trusses of small, golden orange fruit. Best grown outdoors in a protected spot.

3 'Totem' is a compact variety, ideal when space is limited because it can be grown in containers and windowboxes, and gives a good crop of sweet fruits.

VINING TOMATOES

4 'Gardener's Delight' produces a heavy crop of intensely flavored, bite-sized orange-red fruit. This vining variety is suitable for growing in a greenhouse or a garden bed.

5 'Sungold' matures golden-orange, giving a bright splash to salads. This tall indeterminate variety produces small, abundant fruit, which is reputed to be the sweetest available.

6 'Sweet Olive' produces small, fleshy, olive-shaped fruits with a rich flavor. The tall plants grow well inside and out, and require no pruning.

7 'Tigerella' is an early variety that gives a good crop of tangy fruit, with distinctive yellow-striped, red skin. It can be grown indoors or out.

8 'Marmande' produces large, fleshy, ribbed fruits with a distinctive rich flavor. These plants should be stopped at three trusses to allow fruit to ripen.

9 'Moneymaker' is a reliable variety that gives a good crop of tasty, midsized fruit. It can be grown inside or out, and is suitable for beginners.

Other varieties to try:
'Big Beef'—vining
'Black Russian'—vining
'Brandywine'—vining
'Early Girl'—vining
'Suncherry'—vining
'Sweet Million'—vining

TOMATOES

March: what to plant

A BUNCH OF CAULIFLOWERS

Early summer cauliflowers, sown in fall and overwintered under cover (p.184), are now ready for hardening off and planting out into their final positions. Choose good, firm soil, with a pH of 6.5–7.5, avoiding beds manured the previous fall or those where brassicas have recently been grown. Plant each cauliflower about 20 in (50 cm) from the next because they will develop into large plants. Place collars around the base of each to protect against cabbage maggot fly and net against birds, if necessary.

HARVEST: **JUN–AUG**

SPRING SPINACH

Spinach plants sown under cover last month (p.41) should be planted out now, after hardening off, to be ready for harvest later in spring. Plants can reach a good size, so space them 6 in (15 cm) apart with a distance of 12 in (30 cm) between rows, and protect them again with cloches if conditions turn cold. The lushest growth is produced on plants growing in rich, moist soil in full sun, so site plants accordingly.

HARVEST: **APR–NOV**

PLANT

CAULIFLOWERS

SPINACH

PEAS

GRAPES

SUMMER PEAS

Harden off young peas, sown in January, and plant in fertile soil and full sun. Dig a shallow trench for those sown into gutters (p.27), and slide the plants in all at once, to reduce root disturbance. Peas in peat pots should be planted 2–3 in (5–8 cm) apart. Insert supports, such as brush or stakes and netting (pp.88–89).

HARVEST: **JUN–OCT**

GROW GRAPES

On a sheltered site in full sun, fix horizontal support wires to a wall or to sturdy wooden posts—a south-facing wall is ideal. Improve the soil with compost. Plant vines 4 ft (1.2 m) apart and 10 in (25 cm) from the support base, and firm in well. Ensure that the graft union is above soil level.

HARVEST: **OCT–NOV**

BUDDING BROAD BEANS

After a short period of hardening off, plant out broad bean seedlings, sown in February, 6 in (15 cm) apart with 9 in (23 cm) between rows in full sun and good rich soil. In sheltered spots dwarf varieties may not need support, but if in doubt a simple system of stakes along each side of the row, with string or wire between them will be enough to keep mature plants from toppling over. Remember not to plant broad beans where they, or other peas or beans, have recently been grown.

HARVEST: **MAY–AUG**

PLANT BERRIES

Blackberries are tough plants and will tolerate slightly poor drainage, some shade, and even late frosts, but such hazards are best avoided. Improve the planting area with plenty of compost, and plant each cane to the depth it was in its pot, spaced 12 ft (4 m) apart. They require post and wire supports to keep the growth manageable.

HARVEST: **JUL–OCT**

FIRST EARLY POTATOES

BROAD BEANS

BLACKBERRIES

PLANT POTATOES

HARVEST: **JUN–SEP**

Plant early varieties if the soil isn't frozen. Their roots help break up newly cultivated earth and they like a sunny site, with deep, fertile soil.

1 PRESPROUTING
Presprouted tubers provide a jump on the harvest. Dig 6 in (15 cm) deep rows, 15 in (38 cm) apart to give them plenty of room.

2 PLANTING
Carefully place a potato 'rose-end' up in the bottom of the row every 12 in (30 cm), trying not to damage the shoots.

3 COVERING
Rake soil over to cover the row. If the weather is cold, a thick mulch of compost or well-rotted manure will help protect the tubers.

DON'T FORGET

Frosts may be less severe this month but keep cloches, row cover, and even sheets of newspaper handy to protect emerging crops on cold nights. Also protect young plants from slugs and snails.

See FREEZING FRUIT pages 150–151

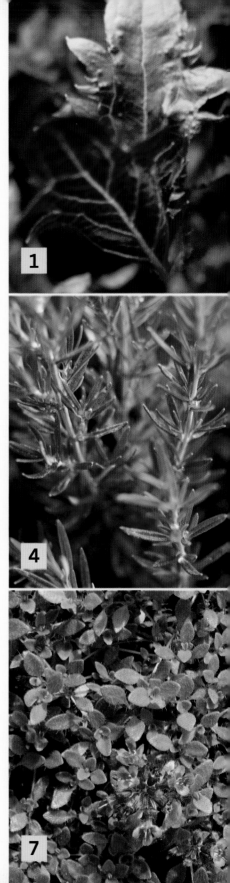

1

4

7

Herbs

If you grow only one edible thing, make it herbs. It's easy to buy culinary herbs, but picked fresh from the garden they have a more intense flavor. Many need little attention and with their colorful, aromatic foliage, and, in some, attractive flowers, they are ideal not just in dedicated herb gardens, but also in flower beds and pots.

TAKE YOUR PICK

Where to grow herbs

A number of favorite garden herbs, such as rosemary, thyme, and marjoram, come from the Mediterranean, and love growing in free-draining soil in full sun. These plants have evolved to cope with dry conditions and relatively poor soil, where many other plants would struggle, so they are perfect for placing in awkward spots, such as the base of a sunny wall. There are also herbs that prefer moister conditions and will tolerate some shade. Parsley, mint, and chives all fall into this group and produce the lushest growth in soil that has been improved with plenty of organic matter. Whether you are planning an herb garden or just experimenting with one or two varieties, these requirements are worth bearing in mind.

Containers

Herbs do well in containers. In fact, if you have heavy soil they are likely to grow better in free-draining potting mix than they do in the ground. Make sure the pots have plenty of drainage holes and that you use a mix with perlite or vermiculite to improve drainage. Pots can be placed close to the kitchen door, so that when you want to add an aromatic flourish to your cooking, you can step right outside and pick what herbs you want.

Planting and maintenance

The simplest herbs to grow in the garden are perennials, such as sage and marjoram, which are usually bought as small plants. Once in the ground, they flourish year after year with minimal attention. Most perennials benefit from cutting back in summer, after flowering, which helps keep the plant compact and encourages a fresh flush of growth that is ideal for picking.

Mint, another perennial, has shoots that spread just below the soil surface, which allows it to rapidly become invasive. To help prevent this, plant mint in sunken pots and regularly remove any escaping shoots.

Basil and cilantro are annuals, which flower in their first season and then die. They must be grown from seed each year. Sow every 3–4 weeks from spring onward so that you have a succession of plants to pick throughout the summer. Biennial herbs, such as parsley, flower in their second year, but any biennials that you use frequently are best sown every year in the same way as annuals.

1 Basil Deliciously sweet with a hint of anise, basil is a tender annual that can be sown between mid-spring and midsummer, in full sun and heat.

2 Cilantro Perfect for dishes with Asian flavors, this annual should be sown successionally from early spring until late summer, because it often goes to seed quickly.

3 Mint A vigorous perennial, mint comes in many interesting varieties, all of which can be invasive. Grow it in well-watered pots or a container sunk into the soil.

4 Rosemary Easy to grow, this perennial Mediterranean shrub looks good in flower beds. To keep plants bushy, cut them back after their light blue spring flowers have died down.

5 Parsley Curly or flat-leaved, this hardy biennial herb grows well in pots and tolerates some shade. Sow it at regular intervals from spring into summer.

6 Marjoram Loved by butterflies and bees, perennial marjoram has pink summer flowers and grows best in full sun, although the attractive golden-leaved varieties appreciate a little shade.

7 Thyme This low-growing perennial is available in a huge range of varieties, all of which thrive and develop the fullest flavor in dry, sunny conditions.

8 Sage A beautiful perennial garden plant that thrives in sunny conditions, sage benefits from being pruned in late spring after its blue flowers have finished, to keep it compact.

9 Chives Easy to grow from seed or as divisions from existing plants, chives appreciate a moist soil. They make a lovely edging plant with pink pom-pon flowers in spring, and sometimes a second flush of flowers in summer.

Other varieties to try:
Dill—annual
Fennel—perennial
French tarragon—perennial

HERBS

March: what to do

CLEAR FOR CULTIVATION
Mulches help suppress weeds in beds where crops are growing or in areas being cleared for cultivation. Black paper mulch (see left) is permeable to rain, so it is useful for growing crops through, but you might need to irrigate beneath it. You could also cover large weedy areas for a few months with old carpet to kill off perennial weeds before cultivation. Organic mulches, such as compost or straw, should be laid at least 2 in (5 cm) thick. In addition to discouraging weeds, they add organic matter to the soil.

WAR ON WEEDS
Weeds compete with seedlings for light, moisture, and nutrients, so give your vegetables a head start by removing all weeds from seedbeds and planting areas. Annual weed seedlings can simply be hoed off and the debris raked up. Perennial weeds need to be dealt with more rigorously. Dig them out with a fork and make sure you remove every scrap of their roots. If you don't, most of them will regrow in a short time.

TEND

SUPPRESS WEEDS

DIG OUT WEEDS

HERBS

MULCH

HELP FOR HERBS
Encourage a fresh flush of fragrant leaves on perennial herbs such as rosemary, marjoram, sage, and thyme, by pruning them back before growth starts. This treatment also helps keep plants compact and an attractive shape. With perennials that die right back, such as mint and fennel, clear away any of last year's dead stems to make way for new shoots.

IMPROVE SOIL
To get the best from your fruit trees and bushes it's important to keep the soil in good condition, especially if your soil is light nad sandy. Lay a generous mulch of compost or well-rotted manure, at least 2 in (5 cm) thick, at the base of each one, allowing space around the canes or trunk to avoid the risk of rot.

SPRING BOOST

Crops that have come through a hard winter can look distinctly the worse for wear at this time of year. If your cabbages, purple sprouting broccoli, kale, or overwintered onions have yellowing leaves, it's a sure sign that they could do with an early spring boost. To perk them up, apply a balanced fertilizer this month.

BEDS FOR BEANS

Pole beans and celery grow best on a rich soil that retains plenty of moisture. To encourage strong growth, prepare their beds in advance of planting. A traditional way to provide the right conditions involves digging a trench about 12 in (30 cm) deep and 18 in (45 cm) wide. Work in plenty of well-rotted manure or household compost as you backfill the trench. Beans are legumes and supply their own nitrogen, so if manure and compost are scarce, use kitchen peelings to help retain moisture.

FEED

PREPARE THE SOIL

SEEDLINGS

PRICK OUT SEEDLINGS

If your seed-starting kit (p.42) or windowsill is full of tomato, pepper, celery, or other seedlings, start pricking them out into individual pots.

1 REMOVE FROM TRAY
Using a small dibble or pencil, loosen the roots of each seedling and lift it from the soil by the first pair of leaves, not by its stem.

2 REPOT
Plant out in separate cells or pots. Make a hole with the dibble and replant the seedling. Gently firm the mix and water in.

3 HARDEN OFF
To acclimatize the seedlings to outdoor conditions, harden them off in a cold frame with a lid that can be opened and closed.

DON'T FORGET

Pests are beginning to emerge this month, so look out for snail trails and signs of marauding insects. Decide how you want to approach pest control (pp.104–105) and be ready to take action.

See START A COMPOST HEAP pages 190-191

GROWING IDEAS

Growing mushrooms

Mushrooms are an unusual crop but once you've grasped the basic technique, they're easy to grow and can provide a worthwhile harvest from unused spots outdoors, or in a dark corner inside. The familiar white and brown cap mushrooms are the quickest and easiest, but you can also grow more exotic species, like oyster mushrooms.

1 **It's simple to grow** your own white cap mushrooms from a kit at any time of year, as long as you have the correct growing conditions. Pour the specialized soil into the tray or container provided. Break up lumps.

2 **Moisten the soil** thoroughly. Carefully open the package of mushroom spawn and scatter it evenly over the soil. Gently mix it into the surface using your hand or a hand fork. Don't mix the spores in deeply.

3 **Cover the container** with the lid or use layers of damp newspaper. Place it somewhere at around 59°F (15°C) and keep it moist. Mushrooms don't need to be in the dark, just out of direct sunlight; a shed would work.

4 **After about 14 days**, weblike mycelium should be visible on the surface. Remove any newspaper and cover the mycelium with 1 in (2.5 cm) of soil, keeping it moist. The first mushrooms will appear in 10 weeks.

TRY THESE

There are many different types of mushrooms and growing kits to try at home. Some are more complicated than others—just follow the instructions given.

White cap mushrooms—Much tastier when home-grown, these are quick and easy to grow throughout the year.

Oyster mushrooms—Grown outdoors on logs, you'll need patience until these bear fruit in spring and fall.

Shiitake mushrooms—These are grown on logs, shocked into fruiting by soaking in cold water for 48 hours.

Brown cap mushrooms—Also known as chestnut mushrooms, these are grown in the same way as white caps.

GROWING MUSHROOMS

March: what to harvest

TASTY FLORETS
After a May sowing and the winter spent outside, hardy cauliflowers, such as 'Maystar', should start developing their large, white curds this month. Cauliflowers are best cut while the curds are still firm and healthy, or else the heads can yellow and open. They do, however, have a tendency to mature all at once. Split into florets and freeze surpluses (pp.148–149) or pickle them (pp.176–179).

RED STALKS
In good weather, rhubarb will start sending up tasty red-tinted stems. Only harvest from mature plants over 2 years old, picking what you need by gripping them near the base and pulling. Don't cut the stems because the stump left can encourage rot to set into the crown.

HARVEST

WINTER CAULIFLOWER

RHUBARB

CHICORY & RADICCHIO

CABBAGE & SPROUTS

THE BITTER END
Bitter-leaved radicchio and endive sown in late summer and grown under cover through the winter, will be coming to an end this month. Radicchos, such as 'Palla Rossa Verona', can be harvested by snipping off individual leaves, or cutting the whole head with a sharp knife just above ground level. Cut the entire heads of broad-leaved endive. Even at this late stage both types may resprout to provide further harvests, so if their space isn't needed for another crop, leave them in the ground to grow on, but water them well to encourage new shoots.

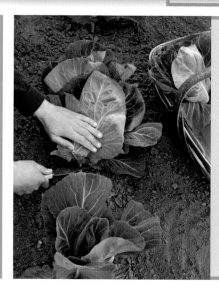

LAST BRASSICAS
New spring crops may be just around the corner but don't be tempted to overlook the last of your hardy winter brassicas. Having started at the bottom, you'll probably be picking near the tops of the stems of late sprout varieties, such as 'Exodus' and 'Trafalgar', by now. When the sproufts are finished, remember to cut the delicious leafy tops, too. You should also pull up or cut winter cabbages as required, trimming away any weather-damaged outer leaves. After harvesting, dig up the roots. If there are any signs of disease, such as clubroot, burn them—don't compost them.

GROW BETTER SWISS CHARD

Swiss chard sown in late summer (p.154) will survive most winters outdoors and start growing again this month, with fresh leaves to crop. Cut back old battered growth and pull bright new leaves away at the base. The succulent stems are good to eat.

'RHUBARB CHARD'
As its name suggests, this variety has ruby-red stems and purple-flushed foliage, much like rhubarb. It is also good for winter color.

'LUCULLUS'
This is a prolific chard that gives a good crop of white-stemmed leaves. Like all chard, its stems can be cooked and served like asparagus.

'BRIGHT YELLOW'
All chard resprouts early in spring, providing tender new leaves. Use this variety raw to add a cheery splash of color to your salads.

PERPETUAL SPINACH
Easy to grow, this thin-stemmed variety is hardier than true spinach, and gives a reliable, tasty crop. It is a good choice for drier soil.

SWISS CHARD

STORED ROOTS

GREEN ONIONS

ROOT CHECK

All of your stored winter root crops (pp.210–211), like carrots and beets, should be used up in soups and stews as soon as possible. Check through them and discard any that are showing signs of decay. Don't be tempted to bring what's left indoors to keep in the refrigerator, because they will shrivel up and spoil much faster there than in their original stores.

EARLY ONIONS

Start harvesting hardy varieties of green onions, such as 'Evergreen Hardy White', sown in late summer or early fall, and over-wintered outside. If the soil has become compacted around the bulbs, loosen it with a hand fork before picking—onions can easily break if pulled too hard.

April: ready to eat

Enjoy a wintry feast and finish up the vegetables such as brussels sprouts and leeks that have fed you during the lean winter months. Pea shoots, spinach, and other spring crops will begin to take their place.

New **lettuces** grown under cover can be harvested as loose leaves

Last year's **jam** *pages 128–129* is still useful for pies or scones

Colorful **Swiss chard** is both good to eat and ornamental

Purple sprouting broccoli will finish producing this month

Whatever the season, there are always **cut-and-come-again crops**

Check in your cabinet for any **pickles** *pages 176–179* that need eating

Pick the last **brussels sprouts** and also harvest the tops as an alternative to cabbage

Shallots, onions, and **garlic** are handy to have in storage

It's end of season for **kale**, so freeze any surpluses for later

Mushrooms *pages 68–69* grown earlier this year should be popping up now

End of winter spell the last of the fresh **leeks**

New-season **spinach**— a welcome spring crop

If you haven't finished your **celeriac**, pickle what's left for later in the year *pages 176–179*

Spring cabbage comes in as winter cabbage bows out

Sprouting seeds *pages 36–37* are the easiest crop of all

Homemade white wine pages 180–181 matures rapidly. Open a bottle of last year's now.

Make some fresh **mint** sauce to go with spring lamb

There are plenty of delicious recipes for **winter cauliflower**

If you've no fresh herbs to snip, use dried ones in your cooking

Summer radishes are just coming in—sample them at their youngest and freshest

Eat **frozen vegetables** *pages 148–149* from last year to make room in the freezer for new harvests

Too early for peas, but not for picking **shoots** from early pea sowings

It's now or never for eating the last few **Jerusalem artichokes**

Green onions—pick some, leave some for later

Use the last **parsnips**; cut up and freeze any that you don't need right now

Tender new season forced **rhubarb** has an exquisite flavor

Winter cabbage gives way to wonderful spring salad crops

Stored **rutabagas** are still on duty in the kitchen

Salsify will keep going for a little longer

Windowsill **herbs** are coming into new growth

April: what to sow

SOW ON CUE

Sow cucumbers and zucchini at the end of the month to give them a head start, especially those you plan to grow on under cover. Sow cucumbers ¾ in (2 cm) deep in small peat pots and place them on a heated mat or on a warm windowsill, at about 68°F (20°C). Sow zucchini in the same way, but at 59°F (15°C).

● HARVEST: **JUL–OCT**

BEAN FEAST

For an early start for snap and runner beans, warm the soil with cloches and sow beneath them, or sow into small peat pots under cover, 2 in (5 cm) deep, and plant out later. If sowing outside, space pole beans 12 in (30 cm) apart, and bush beans, 8 in (20 cm) apart.

● HARVEST: **JUL–OCT**

SOW

CUCUMBER & ZUCCHINI

BEANS

MELONS

FENNEL & ENDIVE

TRY MELONS

HARVEST: **AUG–SEP**

Sow two seeds, ¾ in (2 cm) deep in small pots at 64°F (18°C). Once germinated, thin the weakest, water sparingly, and grow the plants on a few degrees cooler.

'BLENHEIM ORANGE'
This is a traditional variety, with netted, green skin and orange-red flesh. It has a good flavor, and is suitable for cooler regions.

CANTALOUPE
This is a type of melon, not just a variety, and produces small fruit with yellow skins and flesh. Good in cooler areas, even outdoors.

'ANTALYA'
This is a galia-type melon, with netted, yellow skin and sweet, green flesh. Plant through black plastic mulch for extra heat.

LUXURY VEG

Sow Florence fennel and endive to harvest during the summer. Raise plants in cell packs under cover to transplant later, or sow seed directly outdoors if the soil is above 50°F (10°C)—Florence fennel may bolt in colder soil. Sow seed ½ in (1 cm) deep. Outdoors, sow thinly in rows 10 in (25 cm) apart for endive, 12 in (30 cm) apart for Florence fennel. Thin the seedlings promptly.

HARVEST: **VARIOUS**

GROW GREENS

In areas with cool summers, sow kale this month to harvest in the fall and winter, plus summer and fall cauliflowers. Sow them outdoors in rows or into pots, ½ in (1 cm) deep, thinning those sown in the soil to 3–4 in (8–10 cm) apart. Grow the plants on and transplant them into their final positions in June. Space kale plants 18 in (45 cm) apart, and the cauliflowers 24 in (60 cm), and water well. Cover the seedlings and young plants with nets in areas where birds can be a problem.

● HARVEST: **VARIOUS**

LETTUCE SEASON

You can sow lettuce seed almost all year but now is peak season. Sow seed thinly, ½ in (1 cm) deep, either directly in rows, 8–14 in (20–35 cm) apart, depending on variety, or in cell packs to plant out later. The latter method is ideal for plants to pop into odd gaps or pots. Be vigilant—slugs will find young lettuce seedlings quickly.

● HARVEST: **MAY–NOV**

KALE & CAULIFLOWER

SUMMER LETTUCE

SWEET CORN

SWEET CORN FOR SUMMER

HARVEST: **AUG–OCT**

Sweet corn is a tender crop that germinates better in warm soil. Wait to plant until the soil temperature is above 55° F (13° C).

1 MARKING OUT
Corn make tall plants, so give them space. Sow clusters of seeds 14 in (35 cm) apart, in rows with 24 in (60 cm) between them.

2 BLOCK PLANTING
The flowers are pollinated by wind, which is essential for the ears to form fully. Plant in blocks to help ensure good pollination.

3 SOWING INDOORS
If you live in a cooler area, sow seed singly, 1½ in (4 cm) deep, in cell packs or pots, under a cold frame or in a greenhouse.

STILL TIME TO SOW

Outside sow: leeks, onion (p.26), peas (p.27), parsnips, brussels sprouts, kohlrabi, spinach, (p.41), cabbage, turnips (p.54), carrots (p.55). Indoors: celeriac (p.40), broccoli (p.54), tomatoes, peppers, and eggplant (p.55).

Snap and wax beans

Easy to grow, snap and wax beans are picked young for their pods. Both tall pole varieties and compact bush types are available.

1 'Rocquencourt' is an unusual yellow-podded bush bean that can be grown without support. The flowers and pods make this variety attractive enough to grow in a patio container.

2 'Delinel' produces a large, reliable harvest of pencil-thin, stringless pods when picked regularly. Growing to only 18 in (45 cm) tall, it is suitable for containers. Water and feed well.

3 'The Prince' gives a good crop of flattened pods, similar to young runner beans. This bush variety has a delicious flavor, especially when young, and is a good choice for freezing (pp.148–149).

4 'Blue Lake' is a pole variety that produces a heavy yield of sweet-tasting, stringless pods when picked regularly. A bush-type version of this variety is also available.

5 'Purple Teepee' is a bush variety that gives a good harvest of distinctive purple pods, which turn green when cooked. Young beans can be eaten raw and added to salads for extra color.

6 'Cobra' is a pole bean that gives a plentiful supply of slender, stringless pods. Its purple flowers are especially attractive, allowing it to be grown in mixed borders—ideal for small yards.

Other varieties to try:
'Fortex'—pole
'Kentucky Blue'—pole
'Provider'—bush
'Rocdor'—bush
'Tavera'—bush

TAKE YOUR PICK

Runner beans

Eaten as pods, sliced or whole, runner beans are a must for every vegetable patch. Some types are also good for dried beans.

1 'White Lady' gives a good crop of thick, succulent pods. The white flowers are not as attractive to birds, which make them less prone to damage. The plant sets beans in hot, dry conditions, unlike many others.

2 'Polestar' is a stringless variety, making the beans easier to prepare in the kitchen. If picked regularly, it gives a good crop until the end of summer. The smooth beans freeze well.

3 'Painted Lady' has very attractive bicolored flowers, and is almost as good to look at, as it is to eat. It produces delicious beans, and is a good choice to grow in mixed garden borders.

4 'Desiree' produces a heavy crop of fleshy green pods, making it a good choice for where space is limited. You'll only need a few plants to stay supplied with beans all summer.

5 'Lady Di' gives a very heavy crop of long, stringless pods. The beans inside are slow to develop, which means the pods can be left to grow for longer without becoming too tough.

Other varieties to try:
'French Horticultural'
'Hestia'—bush variety
'Nightfall'
'Scarlet Emperor'
'White Apollo'

BEANS

Zucchini

Just two or three of these vigorous plants will supply you with plenty of tender fruit in a wide variety of shapes and colors. You can harvest the flowers too.

1 'Elite' is an early variety that matures 2 weeks sooner than standard crops. The shiny green fruits are best picked when 6 in (15 cm) long.

2 'Jemmer' is a productive variety. The long golden fruits are easy to spot among the leaves, so fewer will be accidentally left behind.

3 'Venus' is a compact variety that produces dark green fruits from July until the first frosts. Harvest regularly to encourage a sustained crop.

4 'Defender' produces a very high yield, making it a good choice if you only have room for a few plants. It is resistant to cucumber mosaic virus (p.241).

5 'Parador' is a golden-fruited variety that matures early, and will bear prolifically through summer. Harvest young for salad-sized zucchinis.

Other varieties to try:
'Eight Ball'—round
'Gold Rush'—bush
'Patriot'—bush
'Raven'—bush
'Tigress'—bush

Sweet corn

These tall plants look good in a border as well as in the vegetable bed. Other crops will also grow between the stems, making this a useful crop in smaller plots.

1 'Lark' produces, sweet-tasting kernels that are thin skinned and tender enough to eat raw or cooked. It is a mid-season variety that performs well in cool areas.

2 'Indian summer' produces white, yellow, red, and purple kernels, giving its ears a multicolored appearance. This sweet-tasting variety performs best in warmer areas.

3 'Swift' is a dwarf sweet corn that produces thin-skinned, sweet-tasting ears that reach up to 8 in (20 cm) long. This variety matures early and performs well in cooler climates.

4 'Sundance' is a good choice for cooler regions, and reliably produces an early crop of 7 in (18 cm) long, yellow ears. The kernels are sweet and creamy.

5 'Butterscotch' is as early-maturing variety with tender kernels that stay sweet even after freezing. It grows to just 5 ft (1.5 m) tall, shorter than many.

Other varieties to try:
'Butter & Sugar'
'Honey Bantam'
'Minipop'
'Silver Queen'
'Sugar Buns'

ZUCCHINIS AND SWEET CORN

Cucumbers

Home-grown cucumbers are so much better than those from the store. Provide a sunny, warm spot and a trellis or other support for the best harvest.

1 'Marketmore' is a favorite variety, and gives a prolonged crop of fruits, each measuring up to 8 in (20 cm) long. It is resistant to both downy and powdery mildew (p.241 and p.243).

2 'Crystal Apple' can be grown outside, and has pale yellow-green fruit the size of apples. These are sweet and juicy, and appeal to children. They're also suitable for pickling (pp.176–179).

3 'Masterpiece' is a standard variety that produces a steady supply of slightly prickly, dark green fruit. These are best harvested at 8 in (20 cm) long. Plant two or three for a summer-long harvest.

4 'Carmen' is an all-female greenhouse cucumber that produces long green fruit throughout the summer. It is disease-resistant, making it a good choice for organic gardeners.

5 'Burpless Tasty Green' produces lots of crisp, tasty fruit that can be harvested at 10 in (25 cm) long. As its name suggests, the fruit won't cause indigestion. It is very easy to grow.

6 'Passandra' is a miniature, indoor variety and bears fruit, half the normal size, on every flower. It is resistant to downy and powdery mildew, as well as cucumber mosaic virus (p.241).

Other varieties to try:
'Northern Pickling'—pickler
'Suyo Long'—burpless
'Diva'—seedless
'Sweet Success'—seedless
'Regal'—pickler

Lettuce

Some types of lettuce have dense hearts, others do not. All grow fast from seed, and can be sown under cover in winter or outside from spring onward.

1 'Tom Thumb' is a butterhead variety, and quickly forms a solid head of soft, ruffled, tasty leaves. It is a compact plant and can be grown closely packed together. It is suitable for containers.

2 'Winter Density' is a hardy cos lettuce, that in mild areas, can be sown outside in fall (p.166) ready to harvest in spring. It is also suitable for spring and summer sowing.

3 'Lollo Rosso' is a highly attractive loose-leaf lettuce. Its frilly leaves are flushed with red and look good in mixed beds or containers. Cut the leaves as you need them, or the whole head.

4 'Sioux' is an iceberg lettuce, and forms a dense head of red-tinted leaves that become brighter into summer. It is good in smaller gardens because it can be treated as an edible bedding plant.

5 'Pinokkio' is a cos variety that produces small, neat heads of sweet-tasting, dark green leaves. Single leaves can be cut 6 weeks after sowing, or the plant can be left to heart-up for another 4 weeks.

6 'Freckles' is a cos lettuce with bold, red-splashed leaves. It is very attractive in the garden and in salads. Grow it in containers for color and a handy crop. Water well, especially during dry spells.

Other varieties to try:
'All Year Round'—butterhead
'Clarion'—butterhead
'Green Salad Bowl'—loose-leaf
'Little Gem'—cos
'Saladin'—crisphead

CUCUMBERS AND LETTUCE

April: what to plant

SPEEDY STRAWBERRIES
If you're looking for a quick crop from plants put in between now and early summer, then cold-stored plants are the answer. Often available by mail order, these unpromising looking specimens will quickly put on new leaves, send out flowers and should fruit within 60 days of planting. Plant in soil improved with plenty of compost where strawberries haven't recently been grown, or in large pots.

HARVEST: **JUN–SEP**

GROW GLOBES
Harden off and plant out winter-sown kohlrabi before the plants get too big. This decreases the likelihood of bolting; plant out and cover with cloches rather than delay. Space plants 9in (23cm) apart and leave 12in (30cm) between the rows.

HARVEST: **JUN–NOV**

PLANT

STRAWBERRIES

KOHLRABI

HERBS

LETTUCE

HERB PLANTING
Few jobs in the garden are as rewarding as planting up an herb patch. They grow in all shapes and sizes, so pick the right ones for where you want them.

HARVEST: **VARIOUS**

UPRIGHTS
Plant taller, upright herbs, such as bronze- and green-leaved fennel, toward the back of your herb bed, to give it height.

SPREADERS
Some herbs, such as mint, spread quickly and may over-run slower growers. Plant these in sunken pots to restrict their spread.

LOW CREEPERS
Plant a mixture of low, spreading herbs, like thyme and marjoram, at the front of your garden to create a carpet of summer color.

SUMMER SALAD
Lettuces raised from seed under cover (p.26) will be ready to plant out now, either spaced 12–14in (30–35cm) apart in beds or in large pots and growing bags on a sheltered patio. Young plants may also become available in nurseries and garden centers this month, which are ideal for filling gaps before other crops get going. Cover with a cloche if the weather turns cold.

HARVEST: **MAY–NOV**

PLANT OUT ONIONS

Now is the time to plant out the onion seedlings sown in spring (p.26), positioning them 6 in (15 cm) apart using a dibble. Any sets not sown earlier (p.45) can also be planted now at the same distances. Avoid planting larger sets, which are prone to bolting, and only plant them out when the soil is warm and workable. Rake the soil lightly to loosen it and make a shallow row about 1 in (2.5 cm) deep, the length of your row. Push each set gently into the ground so that its tip is just level with the soil surface.

HARVEST: **JUL–OCT**

PLANT POTATOES

Buy certified disease-free seed potatoes, which can be presprouted, but there is thought to be little benefit to late yields. In rows 6 in (15 cm) deep, place a potato "rose-end" up every 15 in (38 cm). Cover with soil and space further rows 30 in (75 cm) apart. Late potatoes are below ground longer than early varieties but store well over winter.

HARVEST: **SEP–OCT**

ONIONS

POTATOES

ASPARAGUS & ARTICHOKES

PLANT OUT PERENNIALS

HARVEST: **VARIOUS**

Spring asparagus and summer globe artichokes need fertile, well-drained soil in full sun. Buy artichokes as young plants, asparagus as 1-year-old crowns.

1 DIG FOR ASPARAGUS
Dig a 12 in (30 cm) wide and 8 in (20 cm) deep trench for asparagus and make a 4 in (10 cm) high ridge down the middle of it.

2 COVER ASPARAGUS
Place crowns on the ridge, about 12 in (30 cm) apart, spread their roots and cover with soil. Fill in the trench as the stems grow.

GLOBE ARTICHOKES
Plant artichokes at a depth of about 2 in (5 cm), allowing 3 ft (1 m) between plants. Use row covers if the weather turns cold.

DON'T FORGET

Crop rotation helps prevent the buildup of pests and diseases in the soil. Plan to grow related crops, such as peas and beans, together and find a different bed for them next year.

Patio fruit and vegetables

Don't be deterred if the only area you have for your kitchen garden is a paved patio or backyard deck, because these are often designed to make the most of sunny, sheltered spots that are ideal for growing fruit and vegetables. Many crops thrive in containers, and although the harvests will be smaller, they're no less rewarding.

Container gardening

Growing fruit and vegetables in containers has many advantages over gardening in open soil. For a start there's no heavy digging to do, and you can select the perfect potting mix for every plant. Weeding should be minimal and less back-breaking because the pots raise the soil surface; this makes picking crops easier too. Containers can also be moved to take advantage of summer sun or winter shelter, as required.

Herbs and salads are great for beginners, but tomatoes, chiles, eggplant, and even root crops in deep pots, should all thrive, especially dwarf and patio varieties. Even fruit trees and bushes will produce well in large containers, once established, so don't feel you have to miss out if you're gardening in a small space.

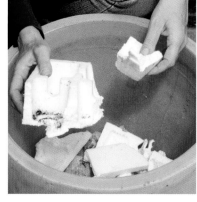

ENSURE GOOD DRAINAGE
Before planting, check that there are adequate holes in the bottom of the container. If not, carefully drill some or use another pot. Place broken foam packing or shards of clay pots in the bottom to improve drainage.

USE THE RIGHT GROWING MIX
Single-season crops, such as lettuce, can be planted into standard mix. Trees, shrubs, and perennial crops such as rhubarb, are best planted into a well-drained potting mix with some compost added.

FOOD AND MOISTURE
To help prevent your crops from drying out, and to keep them well fed, incorporate water-retaining gel crystals and slow-release granular fertilizer into the soil mix before planting.

CLIMBING CROPS IN POT
To grow climbing vegetables, such as peas and runner beans, insert stakes into the soil to form a tepee (p.88). Plant seedlings or direct sow seed at the base of each stake.

Jo's tips

Routine feeding and watering of fruit and vegetable plants in pots is vital if you want a good harvest. Water them generously once or twice a day during summer, and apply a balanced liquid feed to root and leaf crops, or a high potash feed to fruiting crops, weekly during the growing season.

Summer fruit growing in containers can be attractive as well as productive. Even if you have a vegetable garden, plant containers to bring crops closer to the kitchen.

TRY THESE

Almost any large, durable container with good drainage is suitable for crops, so be creative. Try recycling old cans, metal tubs, crates, and bags.

Windowboxes are ideal for herbs and low-growing crops that you might want to pick from the kitchen window.

Growing bags are incredibly versatile, and can be used inside or out for a huge range of fruit and vegetables.

Recycled containers can be as varied as your crops. Try growing potatoes in old trash cans and leeks in grow bags.

Clay and concrete pots look good on the patio, although they can be heavy and prone to frost damage.

April: what to do

GIVE THEM AIR

It's easy to neglect plants when they are hidden away beneath cloches, but they do need extra care if they are under cover. Remember to open the lid of the cloche on sunny days to give your plants ventilation; otherwise, they will overheat. Be sure to tuck them up again every evening to keep out the cold, because nights can still be chilly this month. Weeds grow well under cloches too, so remove them regularly and check for pests while you are at it. Cloches also keep out the rain, so watering is essential.

PRUNING STONE FRUIT

Prune now to fan-train young peach, apricot and cherry trees. After planting and fixing support wires to the wall or fence, cut the vertical leading shoot back to two branches, about 12 in (30 cm) from the ground, one growing to the left and one to the right. Prune them to about 15 in (38 cm) and tie to bamboo stakes attached to the wires. In the second spring, cut back all new growth by one third, and in the third spring by a quarter.

TEND

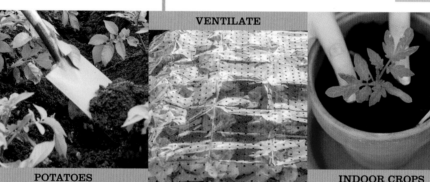

POTATOES   VENTILATE   INDOOR CROPS   FAN TRAINING

HILLING UP

Pulling soil up around the stems of growing potatoes prevents the tubers from turning green and poisonous on exposure to light. Do this once the plants are about 6 in (15 cm) tall. If they are growing in open ground, pull up the soil into a mound to cover the lower leaves, leaving the tops exposed. Hill up container-grown plants in the same way by adding more soil.

MOVING ON

Young plants destined to be grown in large containers are best potted on in stages, in progressively larger pots. Water a plant well before knocking it out of its pot, part-fill the new pot with mix, and position the plant. Fill the pot to about 1/2 in (1 cm) below the top with potting mix, firm gently, and water in.

HARDENING OFF

Seedlings raised under cover (p.42) need to be acclimatized to cooler, breezier conditions before they are planted outdoors. Do this gradually over about 2 weeks. The first step is to increase the amount of ventilation. Then move your plants into a sheltered position outside for longer periods each day. Eventually they will need protection only on cold nights and will be ready to plant out. Check that all danger of frost has passed before you move young plants into their permanent outside position.

CITRUS CARE

Although citrus trees (pp.222–223) need protection in winter, they don't do well in a hot sunroom or greenhouse all summer. As the weather warms up, move them to a sheltered site outdoors. Apply a general fertilizer that contains trace elements, such as iron, copper, and zinc, and repeat every 4 days until fall.

SEEDLINGS

CITRUS

PESTS

WATCH OUT FOR PESTS

A vegetable garden full of tender new shoots will tempt in all kinds of pests (pp.236–239). Be vigilant and deal with them before an entire crop is ruined.

FLY BARRIER
Cabbage maggots feed on cabbage-family crop roots, causing plants to wilt. Barriers keep adult flies from laying eggs near young plants.

SLUG PELLETS
Unless you garden organically (pp.104–105), protect seedlings and young crops with a light sprinkling of slug pellets.

PHEROMONE TRAP
Hang pheromone traps in your apple and pear trees as an organic method to protect your fruit against codling moth caterpillars (p.237).

DON'T FORGET

You might want to net your fruit bushes now, although they are a long way from fruiting. Some birds love the flower buds of fruits such as gooseberries and currants and can do a great deal of damage.

See CITRUS
pages 222–223

GROWING FEATURE

Providing support

Supporting climbing or sprawling plants not only allows them to make healthy, upward growth, but has the advantage of making the most of valuable vertical space in small gardens. Peas, beans, cucumbers, tomatoes, and small-fruited winter squashes all look great scrambling skyward, keeping the crops off the soil.

Choosing supports

Many different materials make perfect plant supports, so take your pick from stakes, trellises, netting, prunings, or anything else you can find. Whichever you choose, make sure that it is strong enough to take the weight of fully grown plants, especially if your garden is exposed to the wind. Also check that the support suits the way that your crops climb, with plenty of places to take hold of, or gaps to grow through.

Climbing plants have different ways of gripping onto supports, all of which suit some materials better than others. Peas and squashes have curling tendrils

(left to right) **Twining beans** twist their stems around supports but need tying in when first planted. **Pea tendrils** look delicate, but hold onto netting or branched sticks very securely. **Cordon tomatoes** need to be tied into their supports regularly.

that wrap around supports, allowing them to make their own way skyward, so they need lots of little places to grasp, provided by well-branched pea-sticks or netting. Beans, on the other hand, twine their stems around the supports, and do best twisting up a smooth stake, although the young plants may need to be tied in to get started. Vining tomatoes have no means of holding on, so they need to be tied in regularly to stakes or taut vertical strings.

Bean tepees

Cane tepees are simple and effective supports, made by pushing up to eight canes firmly into the soil and angling them to a point at the top. To allow climbing beans to reach their full potential, use 8 ft (2.4 m) canes, leaving space at the base of each for plants to grow. Willow and hazel tepees can be bought or made, and their more rustic appearance suits many gardens. Climbing beans are the traditional tepee crops, but there's no reason why outdoor cucumbers, and other climbers including sweet peas, shouldn't scramble over them as well.

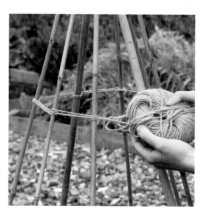

1 SECURE WITH STRING
Fully laden tepees may support a considerable weight, so tie them firmly at the top where the canes cross, and again lower down to keep the tepee from buckling outward.

2 TIE CLIMBERS IN
It's a good idea to tie young bean plants to their stakes with string to get them growing the right way. This also helps prevent them from merging into each other and becoming tangled.

TRY THESE

Using a variety of different supports keeps the full range of climbing crops happy and helps makes the best use of your growing space.

Plastic netting gives effective support to most climbing or sprawling plants. Stretch it between posts or on fences.

Brush can be cut from any stemmy shrubs or small trees around your yard as needed.

Garden fences and trellises provide shelter and support to taller crops. Attach wires for plants to cling onto.

Vertical strings tied to frames or inside greenhouses are ideal for cucumbers, vining tomatoes, and melons.

Finished tepees are ideal for climbing crops, like peas and beans, and make good use of a small space. You can even make them in large containers for patio crops.

April: what to harvest

FIRST SUMMER SPINACH

Start picking the first baby salad leaves now, from spinach plants sown under cover in early spring (p.41). Pick them regularly to encourage further crops but leave some plants to develop unmolested, to give you a harvest of full-sized plants for cooking later in summer. Cooked spinach freezes well but the baby leaves growing now are best eaten fresh. Give time to regrow.

KALE HEARTS

The kale season is about to close but the plants will soon be producing fresh young leaves at their centers, which are far more appetizing than the winter-worn, outer ones. Cut these leaves then uproot and compost the plants as they finish.

HARVEST

SPINACH

KALE

RADISHES

ARUGULA

RAPID RADISH

Hot and peppery, these feisty roots can be ready to eat just 3 weeks after sowing (p.27). They soon spoil quickly, so pull them as soon as they're ready.

'CHERRY BELLE'
This is a quick maturing variety that produces small, rounded radishes that are sweet and mild. They are delicious whole in salads.

'FRENCH BREAKFAST'
This variety takes about a month to mature from sowing, and produces mild, crunchy roots that are just long enough to eat sliced.

'SCARLET GLOBE'
This is a quick-growing variety with bright red skin and crisp white flesh. It is ready to harvest after 6–8 weeks; sow successionally.

ARUGULA SPEED

These delicious, peppery leaves are ready to pluck in as little as 3 weeks from sowing (pp.28–29). Pick leaves individually or use scissors to cut entire rows of plants, 1 in (2.5 cm) above the soil surface. Feed and water to encourage new growth, then reharvest at least once more. If you then let them bolt, you can use the creamy flowers to decorate salads. The leaves and flowers are best eaten fresh.

SPRING GREENS
If you've plenty of spring cabbages, sown last July (p.132), harvest some now as spring greens before they heart up, leaving others to develop. If you don't need the space for other crops, cut the cabbages above their lowest leaves, rather than uprooting the plant. The stalks often resprout to produce a second crop of several small heads.

EARLY STRAWBERRIES
Early varieties of strawberries, brought under cover in January (p.30), should be coming into fruit by the end of this month. Wait until the fruit has turned completely red before picking it with the stalk intact. If you just have a few plants, the berries will be a treat to eat while you're out gardening. If you have a larger crop, they should still be eaten as soon after picking as possible to be at their best. Failing that, use them for early jam (pp.128–129).

SPRING CABBAGE

STRAWBERRIES

SHOOTS & LEAVES

TASTY TIPS
With so much fresh growth around it's worth taking a tour of your vegetable and herb patch for pickings to perk up a plain salad. Most crops won't miss a few leaves and shoots, just pick sparingly so you don't check the later development of your mature crops.

SWISS CHARD
The baby leaves of Swiss chard add color to the vegetable patch with their bright stems. They have a sweet, earthy flavour.

PEA SHOOTS
Peas benefit from being pinched back, and you'll love the delicious, sweet flavor of the shoots. Just snip off the topmost leaves.

HERBS
The young leaves of many herbs often have the most intense flavor. Try picking the new shoots of basil, cilantro, and marjoram.

BEETS
Beets give two crops in one. Pick a few red-veined leaves for salads, and enjoy eating the rich-tasting roots a couple of weeks later.

Try MAKING FRUIT CORDIALS pages 144–145

May: ready to eat

Pick the first irresistible broad beans, peas, beets, carrots, and turnips while they are tiny and sweet. Savor delicious new asparagus and strawberries, and use up last year's jars of jams and pickles, too.

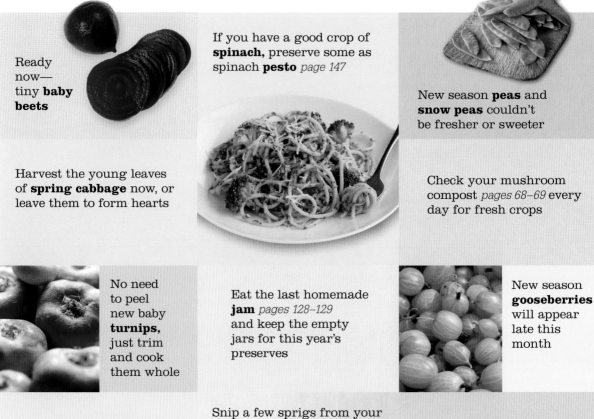

Ready now— tiny **baby beets**

If you have a good crop of **spinach,** preserve some as spinach **pesto** *page 147*

New season **peas** and **snow peas** couldn't be fresher or sweeter

Harvest the young leaves of **spring cabbage** now, or leave them to form hearts

Check your mushroom compost *pages 68–69* every day for fresh crops

No need to peel new baby **turnips,** just trim and cook them whole

Eat the last homemade **jam** *pages 128–129* and keep the empty jars for this year's preserves

New season **gooseberries** will appear late this month

It's the last of the **winter cauliflower**, but summer varieties will soon be ready

Snip a few sprigs from your perennial **herbs**

Hardy **onions** planted last fall can now be harvested

Pull up some finger-sized early **carrots**

Harvest **spinach** and **Swiss chard,** taking leaves from alternate plants down the row

Crispy **summer radishes** add bite to your salads

Pick some **broad beans** while small and cook the pods whole

Cut-and-come-again salads—keep cutting and the leaves will keep coming

Fresh **sprouting seeds** *pages 36–37*, such as mung beans, are tasty and healthy

Finish up last year's homemade **pickles** *pages 176–179*

Pick some slender young **green onions**

Eat the leeks lifted and frozen last month

Cut new **asparagus** spears every few days and freeze the surplus

Lift the very last of the **salsify**—it'salreadytime to sow a new crop

Summer comes early if you have **strawberries** indoors under cover

Drink leftover homemade wine pages 180–181 because you'll need the bottles

Early leaf **lettuces** can be cut now

The distinctive flavor of **arugula** adds interest to green salads

Enjoy the last taste of roast **garlic** stored in oil *page 35*

Pinch out **pea shoots** and **tips** to use in salads

Harvest young **beets** greens as well as the roots

Pick stems of **rhubarb** for pies, crumbles, and fools

May: what to sow

SOW

READY FOR WINTER
Carrots for storage, such as 'Bolero' and 'Danvers', are slower to mature than early varieties. Sow them now until midsummer for crops to store. Sow seed thinly into ½ in (1 cm) deep rows, spaced 6 in (15 cm) apart, then thin to 2–3 in (5–8 cm). Choose well-dug soil in full sun that is not stony or recently manured.

HARVEST: **JUL–DEC**

SOW SQUASH
Summer and winter squash can be sown outside next month but it's worth giving crops a head start in cooler areas. Sow seed ¾ in (2 cm) deep into biodegradable pots set on a heating mat, or on a warm windowsill. Water lightly to prevent damping off.

HARVEST: **VARIOUS**

STORAGE CARROTS

SALSIFY

WINTER SQUASH

RUTABAGAS & TURNIPS

ROOTS TO SUCCESS
HARVEST: **VARIOUS**

Sow rutabagas and turnips ½ in (1 cm) deep in rows, in good soil that stays moist to help keep them from becoming tough.

RUTABAGAS
Slower-maturing and larger growing than turnips, thin the rutabaga plants to 10 in (25 cm) apart. Harvest in fall.

TURNIPS
Fast-growing, sow early varieties now for a midsummer crop. Sow standard varieties in midsummer for a fall and winter crop.

CURIOUS SALSIFY
This unusual root crop has an earthy, nutty flavor, and it can be boiled or steamed. It grows in any soil that is not too stony. On heavier soil, dig a trench to a spade's depth, and fill it with sandy soil or compost to help the long roots develop. Rake the soil to a fine tilth and sow seed thinly in rows 12 in (30 cm) apart. Germination can be slow, but thin seedlings to about 6 in (15 cm) apart.

HARVEST: **NOV–MAY**

STILL TIME TO SOW
You can still sow most crops from last month, indoors and out, if you've had a slow start. Now is your last chance to sow sprouting broccoli (p.54), French and runner beans (p.74), and sweet corn (p.75).

YEAR-ROUND LEAVES

HARVEST: **ALL YEAR**

The closely related leaf crops Swiss chard and leaf beet are very easy to grow, and can be enjoyed raw in salads or cooked. They are a good choice for smaller gardens. Protect the plants during winter, and you can look forward to fresh greens even in the coldest months.

1 PREPARE THE SITE
Neither crop is fussy about the site, but they both prefer soil that has been improved with plenty of well-rotted manure.

2 SOW IN ROWS
The seeds of these crops are large and easy to handle. Sow them thinly in rows ¾ in (2 cm) deep and spaced 15 in (38 cm) apart.

3 COVER AND WATER
Carefully cover the seeds and water them well. Swiss chard can also be sown singly in cell packs and planted out later.

4 THIN SEEDLINGS
As they grow, thin individual plants to 12 in (30 cm) apart. Don't waste the thinned young plants, use them in your salads.

CABBAGE & CAULIFLOWER

BELGIAN ENDIVE & CHICORY

SWISS CHARD & LEAF BEET

WINTER BRASSICAS

Now is the time to sow your winter cabbages and spring cauliflowers, so they have time to grow before the cold, frosty weather comes. Sow outdoors into a seedbed, ½ in (1 cm) deep in rows. Grow on, thinning the young plants to 3–4 in (8–10 cm) apart, then transplant them into their final positions in July. Avoid planting cauliflowers on freshly manured soil, which promotes excess leafy growth.

HARVEST: **VARIOUS**

CHIC CHICORY

For Belgian endive to force in winter (p.216), and summer and fall crops of other chicories, sow from now to early summer. Belgian endive prefers poor soil, other choices need rich soil. Sow both ½ in (1 cm) deep, in rows 12 in (30 cm) apart, thinning to 10 in (25 cm). Chicory can also be sown in cell packs for transplanting.

HARVEST: **VARIOUS**

Winter cabbage

Winter cabbage is hardy enough to harvest and look attractive throughout the coldest weather. Where space is limited, grow some in your flower borders.

1 'Savoy Siberia' is a very hardy variety, ideal for areas where the winters are particularly cold. The heads are packed with sweet-tasting, textured leaves that last well once mature.

2 'Tarvoy' is a useful variety because its heads stay in good condition in the garden for many weeks when mature. It is a good choice if you plan to grow a large crop to cut over a longer period.

3 'Tundra' is a reliable variety that produces sturdy heads of tightly packed green leaves. It is late to mature and very hardy. The heads stay in good condition for weeks until harvested.

4 'January King' is a very hardy variety that produces large heads of blue-green leaves that develop a red flush in cold weather. Quick-maturing, young, small heads can be cut in fall.

5 'Jewel' is a hardy variety that produces loosely-packed heads of dark green, smooth leaves. It is slow to mature and resists bolting, so it can be left in the ground until needed.

Other varieties to try:
'Mammoth Red Rock'
'Bartolo'
'January King'
'Tundra'
'Savoy King'

Chicory

Often expensive or difficult to buy, chicories are crisp, slightly bitter salad crops. Sow them from now to late summer, and enjoy fresh leaves until next spring.

1 'Treviso Precoce Mesola' is a versatile, quick-growing radicchio, also known as a red chicory. It can be harvested throughout summer as salad leaves or left to develop into full heads.

2 'Pan di Zucchero' is a sugarloaf chicory that produces tall, upright heads of loosely-packed green leaves that mature in fall. Plants grown under protection will crop through winter.

3 'Palla Rossa' is a radicchio with a delicate flavor. It can be harvested as salad leaves in summer or as whole heads in fall. It develops its best leaf color as the weather cools.

4 'Variegata di Castelfranco' is a colorful variety that can be harvested as salad leaves or full heads, or forced like a Belgian endive (p.216). It is a tasty crop with a delicious, crunchy texture.

5 'Zoom' is a Belgian endive, grown to be forced and eaten as "chicons" (p.216). The forced heads have a strong, bitter taste and can be eaten cooked or raw. This is a useful winter vegetable.

Other varieties to try:
'Cesare'—red
'Lightning'—Witloof
'Orchidea Rossa'—red
'Trevi'—red
'Variegata di Chioggia'—red

WINTER CABBAGE AND CHICORY

May: what to plant

YOUNG CELERY

Young self-blanching and trench celery plants, sown in February (p.40), can now be hardened off and planted out, once the risk of frost has passed. Celery needs rich, moist soil in full sun to do well. Self-blanching types are often planted in blocks to keep the stems upright, so space plants about 8 in (20 cm) apart. For trench celery, work manure or compost into a 12 in (30 cm) deep and 18 in (45 cm) wide trench and fill in to leave a 2 in (5 cm) dip along the length to retain moisture. Plant the celery in the dip about 12 in (30 cm) apart.

HARVEST: **AUG–DEC**

FLORENCE FENNEL

Florence fennel seedlings sown earlier in April (p.74) should now be full of feathery foliage, ready to be hardened off and planted out. If the weather is still chilly, wait a little longer, or the plants will bolt (go to seed). Florence fennel needs a good moist soil, so work in plenty of compost before planting. Allow space for the swelling stems: about 12 in (30 cm), between each plant. Water well and watch out for snails and slugs.

HARVEST: **JUN–OCT**

PLANT

BROCCOLI

CELERY

LEEKS

FLORENCE FENNEL

BIG BRASSICAS

Brussels sprouts, which bear in fall to winter, and sprouting broccoli, in spring, are tall, wide plants and need to be planted in a firm soil to give the roots a good hold and keep them from toppling over. Transplant them from their seedbed when the plants are 3–4 in (8–10 cm) tall. Space broccoli and dwarf brussels sprout varieties 24 in (60 cm) apart and tall sprout types 36 in (90 cm) apart.

HARVEST: **VARIOUS**

LARGE LEEKS

For large leeks, dig in plenty of compost before planting. Seedlings sown under cover (p.26) should be hardened off and planted out when they are 6–8 in (15–20 cm) tall. Space them 6 in (15 cm) apart and allow about 12 in (30 cm) between rows. To plant, make a 6 in (15 cm) deep hole with a dibble, pop in a leek, and water each row as you finish.

HARVEST: **SEPT–APR**

PLANTING PLUGS

HARVEST: **VARIOUS**

Many vegetable varieties can be bought as small plants from garden centres or as plug plants from mail order nurseries. These are a great way to fill your vegetable beds if you have limited time or no space to raise tender crops indoors. Choose stocky, dark green plants.

1 UNPACK THE PLUGS
If you bought your plug plants through mail order, you should unpack them, plant,and water them as soon as they arrive.

2 PLANT CAREFULLY
If you are planting outside, dig a hole for each plantlet and drop it in. Plug plants need to be hardened off, so protect them at night.

3 MULCH AROUND
After the first watering, put a layer of mulch around each seedling. This helps hold warmth and moisture in the soil.

4 KEEP WELL WATERED
Keep the young plants well watered for 2 weeks or so, while they establish themselves, and protect from slugs and snails.

PLUG PLANTS

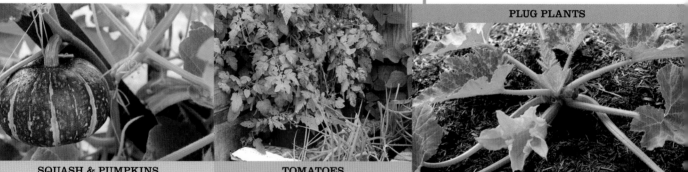

SQUASH & PUMPKINS

TOMATOES

WINTER SQUASH & PUMPKINS

HARVEST: **SEPT–OCT**

These vigorous trailing plants need 3–4 months of warm weather to produce a worthwhile crop.

1 SLIDE FROM POT
Squash and pumpkin seedlings are ready when they have three or four true leaves. Ease the plants gently out of their pots.

2 DIG LARGE HOLE
Plant in rich soil at least 3 ft (1 m) apart, using a trowel to dig a fairly large hole for each seedling. Firm them in and water well.

START TOMATOES

Plant up tomatoes into raised beds, growing bags, or large containers. Bush varieties are attractive for sunny decks and patios. Tall vining varieties can be grown indoors, too, if there is enough space and light. Plant them 18 in (45 cm) apart, or two per growing bag ,and add stake or twine supports to the apex of the greenhouse immediately, because growth is rapid.

HARVEST: **JUL–OCT**

May: more to plant

SUN-LOVING EGGPLANT
Eggplants are heat-loving crops that grow best in areas with long, hot summers. If your growing season is short, plant them through black plastic, in containers, or in a greenhouse. Pot them up into 8 in (20 cm) pots in potting mix, or plant them in the garden beds 12–16 in (30–40 cm) apart, allowing them as much light as possible. If you don't have ideal conditions for growing eggplants, stick with a dwarf variety such as 'Fairy Tale', which is more likely to produce fruit.

HARVEST: **AUG–OCT**

YOUNG CELERIAC
Although mature celeriac plants are extremely hardy, seedlings will bolt (go to seed) if exposed to low temperatures. Don't harden them off until the weather is mild. Plant out celeriac seedlings 12 in (30 cm) apart in soil that has been enriched with organic matter so that it retains plenty of moisture. Water the young plants well after planting and continue to water them regularly to help swell the roots.

HARVEST: **OCT–MAR**

PLANT

EGGPLANT

CELERIAC

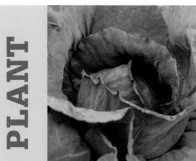

CABBAGE

ZUCCHINI

PLANT OUT CABBAGE
When your summer and autumn cabbages, sown in March (p.54), are about 3 in (8 cm) tall, transplant them into their final positions. Ideally, choose a sunny bed with firm soil. Space summer cabbages about 14 in (35 cm) apart and fall-types 20 in (50 cm) apart. Make holes using a dibble, and lift plants into them gently by the leaves not the stem. Firm the soil around the roots and water well.

HARVEST: **AUG–NOV**

ZUCCHINI
All you need for a plentiful harvest is one or two zucchini plants set into a garden bed improved with compost or well-rotted manure. These plants are large and very hungry and thirsty, so space them at least 36 in (90 cm) apart. A fabric mulch helps retain moisture.

HARVEST: **JUL–OCT**

LATE EARLIES
Late potato varieties are usually planted at this time of year, but if you have limited space and are looking for a quicker crop, then there's nothing to stop you from planting an early variety, as long as you can find seed potatoes this late in the season. Make rows 6 in (15 cm) deep and plant seed pieces 15 in (38 cm) apart with the sprouts pointing upward, leaving 30 in (75 cm) between rows. Allow 12 in (30 cm) between plants, with rows at least 15 in (38 cm) apart. Cover over with soil and water if it is dry.

HARVEST: **AUG–SEP**

CLIMBING CROPS
Once melon and cucumber plants, sown in April (p.74), have two or three leaves, plant them into a sunny garden bed 18 in (45 cm) apart, or in a home greenhouse. Don't plant too deeply, because stems are prone to neck rot. Water in well, keep moist, and shade the leaves from hot scorching sun. Provide support (pp.88–89).

HARVEST: **VARIOUS**

POTATOES

MELONS & CUCUMBERS

PEPPERS

PLANT OUT PEPPERS
HARVEST: **JUL–OCT**

Peppers and chiles thrive in hot conditions. Plant them through black plastic, in pots, or in growing bags. Ideally, provide a vented cover too.

1 WHEN AND WHERE
Peppers and chiles are large enough to plant into a bed once they have their first flowers. Make sure the bed is well drained.

2 SETTING OUT
Ease plants from their pots, handling the rootball not the stem or leaves. Position them in rows, 12–18 in (30–45 cm) apart.

3 FIRM IN AND WATER
Bury the plants at the same depths as in their pots, and firm them in gently. Water them well, and don't allow them to dry out.

TAKE NOTE

On bright, sunny days, greenhouses and cold frames can become very warm. Open vents and windows, and ensure that your plants and seedlings don't dry out.

See PROVIDING SUPPORT pages 88–89

May: what to do

DOUBLE FRUIT CROP
Removing every other fruit from your gooseberry bushes in the second half of this month will give you a crop of smaller berries to cook now and allow the remaining fruit to develop to an impressive size for harvesting in June. This practice is worthwhile only for dessert gooseberries that are going to be eaten uncooked.

SPOTLESS STRAWBERRIES
As the fruit begins to swell on strawberry plants, apply a mulch around them, tucking it right under the berries to keep them clean and away from the soil.

STRAWBERRY MAT
Fiber strawberry mats or collars that fit neatly around the plants are an easy way of protecting the fruit.

PLASTIC MULCH
Cut holes in plastic mulch for the plants to grow through. Keep the mulch taut to avoid water pooling.

STRAW BEDDING
The traditional strawberry mulch is a thick layer of straw. Pack it carefully beneath each plant.

TEND

GOOSEBERRIES

RASPBERRIES

YOUNG PLANTS

STRAWBERRIES

CUTTING CANES
Raspberries are vigorous plants that send up new canes from their base each spring. Summer-fruiting types can become overcrowded, which may lead to a poor and possibly diseased crop. Thin them out by removing the weakest of this year's shoots, leaving five or six strong new canes per plant. Pull out firmly any new canes that sprout outside the row, to prevent unwanted spreading.

STILL DELICATE
Even when hardened off (p.87), seedlings are vulnerable to late frosts. If there is a cold snap, plant out under cloches or supported row covers. Old newspapers make good overnight cover if frost is forecast. Soft new growth is also vulnerable to pests: keep bugs out with barriers such as netting, row cover, or cutworm collars.

PINCH TOMATOES

Tomatoes grow rapidly once planted in their final positions and if you have chosen tall vining (indeterminate) varieties, such as 'Gardener's Delight' or 'Supersonic', they will soon need some support. As they race upward, regularly tie the main stems loosely onto their canes or stakes with twine. At the same time, remove any sideshoots that are developing where the leaves branch from the main stem. Vigorous shoots are often sent up from the base of the plant and these should be removed, too.

BEAT THE BUGS

Cover crops with fleece or net immediately after planting to keep out pests such as carrot rust fly (p.237). Buy or make rigid wire hoops to support the netting and push them into the soil to cover the row, every 12 in (30 cm). Lay the net over the hoops and anchor it into the soil with metal pegs or weight it down with lengths of wood.

TOMATOES

PROTECT CROPS

GREENHOUSES

SCORCHING HOT

In a greenhouse, intense summer sun can scorch the foliage of plants and raise the temperature far too high. Put up shading in late spring and remove it in early fall as the sun's strength diminishes. Blinds are expensive but there are many cheaper options.

PAINT-ON SHADING
Shading paint is cheap and is easy to apply to the outside of glass greenhouses. It will not wipe off some plastics, so check the label.

SHADE CLOTH
Shading fabric may not look particularly attractive, but when attached to the outside of the greenhouse it is highly effective.

EFFECTIVE VENTILATION
Leave doors and vents open all day if it is very hot. Automatic ventilators are available that open and close vents according to temperature.

DAMPING DOWN
Sprinkle water on floors and benches to stop the air from being too dry. Shut doors and vents for a while afterward to increase the humidity.

Organic pest control

Every garden, no matter how well tended, will have its share of pests and diseases to contend with. When you are growing your own food you may prefer not to spray crops with pesticides. Instead, try for natural biological control by encouraging, or introducing, populations of beneficial creatures to prey on persistent pests.

Grow healthy plants

Regularly maintaining your kitchen garden helps minimize problems with pests and diseases. Constantly improving the soil with plenty of organic matter will improve its structure and fertility, and allow plants to grow stronger, making them more resistant to infection and damage. Keeping beds free of plant debris and weeds is also good practice, leaving pests and diseases with nowhere to hide or overwinter, so neaten the area you're cultivating regularly. Keep an eye out for the first signs of pests, such as aphids on shoot tips, and tackle them before you have an infestation on your hands. Simply squashing aphids or other small caterpillars can be remarkably effective.

Friendly predators

Providing food, water, and shelter for a wide range of wildlife will encourage them into your garden, where they will feed on pests and help keep their numbers under control. Feeders will bring in birds that also have a taste for aphids, caterpillars, snails, and other pests. Toads devour slugs, snails, and grubs of all kinds, and are worth encouraging by setting out stones with crevices beneath. Where an insect pest does take hold, it's possible to introduce a biological control, such as nematodes, to combat them.

APPLY NEMATODES
Microscopic, parasitic nematode worms effectively control a range of pests, including slugs, snails, caterpillars, and weevils. They come in a powder, which is watered into the soil using a watering can.

GROW FLOWERS
Growing flowers among your crops not only adds color, but also encourages pollinating insects to visit. These often feed on pests, too. The scent of flowers may also prevent pests locating crops.

CREATE HABITATS
Creating different habitats entices all kinds of beneficial creatures to take up residence. A small pond will bring frogs, toads, insects, and hungry and thirsty mammals and birds.

MAKE HIDING PLACES
Hiding places, such as log piles, pieces of old carpet, or propped up slates, provide shelter for beneficial creatures like snakes and frogs. If you find pests sheltering too, just remove them.

BENEFICIAL BUGS

Many insects pollinate crops and some feed voraciously on common insect pests, so it's a good idea to make your garden attractive to them.

Lacewings—Larvae and adults feast on aphids and other insect pests. Attract them with nectar-rich flowers.

Ladybugs—Adults and larvae prey on aphids. Provide dry places, such as seedpods, for them to overwinter.

Hoverflies—These wasp look-alikes devour aphids and pollinate crops. Encourage them with colorful flowers.

Centipede—At home in leaf litter and log piles, centipedes have an appetite for all kinds of insect pests.

Sacrificial planting—Grow plants that pests can't resist, to distract them from crops or to alert you to the problem so you can control it. For example, aphids love nasturtiums.

ORGANIC PEST CONTROL

May: what to harvest

PEAK TIME FOR HERBS
Annual herbs sown in April (p.82), and perennial ones planted last fall (p.199), should be ready for the kitchen in the next few weeks. Many herbs need pinching out now to encourage bushier growth, so take advantage and use the shoots in your cooking. Most of the soft new growth should be tender enough to pinch off between your fingers, but scissors are better for woodier plants like rosemary and some thymes, and neater for chives. Pick the large leaves of basil as required and pinch out the flower shoots as they appear.

SALAD SEASON
Sown outside in April (p.75), now is the start of the main lettuce season, with non-hearting, loose-leaf varieties, such as 'Green Salad Bowl' and 'Sergeant', ready first. To keep them cropping over several weeks, pick off the outer leaves as required, or cut the leaves with scissors about 1 in (2.5 cm) from the soil and allow them to resprout. Heading types follow, and can be pulled up by the roots or cut at the base with a knife.

HARVEST

GOOSEBERRIES

HERBS

LETTUCE

GALLERY OF GOOSEBERRIES
Gooseberries (p.185) harvested this month are likely to be acidic, and perfect for cooking. Fruit left to ripen will soften and yellow, signaling that they are sweet enough to eat raw. Unless you have thornless varieties, watch out for the fearsome spines when picking fruit.

'HINNOMAKI RED'
Slow-growing variety that produces a heavy crop of large fruit that ripen red. It has good resistance to mildew. Good for small gardens.

'HINNOMAKI YELLOW'
A strong variety that bears a good yield of large, sweet, yellow fruit. It also shows good mildew resistance. Dessert variety, it's good eaten raw.

'INVICTA'
Widely available, this reliable dual-purpose variety can be eaten straight from the bush or cooked. It has good mildew resistance.

'CAPTIVATOR'
An almost thornless variety, good for gardens with children. Its sweet fruit ripen red and can be eaten from the bush. Good mildew resistance.

ASPARAGUS CROWNS

If you have planted asparagus crowns this year (p.83), patience is the order of the day. To allow plants to become established and build up strength, leave spears uncut in their first and second seasons. In subsequent years harvest the spears when they reach around 6 in (15 cm) tall, cutting them with a sharp knife, 2 in (5 cm) below the soil surface. Harvest them over a period of 6 weeks but leave at least six strong spears per plant to grow on. These will supply the all-important energy for the following year's crop.

ROOT TREATS

It's a real treat this month to be able to harvest the first salad beets and baby carrots, sown in March. Do this carefully, loosening heavy soils with a hand fork first to avoid damaging the roots, especially carrots. Twist rather than cut the leaves off your beets to prevent them from bleeding. Remember, their leaves are good to eat, too.

ASPARAGUS

BEETS & CARROTS

TURNIPS

BROAD BEANS

TENDER TURNIPS

There's no denying that turnips are a quick crop to grow. Early varieties can be ready for harvest in just 6–7 weeks after sowing, so make sure you catch them at their best—while they're still sweet and tender. For perfect baby turnips, pull them when they are less than 2 in (5 cm) in diameter. If left to grow much larger, they soon become tough and unappetizing.

BROAD APPEAL

Broad beans sown in fall or late winter should start to yield fleece-lined pods full of delicious, sweet beans this month. Pick frequently, because the beans are at their best when small and tender. If you've a glut, harvest the beans small and freeze them. Don't leave them to become big and starchy.

June: ready to eat

The summer bounty starts with waxy new potatoes, mild green garlic, and a dazzling array of just-picked salad leaves. Pounce on strawberries and gooseberries to eat fresh or to make into jams and desserts.

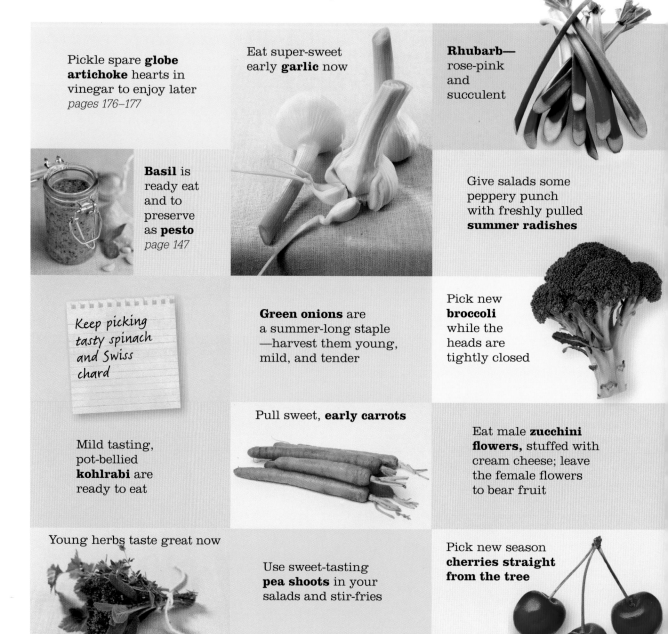

Pickle spare **globe artichoke** hearts in vinegar to enjoy later
pages 176–177

Eat super-sweet early **garlic** now

Rhubarb— rose-pink and succulent

Basil is ready eat and to preserve as **pesto**
page 147

Give salads some peppery punch with freshly pulled **summer radishes**

Keep picking tasty spinach and Swiss chard

Green onions are a summer-long staple —harvest them young, mild, and tender

Pick new **broccoli** while the heads are tightly closed

Mild tasting, pot-bellied **kohlrabi** are ready to eat

Pull sweet, **early carrots**

Eat male **zucchini flowers,** stuffed with cream cheese; leave the female flowers to bear fruit

Young herbs taste great now

Use sweet-tasting **pea shoots** in your salads and stir-fries

Pick new season **cherries straight from the tree**

Fresh **asparagus**—indescribable!

Just ready—the first **new potatoes** are a sign of summer

Pick your first **summer cauliflower**

Full-sized **beets** are ready now—add one to your chocolate cake mix for something special

Beet greens make a tasty and colorful addition to your salads

Enjoy sweet heads of **spring cabbage**

Fresh **gooseberries** are delicious; freeze surpluses to enjoy later in the year

The first summer **turnips** are ready now—ideal for mashing

Keep **sprouting seeds** *pages 36–37,* they're packed with goodness

Give **peas** a chance

Jam made with newly picked strawberries is a highlight this month

You won't go short on salads, with **lettuce heads** and **cut-and-come-again** crops

Plenty of **broad beans** to pick for a few more weeks yet

Eat aniseed-flavored **Florence fennel** now

Indoor **mushrooms** provide a welcome supply all summer, so keep picking

Perpetual spinach will keep you in greens

June: what to sow

LATER LETTUCE

Sow now for late-summer and fall crops. Choose butterhead, cos, or crisphead-types for head lettuce; loose-leaf varieties to use as cut leaves. In hot weather, lettuce might fail to germinate or wilt once growing. Sow in lightly shaded beds, and if the weather is very hot, sow in the evenings and cool the soil first with water.

HARVEST: **JUL–NOV**

SOW AND SOW

Don't forget to continue sowing cut-and-come-again salad crops for a constant supply. A range of baby leaf crops are suitable (pp.28–29). Weed the soil and sow seed thinly in rows, 4–6 in (10–15 cm) wide, to give a mass of foliage to cut in a few weeks time.

HARVEST: **ALL YEAR**

SOW

EDIBLE FLOWERS   **LETTUCE**   **CHINESE GREENS**   **CUT & COME AGAIN**

BLOOMING TASTY

HARVEST: **JUL–OCT**

Annual flowers are often overlooked in the productive garden, but many are edible as well as beautiful, and have their own distinctive flavor. Direct sow now.

CALENDULA
Also known as pot marigold, this cheerful plant flowers in shades of yellow and orange. Use the petals to add color to your salads.

NASTURTIUM
The leaves, flowers, and seed pods of this colorful, spreading plant have a delicious but strong peppery taste. It is best used sparingly.

FRENCH MARIGOLD
This summer bedding plant has a very pungent flavor. Use the flowers in salads, and add the petals to rice dishes for color and a spicy kick.

FAR EAST FEAST

Chinese cabbage and bok choy can handle heat better than many other salad and cooking greens. Both need moist, fertile soil, and will tolerate light shade. Sow seed thinly in rows 12 in (30 cm) apart for Chinese cabbage, 10 in (25 cm) for bok choy. Repeat sow, thin seedlings, and harvest in 6–8 weeks, when ready.

HARVEST: **JUL–NOV**

HURRY NOW FOR HERBS

HARVEST: **JUL–OCT**

This is the last chance to sow most annual herbs. If you leave it any later, they rapidly run to seed at the expense of the leaves you want for the kitchen.

1 SOWING OUTDOORS
Sow tougher herbs, such as dill, parsley, and cilantro, directly into the soil outside in rows or patches. Space evenly.

2 GROWING ON
Keep the seed well watered and thin seedlings to 8 in (20 cm) apart as they develop. Protect from slugs and snails (p.239).

SOWING INDOORS
Sow more basil in pots now, let seedlings grow for a few weeks, then plant them out for a second crop in late summer.

STILL TIME TO SOW

Sow outside now: peas (p.40), kohlrabi (p.41), turnips, sprouting broccoli, beets, broccoli (p.54), Florence fennel (p.74), kale (p.75) carrots (p.94), Belgian endive and chicory, and chard (p.95).

SQUASHES & CUCUMBERS

SNAP & RUNNER BEANS

ANNUAL HERBS

SQUASH FAMILY

Even in short season areas, summer cucumbers and zucchini can be sown under cloches in their final positions outside, as can summer and winter squashes, and pumpkins. All they need is a sunny site, sheltered from the wind, and soil that has been improved with plenty of well-rotted manure or compost. Sow two seeds per hill, 1 in (2.5 cm) deep, spaced 3 ft (90 cm) apart for cucumbers and zucchini, and at least 5 ft (1.5 m) apart for squashes and pumpkins.

HARVEST: **VARIOUS**

LATE BEANS

For late crops of snap and runner beans, sow now, directly into soil prepared with plenty of rich organic matter. If you're growing climbing varieties, remember to put the supports in first (pp.88–89). Sow two seeds per station, 2 in (5 cm) deep, 6–8 in (15–20 cm) apart. Thin out the weaker plant.

HARVEST: **AUG–OCT**

Winter squash

A standard in most home gardens, these vigorous plants produce late-summer fruit in a huge range of sizes, colors, and shapes. Most store well into winter.

1 'Uchiki Kuri' looks like a small pumpkin and produces an early crop of orange-red fruit. The flesh has a sweet, nutty flavor. Plants can be trained upward where space is limited.

2 Butternut is a type of squash, rather than a variety, and is widely sold in supermarkets. Varieties include 'Harrier', 'Hunter', and 'Waltham Butternut', which all have, sweet, nutty fruit.

3 'Queensland Blue' produces large, heavily ribbed fruit that mature to a distinctive blue-green color. Best grown in larger plots, where the plants can be allowed to trail across the soil.

4 'Turk's Turban' is a smaller variety that produces highly attractive, edible fruit. Once peeled, there is little left to eat, so grow more than one plant to make up a worthwhile quantity.

5 'Sweet Dumpling' produces small, attractive fruit the size of tennis balls, which are delicious roasted. This variety can be grown in containers, with the stems trained vertically up a tepee.

6 'Crown Prince' is a blue-skinned variety with sweet-tasting, bright orange flesh. All squash keep well, but if stored properly, fruit of this variety will stay in good condition well into spring.

Other varieties to try:
'Bon Bon'
'Burpee's Butterbush'
'Festival'
'Golden Hubbard'
'Golden Nugget'

TAKE YOUR PICK

Pumpkins

Many pumpkins are grown for carving at Halloween, but sow a good culinary variety and the flesh is fabulous cooked. Some also have tasty, edible seeds.

1 'Jack Be Little' is a miniature variety, with the plants each producing several palm-sized fruits. These are edible and delicious roasted, or they can also be used for decoration. This variety is suitable for pot-growing.

2 'Dill's Atlantic Giant' is among the largest of the pumpkins, especially if fruits are thinned to one per plant. Pick young to eat, or allow the fruits to grow on for over-sized decorations.

3 'Rouge Vif d'Etampes' is an old variety with large, flattened, deep orange fruits that are heavily ribbed. Harvest when plate-size and enjoy them roasted, or grow them on for decoration.

4 'Baby Bear' produces bright orange fruit the size of a basketball. It is a good variety for smaller gardens because it doesn't need too much space. The thin-hulled seeds are especially good to eat.

5 'Hundredweight' is a giant variety that can be grown to eat or for decoration. Water and feed plants well for the largest fruit, although they may become too tough and heavy to cook.

Other varieties to try:
'Connecticut Field'
'Jack O'Lantern'
'New England Pie'
'Spellbound'
'Wee B Little'

WINTER SQUASHES AND PUMPKINS

June: what to plant

PLANT CAULIFLOWER

Spring-sown summer and autumn cauliflower should be ready to transplant from their seedbed now. Using a dibble, lift the seedlings carefully and transplant them into fertile soil that hasn't been manured recently. Space 24 in (60 cm) apart in each direction and water well and protect them where birds are a problem.

HARVEST: AUG–NOV

PLANT GREENS

It's now time to plant out kale and sprouting broccoli, sown in spring. Both crops grow outside through winter in most regions, although they do best under cover in very cold winters. Transplant them from their seedbed in the same way as cauliflowers.

HARVEST: DEC–APR

PLANT

EGGPLANT   CAULIFLOWER   SUGARLOAF CHICORY   KALE & BROCCOLI

EGGPLANT, PEPPERS, & TOMATOES   HARVEST: JUL–OCT

Once plants raised indoors have been hardened off, and have their first flowers showing, these heat-loving crops can be planted outside in sunny, sheltered spots.

EGGPLANT
Eggplant give a better harvest when planted into large containers. Keep them well fed and watered. Harvest August – October.

PEPPERS
Plant in beds, containers, or growing bags, in full sun, and support with stakes. They need good light and warmth to ripen fully.

TOMATOES
Suitable for beds, containers or grow bags. All upright varieties require staking, and tall vining varieties do best in cages. Crop from July.

PLANT CHICORY

Sown last month (p.95), plant out your sugarloaf chicory seedlings now. This type of chicory forms dense heads that are larger than other forms, and they appreciate soil that has had compost dug into it recently, to encourage leafy growth. Harden off the plants and space them out evenly at 10 in (25 cm) intervals. Water in well.

HARVEST: JUL–OCT

FAMILY FRUIT

HARVEST: **JUL–OCT**

These related crops are hungry plants, so work in plenty of compost when you plant out, once hardened off. Cover with cloches if the weather is cool and damp.

ZUCCHINI
These are large, quick-growing plants that need plenty of space. Position them 36 in (90 cm) apart. Can also be grown in large pots.

CUCUMBER
This crop is usually trained on a trellis, and can be grown in large containers. Keep them well watered and ventilated.

SQUASH
Summer squash crop from July, winter varieties from September. Support squash vines on a trellis where space is limited.

DON'T FORGET

When planting out, always water plants in well, and continue to keep them moist during dry spells.

Water under cloches regularly and prop them open to allow air to cool plants on sunny days.

SWEET CORN

SNAP & RUNNER BEANS

CUCUMBERS, ZUCCHINI, & SQUASH

SWEET CORN

HARVEST: **SEP–OCT**

Plant out your seedlings or sow seeds outdoors now in fully warmed, enriched soil in full sun.

PLANTING OUT
Sweet corn doesn't do well if its growth is checked, so plant while the young plants are still small. Water thoroughly before planting.

WORK IN BLOCKS
Pollination is vital for full ears, so plant in blocks with plants 18 in (45 cm) apart each way. This makes wind pollination more effective.

SUMMMER BEANS

Now is the time to sow seeds or plant seedlings of snap beans and runner beans, as soon as their supports are in place (pp.88–89). Plant one per stake, or space them out 6–8 in (15–20 cm) apart along rows of netting or wire. Bush varieties require a similar spacing, but no supports. Try planting sweet peas to cling alongside runner beans to help attract pollinating insects.

HARVEST: **AUG–OCT**

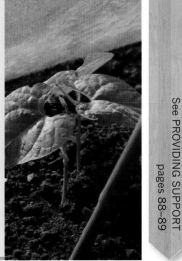

See PROVIDING SUPPORT pages 88–89

PLANTING IDEAS

Productive baskets

Hanging baskets are usually planted with flowering annuals but they can be just as attractive, and productive, when used to grow dwarf or trailing vegetables and herbs. This is not only a great way to make the best use of a smaller plot, but it also allows you to bring your crops within easy picking distance of the kitchen.

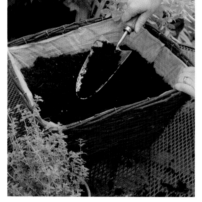

1 LINE YOUR BASKET
To help retain moisture, line your basket with plastic, or a specially made liner, before filling the base with potting mix. Now add water-retaining crystals and slow-release fertilizer.

2 CHOOSE PLANTS
Position upright herbs and vegetables in the center of the basket, with trailing varieties around the edge. In large baskets, add flowering annuals for extra color. Plant closely together.

3 ADD SOIL
Vegetables are thirsty plants; make sure there are no large pockets in the soil mix between plants and only fill to 2 in (5 cm) below the basket rim, so you can water it thoroughly.

4 WATER AND FEED WELL
Water the plants in well and position the basket in a sheltered, sunny spot. To encourage a good crop, water twice daily during summer, and apply a liquid feeding every week.

TRY THESE

The best crops to grow in baskets are dwarf or trailing varieties, or those that you can either harvest quickly or pick while the plants are young.

Salad—Loose-leaf lettuce (p.81), arugula, and cut-and-come-again crops (pp.28–29) flourish in hanging baskets.

Peas—Dwarf, early peas, such as 'Sugarbon', grow well in baskets if kept watered and fed. Pick them frequently.

Tomatoes—Choose trailing bush varieties, like 'Tumbling Tom Red'. Most baskets will hold only one plant.

Herbs—Many compact herbs grow well in baskets. Try marjoram and thyme, which tolerate dry conditions.

PRODUCTIVE BASKETS

June: what to do

SUMMER PRUNING
This is a quick job that is worth carrying out after gooseberries, redcurrants, and whitecurrants have been harvested. Prune all of this year's new growth back to five leaves, cutting with sharp pruners just above a leaf. Removing the tips of soft new growth stops the plants from being colonized by aphids or infected with mildew and opens up the bush to improve airflow.

WATER AND HOE
Container-grown plants need frequent watering in hot weather, but so do plants in the soil. Keep an eye on plants that are prone to bolting and soak them well, perhaps once a week. Hoe between crops to remove weeds, leaving them to shrivel and die.

TEND

FRUIT BUSHES

MAINTENANCE

TOMATOES

SUMMER BERRIES

KEEP UP THE SUPPORT
Your tomatoes will still be heading skyward, so continue to tie them in to sturdy stakes or wires and pinch out sideshoots.

1 REMOVE SIDESHOOTS
Pinch out sideshoots that form where leaves join the main stem, because they will take energy away from flowering and fruiting.

2 TIE LOOSELY
When you attach the main stem of a tomato plant to its support, tie the twine loosely to allow the stem to expand.

CANE CONTROL
New canes sent up this year from the base of summer-fruiting raspberry and blackberry plants will now be getting long and unruly. Tie them in to keep them out of the way and prevent them from getting damaged. The older canes that will fruit this year should be spread across the supporting wires; keep the new shoots close together for now and spread them out once the older canes have been cut back.

WATCH THEM CLIMB

As they grow, climbing varieties of snap and runner beans twist their stems around their supporting stakes (pp.88–89). Once established, they can hang on tightly without your help. Sometimes, however, seedlings need a hand to get started, especially if they are getting tossed around in breezy conditions or flattened by heavy rain. Once the young plants are tall enough, tie each one loosely onto its support with garden twine, taking care not to damage the delicate stem, then watch them take off without tangling.

TRIM HERBS

Many shrubby and perennial herbs, such as rosemary, sage, and thyme, finish flowering during early summer, which gives you the opportunity to cut them back and keep them tidy. Trimming also encourages new growth that will quickly be ready to harvest. Use pruners or shears depending on the size of the job.

RUNNER BEANS

HERBS

STRAWBERRIES

NEW PLANTS FROM OLD

Strawberry plants are easy to propagate from the long runners that they all produce. At no extra cost, you can increase your stock and replace old plants.

1 CHOOSE RUNNERS
Choose four or five strong runners and cut off the rest. Also remove runners from plants you don't want to use for propagation.

2 PEG DOWN IN POTS
Set the runners in buried pots and peg down with wire. Once the plantlets have grown on, cut the runners and plant out.

3 PROPAGATE IN SOIL
You can also let the runners grow directly in the soil. Reposition the plantlet if necessary, peg it down, and sever when established.

DON'T FORGET

The weeks that follow are likely to be hot and dry. If you haven't already laid an organic mulch around your plants to conserve moisture, do it now.

June: more to do

HILL POTATOES

When late potatoes reach about 8 in (20 cm) tall, hill them up by pulling soil around their stems, leaving the top leaves showing. This not only prevents tubers from turning green and inedible in the light, it can help protect them from the spores of potato blight (p.243). This fungal disease thrives in warm, wet summers. Look for brown patches at leaf edges, and remove and destroy infected growth.

REGULAR MEALS

Whether your tomatoes, peppers, chiles, and eggplant are grown in the soil or in containers, they need regular feeding once the first fruit begins to set. Apply a high-potassium tomato fertilizer every week. Use a sunken pot to help deliver the nutrients straight to the roots.

TEND

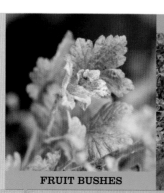

POTATOES

TOMATOES

FRUIT BUSHES

SOFT FRUIT

MILDEW ALERT

If powdery white patches appear on your gooseberry and blackcurrant bushes, it probably means they have been infected with American gooseberry mildew. This fungal disease particularly affects young growth, which becomes misshapen and dies. The mildew also appears on the fruits, which are still edible, although unappealing. Gooseberry mildew thrives in environments where air circulation is poor. The best control is to remove and destroy affected leaves and fruits, and prune the bushes (pp.140–141) to thin out growth and allow free air circulation.

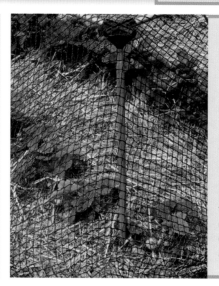

PROTECT SOFT FRUIT

Birds love ripe, soft summer fruits as much as we do. To stop them from feasting on your crops of berries and currants, protect the fruit with netting. The easiest way to do this is to plant bushes together and build a permanent fruit cage around them, but this is not always practical in smaller gardens. To net individual bushes, drive in four stakes around each one to hold up the net. Cover them before the fruit ripens and changes color. Ensure that the net is weighted down at the edges because birds are adept at getting in and can become trapped.

SPOT CHECK FOR PESTS AND DISEASES

Spotting pests (pp.236–239) early, before they have a chance to multiply and damage crops, is key to keeping problems under control.

Check under leaves as you pass, and if plants are unexpectedly wilting, try digging one up to look for pests that attack the roots.

APHIDS
These aphids can rapidly smother foliage, sucking the sap and excreting a sticky substance that causes a black mold to develop.

CARROT RUST FLY
The white maggots of this fly will destroy your carrot crop. Protect your plants with row cover to prevent the female fly from laying her eggs.

ASPARAGUS BEETLE
Both the brightly colored adult beetles and their dark gray larvae rapidly strip asparagus stems. Pick them off by hand and destroy them.

ONION MAGGOTS
The maggots feed on the roots and bulbs of onions. Signs are yellow, collapsing plants. Onion sets are less vulnerable than seedlings.

PESTS

APPLES & PEARS

BROAD BEANS

THE JUNE DROP
Many apple and pear trees shed fruitlets in late June or early July. This 'June drop' may alarm first-time fruit growers, but it is the tree's way of ditching unhealthy fruit and leaving a smaller crop that is easier for it to carry. Do your own thinning after the June drop for a crop of large, healthy fruit, especially on young trees that need to make plenty of strong growth too.

BEAN TOPS
Young shoots at the top of broad bean plants are a magnet for aphids. Infestation can be preempted by pinching out the soft tips of these shoots between your fingers when the plants are in full flower. This also helps direct the plant's energy into swelling the beans rather than producing more leaves.

See COMMON PESTS pages 236–239

Effective irrigation

Gardeners look for rapid growth and copious flowering and fruiting from their crops. Plants can achieve this only if they have a consistent supply of moisture at their roots. In all but the lightest of soils or drought conditions, most outdoor plants do well with moderate watering, but those under cover need more attention.

When to water

Apart from container-grown or greenhouse crops, the plants that require the most careful watering are those that are newly planted or transplanted. Until their roots have become established, they are highly vulnerable to drying out. Watch your young plants for the earliest hints of wilting and leaf-yellowing, and water them promptly if danger signs appear.

Water is often in short supply, especially in summer, so use it efficiently. Watering in the middle of the day can be highly inefficient; much of the stream of water from a hose or sprinkler may evaporate before it can soak

(left to right) **Half plastic bottles** make excellent funnels, channeling water directly to plant roots, where it's most needed. **Mulching** shields the soil around the plant from the sun, keeping it cool and preventing moisture from evaporating so readily.

into the soil. It's better to water in early morning or evening, when the water can penetrate deep into the soil and reach the roots of your plants. A layer of mulch on the soil surface helps prevent evaporation. Make sure that the soil is damp before you add a thick layer of organic material, such as well-rotted compost or manure, or a material that can be planted through, such as black plastic.

WATER AT THE BASE
Concentrate your efforts at a plant's base when watering because the water will then soak down directly to the roots. Be careful that water pressure from a hose doesn't erode the soil.

SOAKER HOSE
This is a long perforated pipe that leaks water along its length. Soaker hoses can be buried in beds or laid on the surface, and are particularly useful for watering under plastic mulch.

WATERING KITS
Greenhouse watering kits are irrigation systems that connect to a main water faucet. A timer controls the supply of water through narrow pipes to drip-feeders placed near the plants.

Give the soil a good soaking when you water. A light sprinkling is wasteful—the water will go no farther than the soil surface and cannot reach the plant roots, where it is needed most.

WATERING PROBLEMS

Inadequate watering leaves plants more susceptible to disease, as well as harmful disorders caused by a lack of essential nutrients.

Blossom end rot on tomatoes (p.240) is caused by calcium deficiency, resulting from inadequate watering.

Mildew on plants is commonly caused because they are kept too dry, leading to white fungal growth on the foliage.

Erratic watering, where plants are kept too dry before watering, often results in fruit with split or corky skin.

Bitter pit on apples (p.240) is caused by calcium deficiency, resulting from inadequate watering. It is easily cured.

Space efficiency

However large your garden, you'll want to make the most of the space. This could be as simple as finding gaps in the flower border for fruit and vegetables, but by planting fast-growing crops, you can squeeze extra harvests out of the vegetable garden as well. Sow them in empty soil is waiting for the next crop to be planted (catch-cropping), or grow them between slow-maturing plants (inter-cropping).

Catch-cropping

Even with meticulous planning it's inevitable that sometimes you will be left with bare soil during the growing season—after one long-term crop is harvested and before the next is ready to plant. This gives you an opportunity to sow a fast-growing crop that will use the space in the meantime, and will finish in plenty of time to prepare the ground in readiness for the crop to follow.

Catch-cropping is particularly useful to fill the gap between winter brassicas, the last of which are often picked in early spring, and tender summer crops that

(left to right) **The last early potatoes** are lifted in summer, leaving the bed temporarily empty. **Sow radishes next**, to harvest in 6–8 weeks, just in time to make way for new spring cabbage seedlings, transplanted from their bed.

can't usually be planted outdoors until the end of May. Another break may come between lifting early season potatoes and planting spring cabbages in late summer. Keep a stock of seeds handy of quick-growing crops that are ready to harvest in 6–8 weeks, such as radishes, beets, and bok choy, right through the growing season and your garden will always be full.

Inter-cropping

Effective inter-cropping takes advantage of the fact that some crops are quicker growing than others, and that they can be grown closely together without competing. Slow-growing crops, such as brussels sprouts and parsnips, take months to mature, locking up your beds for long periods. In contrast, turnips and beets are ready to harvest in just 8–10 weeks, so it's a good idea to make use of their speedy growth. To achieve multiple crops from the same bed, water and feed the plants regularly, and try not to disturb the other crop plants.

1 MAIN CROP FIRST
Plant out maincrop vegetables, such as corn, into their final positions. Firm them in and water well. Insert any stakes at this stage to avoid damaging the intercrops later.

2 SOW INTERCROPS
Make furrows in between the young transplants, and sow intercrops directly. Sow later crops around the developing main crops to prevent them from being shaded.

Don't waste space in the vegetable garden. In the scheme shown here, zucchini and several varieties of fast-growing salad crops have been planted around bean tepees.

TRY THESE

Inter-cropping and catch-cropping requires fruit and vegetables that mature quickly, to avoid interrupting the growth of your main crops.

Lettuce can be harvested as leaves in a matter of weeks. If time allows between crops, let them form heads.

Turnips can be ready in just 6 weeks, making them ideal for inter-cropping between onions, shallots, and beans.

Bok choy matures quickly and can also be cut as baby leaves, allowing you to sow new crops until the last minute.

Green onions are ideal as an extra crop between bulbing onions and shallots, as well as rows of carrots.

SPACE EFFICIENCY

June: what to harvest

TASTE OF SUMMER
June is the peak month for strawberries, when early varieties, like 'Honeoye', bear fruit. Pick berries with their hulls attached, when fully ripe and entirely red. Fruit will ripen every day or two, so keep picking them at their best. Eat fresh, or use in jams (pp.128–129) or cordials (pp.144–145).

CUT ARTICHOKES
Globe artichokes are ready to cut now. Cut them young if you like them tightly closed and tender, or let them mature more if you prefer a fuller flavor. Don't leave them too long or they become hard and inedible. Planted in April, fully mature specimens will often produce a second flush of flowerheads in late summer.

HARVEST

STRAWBERRIES

GLOBE ARTICHOKE

PEAS

FLORENCE FENNEL

PEAS OFFERING
Peas are at their best for a short time, and should be picked often and eaten soon, before their sweetness fades. Pluck the pods of shelling peas when they look full, but not solid, and are still bright green. Snap pea varieties snap cleanly in half at their prime, but might still need strings removed from pods. When the harvest is over, cut the plants down, leaving the nitrogen-rich roots in the soil.

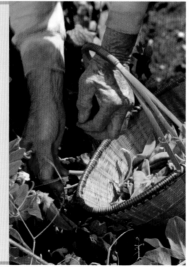

FIRST FENNEL
Harvest Florence fennel once the bulbs reach a useful size. Either cut them with a knife as close to soil level as possible, or cut 1 in (2.5 cm) above the soil, leaving the stump. Crops sown in April may give a second flush of flavorful shoots. Don't forget, the ferny leaves pack a delicious aniseed punch, too.

VEGETABLE FEAST

Pull kohlrabi and turnips, sown in spring, once they reach the size of a golf ball. Standard turnips are good to eat when much larger, but early varieties can become woody. Bok choy is often ready just 6 weeks after sowing, when it can be uprooted or cut about 1 in (2.5 cm) from the base and left to grow back. Broccoli and the first summer cauliflowers are also ready to harvest now, and mature rapidly. Cut the heads while the buds are tightly closed. Split surplus heads into florets for freezing (pp.148–149).

BULB BOUNTY

Planted in the fall, garlic is usually dug in August, but uproot some now for juicy bulbs, milder than any in the stores, and use immediately. Garlic bulbs can grow deep in the soil, so lift them with a fork. Overwintered onion varieties, planted last year (p.167), will also be ready to harvest now. Loosen the soil at their roots and lift as required.

NEW POTATOES

BRASSICAS

GARLIC & ONIONS

TASTY NEW POTATOES

Harvest new potatoes (pp.48–49) when the plants flower, loosening the soil with a fork. Lift all the tubers—any left may sprout and encourage disease.

'FOREMOST'
Good for salads, boiling and baking, this first-year variety is white-skinned and has an excellent waxy texture.

'RED DUKE OF YORK'
A good all-rounder in the kitchen, this variety has a red skin, yellow flesh, and a dry texture. It also has a wonderfully strong flavor.

'INTERNATIONAL KIDNEY'
This is the variety widely sold in supermarkets as 'Jersey Royal'. Best boiled, it has a waxy texture and delicious, yellow flesh.

DON'T FORGET

Check your new potatoes are ready to harvest by scraping away soil from the base of the plants to reveal the tubers. If they look small, cover them again and give them longer to grow.

Try MAKING SOUP pages 226–227

Making simple fruit jam

Easy to make and convenient to keep, homemade jams are one of the best ways to preserve soft fruit crops. All you need are surplus fruit and plenty of sugar to make delectable preserves that will retain the flavor of the fresh fruit much better than any mass-produced equivalents. Stick to single-fruit classics, such as raspberry, blackcurrant, or plum, or mix what you have grown to create something unique.

Raspberry jam

Makes 1 lb (450 g) of jam
(2 small jars)
Takes 25–30 minutes, plus standing time
Keeps 6 months

Ingredients
1½ lb (650g) fresh raspberries
Juice of ½ lemon
1lb 2oz (500g) granulated sugar

Equipment
Large, deep, wide-based saucepan or preserving pan
Wooden spoon
Jars with lids
Waxed paper covers
Labels

1 Wash the fruit, let it drain thoroughly, and pick through it, removing any damaged berries. Place the berries in a large saucepan or preserving pan. Add the lemon juice and about 5 fl oz (150 ml) of water.

2 Simmer the fruit for 3–5 minutes until it has softened and the juice starts to run. Add the sugar to the pan, and stir over a low heat until it dissolves completely. Take care not to let the sugar burn.

Jo's tips

Jam sets because of the interaction of sugar and fruit acids with a substance called pectin, a setting agent which occurs naturally in plant cells. Some fruits, such as apples and plums, contain a lot of pectin, so jam made with these will set more easily than jam made with berries.

To sterilize your jars, wash them in hot soapy water, place them on a rack in a moderate oven, and let them dry thoroughly.

3 Turn up the heat and boil the mixture for 8–10 minutes. To test the setting point, put a little jam on a cold saucer. If it develops a jellylike skin it is ready, you can turn off the heat; if not, boil for a few more minutes.

4 Let the jam stand in the pan for 15 minutes and remove any scum with a spoon. Ladle the mixture into sterilized jars while they are still warm (see Jo's Tips, left), top with the waxed disks, and screw on the lids.

Once you have opened the jam, it will keep in a refrigerator for about 1 month.

TRY THESE

Use this jam-making recipe with other fruit. The amount of sugar added varies according to the fruit used, but the ratio is always about 50:50 sugar to fruit.

Blackcurrant—This jam has a rich, dark color and lovely sharpness. It's also one of the easiest to make.

Strawberry—The essential topping for scones can be tricky to set, so add lemon juice or use preserving sugar.

Gooseberry—Its natural tang counters the sugar perfectly, giving a delicious jam that's an unexpected pink color.

Plum—Use a glut of fruit to produce plenty of firm-textured jam, but remember to remove the stones first.

MAKING SIMPLE FRUIT JAM

July: ready to eat

Revel in the bonanza of berries and currants, and remember to preserve plenty for leaner months ahead. Tasty tomatoes, peppers, and cucumbers will be ready to harvest, along with crisp snap and runner beans.

Kohlrabi is best diced and boiled

Enjoy a cornucopia of **currants**

Globe artichokes make elegant eating

Eat fresh **onions** and **shallots**

Make the most of **broccoli** and **summer cauliflower**

Snip **herbs** often to encourage tasty new shoots

Snap and **runner beans** are ready to pick, cook, and eat

Eat new season **summer raspberries**

Gooseberries are finishing soon, so pick what you can

Rhubarb finishes this month—make pies and crumbles

First **tomatoes**— a summer high

Steam **spinach** and fresh **summer cabbage**

If you've run out of spinach, use colorful **Swiss chard** instead

Green onions, cooked or raw, add flavor to many dishes

Strawberries—don't miss a single berry

Pick your **zucchini** often for a long crop

Cut-and-come-again salads do just that, again and again

Don't forget what's underground—tasty roots like **beets** and **turnips**

Cucumbers right on cue

Delicious **new potatoes** are best cooked simply, and eaten often

Salad is the essence of summer and now is peak **lettuce** season

Fiery **summer radishes** are so easy to grow

Eat fresh **bok choy** and crisp **Chinese cabbage**

Curiously-shaped **summer squash** are delicious roasted

Florence fennel adds a sweet aniseed-tang to a variety of summer dishes

Add **edible flowers** to your salads for extra color

Pick **peas** and **snap peas** when young and tender, and freeze a surplus *pages 148–149*

The first **blackberries** are a must

Cherries and **apricots** don't keep; eat quickly or preserve them now *pages 162–163*

New **peppers** are a sweet treat

July: what to sow

STILL TIME TO SOW

Outdoors, sow: radish (p.27), kohlrabi (p.41), turnip, broccoli, (p.54), Florence fennel, endive (p.74), kale, lettuce, cauliflower (p.75), carrots (p.94), chicory, chard (p.95), and Chinese cabbage (p.110). Plant late maincrop potatoes (p.83).

BETTER BEETS

HARVEST: AUG–OCT

This is a good month to sow beets outdoors for an fall crop. Choose round varieties, and sow ¾ in (2 cm) deep, thinning to 4 in (10 cm).

'RED ACE'
A popular variety, it produces dark red roots, and grows well in drier weather without bolting.

'CHIOGGIA PINK'
The plump, red and white striped roots fade to pink when cooked, but are sweet and tender to eat.

'PABLO'
This variety is a good all-rounder that can be grown for early baby roots, as well as fall crops.

SOW

BEETROOT

LATE SEASON PEAS

SPRING CABBAGE & WINTER RADISH

SOW FALL PEAS

HARVEST: SEP–OCT

Act now, and there's still time go grow a fresh crop of peas in time for fall. Choose dwarf varieties of shelling-types or snow peas, and sow them direct.

1 PREPARE THE SITE
To avoid summer heat, pick a slightly shaded spot and prepare the soil for planting. You can also use large containers, kept shaded.

2 SOW THE SEED
Sow seed 1½ in (4 cm) deep in rows, spaced 6–8in (15–20 cm) apart. Sow clusters in pots at the same depths and distances.

3 GROW THEM ON
Cover the seed with soil and insert pea sticks or plastic netting for support. Keep well watered and tie new growth to supports at first.

COLD SEASON CROPS

There always seems to be a cabbage to sow and this month it's spring varieties, like 'Pixie'. They can be sown in a seedbed, but if space is tight, try sowing them in cell packs outdoors to plant out later, once mature enough. Large winter radishes should also be sown outside now, ½ in (1 cm) deep, in rows spaced 12 in (30 cm) apart. Thin to 6 in (15 cm) spacing for good-sized roots.

HARVEST: **VARIOUS**

July: what to plant

PLANTING LEEKS OUTSIDE

HARVEST: **DEC–APR**

Late varieties of leeks, such as 'Musselburgh' (p.225), sown in late spring into flats or in a seedbed, should be large enough to plant out.

Prepare the site by weeding it thoroughly, and dig in plenty of well-rotted compost to encourage strong, leafy growth.

1 LIFT AND SEPARATE
Carefully lift the young leeks from the seedbed, or tip them from their flat, and separate the roots.

2 PLANT DEEPLY
Leeks need to be planted into holes, 6 in (15 cm) deep, to give them blanched, white stems. Use a dibble.

3 PROVIDE SPACE
Leave room to grow. Space the plants at 6 in (15 cm) intervals, in rows 12 in (30 cm) apart.

4 ALLOW TO SETTLE
Water well but don't firm the soil. Let the holes naturally fill with earth, blanching the stems.

LEEKS

STRAWBERRIES

ENDIVE & WINTER CABBAGE

PLANT

SUMMER BERRIES

Strawberries do well on a free-draining, sunny site, where plenty of well-rotted manure has been added. Avoid beds where strawberries have been grown recently because they're prone to soil-borne diseases. Plant until early fall for fruit next year, spacing the plants about 18 in (45 cm) apart, with 30 in (75 cm) between rows. Position the crown at the base of the leaves level with the soil.

HARVEST: **JUN–SEP**

TASTY LEAVES

Plant out endive and winter cabbage, sown April (p.74) and May (p.95). Both crops like a sunny bed and moist, fertile soil. Space the cabbages 20 in (50 cm) apart each way, and the endive, 12 in (30 cm). Cover cabbages with row covers to keep out butterflies. Crop them December – March. Harvest endive September – March.

HARVEST: **VARIOUS**

Strawberries

Strawberries are the ultimate summer fruit treat and it's possible to grow them in any garden, either in the soil or containers. They are prone to disease, so plants are usually replaced, and beds moved, every 3 years. To extend the fruiting season, grow strawberries under cover, and plant everbearing and day-neutral types.

Junebearers

These are the strawberries that are worth waiting for. Warmed by the early summer sun, their syrupy sweet aroma and smooth juicy flesh must be one of the best things it's possible to produce from your own garden.

The trouble with June-bearing varieties is that each one only fruits for 2–3 weeks. Where you have space, grow a combination of early-, mid- and late-season varieties for a succession of fruit from late May until the middle of July. They can also be moved into the greenhouse or cloched in late winter, which should give you a crop of berries 3 weeks earlier than unprotected plants.

If you are looking for a crop in the first year, buy cold-stored runners in late spring, plant them right away, and if all goes well you should have a harvest in July. Ordinary field-grown plants that are potted up for sale in late summer should bear well the following year if planted before fall sets in.

Everbearers

Although they don't produce many runners, these varieties produce sporadic bursts of fruit from late summer until they are stopped by the first fall frosts. If the weather is not too cold, and you can cover them with cloches, plants may continue fruiting into midwinter, especially container-grown plants moved under cover. Their flavor and texture are rarely considered a match for June-bearing strawberries, but modern varieties are starting to come close, and their yields are improving too. Plant them in late summer or early fall for a crop the following year. Replace plants annually if possible, because they won't produce as many berries in following seasons.

All-season strawberries

Different again are day-neutral strawberries, which have been bred especially to be insensitive to daylength. They can grow and fruit at any time of year, as long as the temperature is kept at a minimum of 50°F (10°C). Because of their dry, firm flesh, they are no real competition for June-bearing varieties, but they are worth planting in pots during midsummer and moving into the greenhouse in mid-fall for flushes of fruit right through winter. Try them indoors on a bright windowsill.

1

4

7

STRAWBERRIES

JUNEBEARERS

1 'Honeoye' is a reliable variety that gives a good crop of juicy, bright red fruits in early summer. Disease-resistant, it is a good choice for beginners. Try growing it in containers.

2 'Symphony' is a late-season variety that fruits mid-July, giving a good crop. The firm fruit have a rich flavor, and are delicious fresh or cooked. Grow it with an early variety for a longer harvest.

3 'Pegasus' gives a large crop of sweet, juicy berries, mid-season, June to July. The fruit are firm and last well once picked, but are best eaten fresh. This variety has good disease resistance.

4 'Florence' is a straightforward variety to grow that gives a good crop of large, firm, dark red berries in midsummer. It is resistant to pests and diseases, so it is a good choice to grow organically.

5 'Korona' is a reliable, early variety that gives a generous harvest of large, red, sweet-tasting fruit in June and July. It is disease resistant. Plant it with a later variety for a prolonged crop.

EVERBEARERS

6 'Mara de Bois' produces sweet, fragrant fruit, with a delicious wild strawberry flavor. It fruits twice, early and late summer, or you can remove the earlier flowers for a stronger late crop.

7 'Flamenco' bears in early and late summer, producing occasional fruit in between. The fruits are large, firm, and juicy, with a good flavor. They are very good for freezing (pp.150–151).

ALL-SEASON STRAWBERRIES

8 'Fern' will fruit whenever it's warm enough, producing good-sized, bright red fruit. Plants have berries at different stages, making them attractive to grow in pots. Good for freezing.

9 'Selva' gives a good crop of large red berries throughout summer and into fall. The fruits have a dry texture and a mild flavor, and are best used for making jam (pp.128–129).

July: what to do

HILL UP BRASSICAS

Lofty winter brassicas, such as purple sprouting broccoli and brussels sprouts, can be rocked or pulled out of the soil by fall and winter winds. Now is the time to get them well anchored in the ground, ready for a change in the weather. Draw up soil around the base of their stems and firm it as they grow. In exposed gardens it is worth staking each plant as well.

PINCH OUT

Climbing snap and runner beans will keep going upward for as long as you let them, so pinch out their leading shoots when they reach the top of their supports. This helps divert energy into the production of flowers and beans, and prevents tangled stems.

TEND

BRASSICAS

BEANS

BRASSICA PESTS

TOMATOES

CABBAGE WHITE CAUTION

When you see white butterflies flitting above brassica beds, be sure that they are laying eggs. Only fine netting will keep them out.

EGGS
Check the undersides of brassica leaves. If you have good eyesight, you will see clusters of the cabbage white butterfly's tiny pale eggs.

CATERPILLARS
Hoards of hungry green or black speckled caterpillars will soon hatch out. Pick them off before they start to devour your crops.

STOP YOUR VINES

In short-season areas, it's now time to "stop" vining tomatoes (pp.60–61) so they develop fruit rather than leaves. Pinch out the tops of plants when they reach the top of their canes or the apex of the greenhouse. Stop outdoor plants after they have formed four or five trusses of flowers and fruit. Water your plants regularly to help prevent the fruit from splitting (pp.122–123) or developing blossom end rot, right (p.240).

TRIM TRAINED TREES

Apple and pear trees that have been trained into espaliers or other formal forms, need pruning this month. A trim will maintain the shape of the tree and prevent new growth from taking up space needed by the developing fruit. Use clean, sharp pruners to cut back new shoots coming from the main stem to three leaves from their base. Also cut back shoots arising from existing fruiting spurs or sideshoots to one leaf.

SUMMER TRIM

Sour cherries fruit mostly on shoots formed the previous year, and established trees must be pruned now to encourage new growth for next year. After harvesting, and into early fall, cut back a quarter of the shoots that bore fruit to a healthy bud near their base. Also cut damaged or unproductive wood from older sour cherry and plum trees.

APRICOT FAN

PRUNE APPLES & PEARS

SOUR CHERRIES & PLUMS

SUMMER FAN PRUNING

Summer pruning of established, fan-trained apricots, plums, and cherries is important, because it helps form fruiting wood for future years.

1 TIE IN
Choose which new shoots you want to grow on for producing fruit and tie them into the fan where they will fill gaps.

2 SHORTEN
Look for new shoots that you don't need to tie in to form part of the framework and shorten them to six leaves from their base.

3 CUT BACK FURTHER
After the harvest ends, the untied shoots that you have already shortened need further pruning. Cut them back to three leaves.

DON'T FORGET

If you are going on vacation, ask friends or neighbors to water your plants. Tell them to reward themselves by picking any fruit or vegetables that ripen during your absence.

July: more to do

PEST WATCH
Treat large infestations of aphids (p.236) on your crops; they can spread cucumber mosaic virus (p.241), causing leaves and fruits of cucumbers and zucchinis to become blotchy and distorted. Destroy any plants showing symptoms. Also look out for imported currantworm (p.237), whitefly (p.239), and caterpillars.

TRAIN GRAPEVINES
Vines, grown indoors or out, are commonly trained as cordons, with a single vertical main stem and horizontal laterals that carry flowers and fruit. In summer, pinch out any weak flowers to leave one truss per lateral, then cut each lateral back to two leaves beyond the flower truss. Cut back any lateral without flowers to five leaves, and any sideshoots from the laterals to one leaf. Thin the fruit in each bunch while small.

TEND

INSECT PESTS

GREENHOUSE CROPS

CURLY ENDIVE

GRAPES

DAILY CARE
In a hot summer, greenhouse crops need daily attention. Container plants need watering once a day and feeding with a high-potash fertilizer weekly once the first fruit has set. Good ventilation is also vital to cool the greenhouse and create air movement to help stop fungal diseases. Open all vents and doors fully on hot days, but close them at least partially at night to keep plants from being chilled by low temperatures.

BLANCHING
Blanching whitens and sweetens stems and leaves. Blanch endive when it is mature. Cover the center with a plate, or put a pot over the whole plant, for about 10 days. With celery (p.98), either tie the stems loosely with twine and gradually hill them up, or tie a collar around them when the stems are about 12 in (30 cm) tall.

ENCOURAGE YOUR BEANS

In hot, dry summer weather, runner bean flowers may be less likely to set, which means that no beans will start to form. To help prevent this, give the plants plenty of water at their bases: soak them well at least two or three times a week if the weather is particularly dry. You can also mist the flowers with water using a fine spray. If you have a persistent problem, it's worth experimenting with white-flowered varieties, such as 'White Lady', which seem to set beans more reliably in hot weather.

THIN OUT FRUIT

The natural "June drop" of fruitlets (p.121) can continue into July. Once this has finished, continue to thin fruit by hand. On apple trees, remove more of the fruitlets to leave one or two apples per cluster. Pears don't require as much thinning as apples. Thin them once the fruit is pointing downward, to two fruits per cluster.

RUNNER BEANS

APPLES & PEARS

WEEDS

UNWELCOME PLANTS

Weed your vegetable beds regularly to prevent annual weeds from seeding into the soil and the perennials establishing large, hard to remove roots. Hoe between crop rows to destroy weeds as soon as they appear, or use a hand fork to tackle stubborn patches.

HAIRY BITTERCRESS
Long seed pods develop when the flowers of this weed die down. Hairy bittercress is fairly easy to pull out when it is still in early growth.

CATCHWEED BEDSTRAW
Also known as cleavers, this plant has sticky leaves covered with tiny clinging hooks. It spreads rapidly and should be dug up by its roots.

GROUNDSEL
The yellow flowers of this plant develop into fluffy white seed heads like those of dandelions. Root it out before the seeds disperse.

BINDWEED
This persistent creeper and climber can quickly smother crops. It is hard to eliminate because it can regrow from any fragment of root.

See PRUNING FRUIT IN AUTUMN pages 206–207

Pruning fruit in summer

Where fall pruning concentrates on the long-term shape and structure of your fruit trees and bushes, the aim of summer pruning is to maintain their immediate size, health, and productivity. Most pruning tasks now are simple to do, and take just a new minutes, and can make all the difference between having neat, fruitful plants; and a messy garden and a disappointing crop.

Cut down to size

The main focus of summer pruning is to control soft new growth, which not only attracts insect pests, but also restricts airflow at the middle of the plant, encouraging diseases such as powdery mildew (p.243). It is also an opportunity to cut out weak or diseased growth. This is also a good time to train vines.

When pruning, always cut just above an outward-facing bud, using sharp pruners, cutting at 45° away from the bud. This drains rainwater away from the bud, preventing disease.

RED- AND WHITECURRANTS
Now is the time to prune all of this year's new growth, except the branch leaders, back to five leaves by midsummer. The main formative pruning is done in the winter (p.206).

GOOSEBERRIES
To help prevent mildew (p.243), prune branches in the middle of the bush to improve air flow. Cut back new growth to five leaves, leaving the leading tips of the branches uncut.

Jo's tips

Gooseberry bushes have a tendency to form droopy branches. To help keep the bush upright, prune to inward- and upward-facing buds, rather than to outward-facing buds, as you normally would with other shrubs and bushes.

Blackcurrants produce their best fruit on last summer's growth, so removing new wood now will affect the following year's crop. Prune these bushes during winter instead (p.206).

SUMMER-FRUITING RASPBERRIES
As soon as each cane has finished bearing, untie it from its support and cut it at ground level to remove it completely. Tie the young canes that will fruit next year into the supports.

FAN-TRAINED FIGS
Pinch back the growing tips of new shoots to five leaves. This will encourage lower buds on the shoot to produce embryonic fruit that will overwinter and ripen next summer.

Grape vine pruning

There are two main techniques used to train and prune grapes. The "single cordon" system involves maintaining a single upright stem, from which multiple fruiting laterals are trained against wires. It is often used for indoor grapes.

The "double guyot" system entails training two new branches horizontally each year, from which upright fruiting shoots develop. This system is widely used for outdoor vines. Whichever method you use, summer pruning is essential for a good crop, and to keep your vines under control.

1 TRAIN SINGLE CORDONS
Tie in the central leader against a cane attached to a framework of horizontal wires. Cut back all lateral stems that have no flowers to five leaves from the central leader.

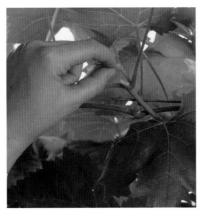

2 CUT BACK LATERALS
On mature plants, cut back flowering lateral stems to two leaves beyond the last truss, and tie them to the wires. Thin surplus trusses and pinch out sideshoots to one leaf.

1 TRAIN DOUBLE GUYOT GRAPES
Tie in new vertical shoots growing from branches trained horizontally in fall (p.205). Remove growing tips at the top wire and any sideshoots. Thin trusses to every 30cm (12in).

2 CHOOSE THREE STEMS
Train three sideshoots upwards from the vine's centre to provide next year's fruiting arms. Tie them into the supporting wires, and pinch back any sideshoots to one leaf as they grow.

PRUNING TOOLS

Choosing the right tool for the job makes pruning easier, and also helps prevent accidental damage, such as tears, occurring to your plants.

Pruners must be clean and sharp. Use them to cut new growth, and woody material up to pencil thickness.

Pruning saws are ideal for thicker stems and branches, although you need good access to saw effectively.

Loppers can be used to cut stems too thick for pruners, but too thin for a saw. Avoid twisting them as you cut.

Bow saws are only suitable for cutting thick branches. They are liable to tear smaller stems, causing damage.

July: what to harvest

PLENTIFUL BERRIES

Blackberries and summer raspberries will start ripening over the next few weeks, so pick every couple of days. Pick raspberries when they've turned a rich pink-red, pulling the soft fruit away from the core. Blackberries should be harvested when entirely black and glossy, and often come away with the core still in place. Both fruits keep fresh for only a day or two, so freeze any extras (pp.150–151).

CUCUMBERS NOW

In warm regions and in greenhouses, the first cucumbers will be ready for picking this month. Cut the fruit with some stalk, once they reach a usable size. Baby fruits are especially delicious. Pick regularly to avoid a glut because cucumbers don't keep well.

HARVEST

RASPBERRIES

CUCUMBERS

BEANS

CURRANTS

PICK BEANS OFTEN

The secret with snap and runner beans is to pick often. Harvest the pods small and tender for the tastiest crop; this will also help keep the plants productive for longer. Some varieties also do well when they get string if you use them as delicious green shelling beans. Whole beans freeze well, if you get overwhelmed (pp.148–149), but let some to develop and ripen for seed (pp.172–173).

CURRANT CROP

Currants of all colors are bearing this month in abundance. Pick sprigs of red- and whitecurrants whole, as they ripen. Usually, blackcurrants develop over a longer period, so pick the berries individually. Currants don't keep; pick and use them quickly, and freeze any that you can't eat right away.

PICK ZUCCHINI AND SUMMER SQUASH

These two crops are closely related and are grown in the same way (p.74 and p.115). They can both be picked when tiny, tender, and at their sweetest, or left to grow larger for stuffing.

'PATTY PAN'
This variety produces a large crop of saucer-shaped fruit that can be eaten whole when small and young, or allowed to grow on to full size.

'SUNBURST'
Produces bright yellow fruit that can be harvested as a baby vegetable or allowed to grow on. They taste delicious when roasted or fried.

'TROMBONCINO'
The elongated fruit can reach up to 3 ft (1 m) long but are best cut when they reach 12 in (30 cm). Allow plants to trail or train upward.

ALSO HARVEST

With lots of fruit and vegetables ready to harvest this month, check your broad beans — and don't overlook leafy crops. Pick bok choy, Chinese cabbage, radicchio, and sugarloaf chicory until fall.

ZUCCHINIS & SQUASHES

TOMATOES

ONIONS & SHALLOTS

TOMATO TIME

Tomatoes are a sure sign of summer, and the first fruit, sown in spring, are ready to harvest. Pick them as soon as the entire fruit turns red or yellow, depending on variety. Cherry-types should ripen first, followed by salad tomatoes, plum varieties, then the mighty beefsteaks. Pick regularly to encourage a prolonged crop. Best eaten fresh; if you have surplus tomatoes, try oven-drying them (pp.160–161).

FIRST ONIONS

Start lifting onions and shallots now as you need them, as soon as they're big enough to use. At this stage the edible leaves should still be green, and the bulbs juicy, with a slightly milder flavor than later, dried harvests. Lift whole clumps of shallots together because they keep well in their fresh state for a week or so.

See MAKING SIMPLE CHUTNEY pages 212–213

Making fruit cordials

What could be better than capturing the essence of home-grown soft fruit in delicious cordials, to enjoy on long, hot summer days? A simple combination of fresh fruit, sugar, and water are all you need to make these quick and easy syrups. Children love the fruity flavors and bold candy colors; just dilute to taste and serve with a straw. You can also freeze the cordial to make refreshing ice pops.

Blackcurrant cordial

Makes 16 fl oz (500 ml) of cordial
Takes 25 minutes
Keeps 1–2 months, refrigerated

Ingredients
1 lb (450 g) blackcurrants
(or loganberries)
12 oz (350 g) superfine sugar
1 tsp citric acid

Equipment
Large saucepan
Wooden spoon
Fine sieve
Measuring jug
Sterilized glass bottles

Jo's tips

If you make more cordial than you can use in 1 or 2 months, try freezing some, undiluted, in ice-cube trays. That way it will keep for up to 6 months, and the ice cubes can be used to cool, brighten up, and flavor glasses of water and other drinks.

Don't just dilute your cordial with plain water, try adding some fizz to it with sparkling water or lemonade. For a colorful and fruity 'Kir Royale' cocktail, mix champagne with homemade blackcurrant cordial.

1 **Place the fruit in a pan** and add just enough water to cover the bottom. Simmer the fruit very gently for the least time necessary to extract the juice, 3–5 minutes only. Pulp the fruit with a wooden spoon as it cooks.

2 **Remove from the heat** and allow the fruit mixture to cool a little, so it's safe to handle. Pour the fruit through a muslin or fine sieve resting over a jug, squashing the cooked fruit to extract as much juice as possible.

3 **Pour the juice into a measuring** cup and add 12 oz (350 g) of sugar to every 16 fl oz (500 ml) of liquid. Add the citric acid, and keep stirring until all the sugar is fully dissolved. Spoon off any floating fruit debris.

4 **Pour the syrup** into sterilized bottles, fasten the caps, and allow it to cool fully before storing it in the refrigerator. Drink the cordial diluted with water, adding plenty of ice cubes. Drink diluted cordial right away.

Homemade cordials are an additive-free alternative to those available in stores, and rich in color and flavor.

TRY THESE

Many different fruits can be used to make delicious summer cordials with the technique shown. Mix fruits and vary the amount of sugar to taste.

Raspberries—A true taste of summer, this cordial is best with lemon juice added to give it a little acidity.

Rhubarb—More of a grown-up treat, rhubarb gives cordial a sharp tang that is wonderfully refreshing.

Strawberries—Cook these delicate fruits very gently to preserve their bright red color and sweetness.

Redcurrants—Although weakly flavored, redcurrants add glorious color to mixed fruit cordials.

MAKING FRUIT CORDIALS

Making relishes and pesto

Relishes are tangy sauces that are easy to make, and the perfect way to use up and store a glut of vegetables and fruit from the garden. You can cook or pickle all kinds of produce in this way to provide delicious homemade accompaniments to burgers, cheese, cold meats, and barbecued food. Experiment with textures and flavors: smooth or chunky, sweet or spicy, fiery hot or mellow and fruity.

RECIPE IDEAS

Corn and pepper relish

Makes 2¼ lb (1 kg) (2 small jars)
Takes 35–40 minutes
Keeps 3 months

Ingredients

4 corn ears

2 red bell peppers, seeded and diced

1 red chile, seeded and sliced

2 celery stalks, sliced thinly

1 onion, sliced

2 cups white wine vinegar

1 cup granulated sugar

2 tsp sea salt

2 tsp mustard powder

½ tsp ground turmeric

1 **Holding the corn cobs upright,** strip off the kernels with a sharp knife. Blanch the kernels in a pot of boiling water for 2 minutes and then drain. Place all the ingredients in a large saucepan and bring to a boil.

2 **Stir the mixture** until the sugar dissolves, then lower the heat and simmer for 15–20 minutes, stirring frequently. Let the mixture thicken until a spoon drawn across the base of the pan leaves little liquid behind.

Jo's tips

Cucumbers make an ideal relish base. Cut out the seeds and salt the cucumber for an hour to draw out excess moisture.

If you want your pesto to last for several months, freeze some of it in ice-cube trays and bag it when frozen.

To sterilize your preserving jars, wash them in hot soapy water, place them on a rack in a moderate oven, and leave them there to dry thoroughly.

3 **Check the relish for flavor,** and adjust the seasoning according to taste, before carefully ladling it into warm, sterilized preserving jars (see Jo's Tips, left). The relish should have a wetter consistency than chutney.

4 **Seal the jars** with nonmetallic lids and leave them to cool. Label, and store your relish in a cool, dark place for up to 3 months. You can use the relish right away; once opened keep it in a refrigerator.

Preserve the taste of your summer garden produce by making a few jars of relish for your pantry.

TRY PESTO

Traditional homemade pesto perks up pasta and adds vibrant flavor to many meat and fish dishes. It is made in minutes and needs no cooking.

Makes 7 oz (200 g) (1 small jar)
Takes 10 minutes
Keeps 2 weeks in refrigerator or 6 months frozen

Ingredients

2½ oz (65 g) basil
1 garlic clove, lightly crushed
1 oz (30 g) pine nuts
freshly ground black pepper
1 oz (30 g) Parmesan cheese, grated
7 tbsp extra virgin olive oil
salt to taste

1 Pull the leaves off the basil and put them in a food processor with the garlic, pine nuts, black pepper, Parmesan, and 2 tablespoons of the olive oil, and blend coarsely.
2 With the blender running, add another 4 tablespoons of olive oil, a little at a time, and blend to a shiny paste. Add salt to taste.
3 Spoon the pesto into a sterilized jar (see Jo's Tips, opposite page) and top with the remaining oil to make the mixture airtight. Put the lid tightly on the jar and store in a refrigerator. If you use a little at a time, cover the rest with more oil.

Freezing vegetables

Freezing is a convenient way to store excess produce. It preserves fruits and vegetables, and their nutrients, for several months. Some freeze well simply cleaned, while some should be blanched—briefly immersed in boiling water—first. Others are only worth freezing once cooked into soups, sauces, or purées. Get to know what works; there's nothing more satisfying than having your freezer filled for winter.

Freezing vegetables

There are two general methods to use when freezing vegetables, depending on how long you want to store them. For short-term storage (for less than 3 months), cut the vegetables into usable-sized pieces and freeze them on a tray. Then bag them up, return them to the freezer, and use them as required.

For longer-term freezing, you need to blanch the vegetables before freezing to destroy natural enzymes that spoil flavor, color, and texture. Freeze root vegetables only after cooking into soups or stews first or else their texture will be spoiled.

1 Bring a large pan of water to a vigorous boil. Immerse smaller vegetables for 2 minutes, and larger ones for 4 minutes only. Drain the vegetables into a large strainer or net, to remove them all at once.

2 Prepare a basin of iced water while the vegetables boil. As soon as the time is up, lift the vegetables from the pan and plunge them into the iced water to stop them cooking further. Leave for several minutes.

Jo's tips

Always wrap food securely, and squeeze as much air as possible out of freezer bags before sealing. This helps to prevent freezer burn, which dries out frozen produce and causes it to spoil prematurely.

Label food clearly, including a date, so you can identify what soup is what in 3 months' time, and also so you can use older produce first.

3 Remove the vegetables from the iced water as soon as they have cooled, and drain them. Allow them to dry in a colander, or spread them out on clean dish towels or paper towels and blot them dry.

4 When dry, divide the vegetables into portion-sized quantities, pack them into freezer bags or sealed containers, label and date them, and place in the freezer. They will keep well for up to 6 months.

Freeze vegetables as individual portions and you can then simply defrost what you need.

TRY THESE

This freezing technique is suitable for a wide range of vegetables, including those listed below. Try to use all frozen vegetables within 6 months.

Snap and runner beans—Best picked young, when they snap between your fingers. Blanch before freezing.

Sprouting broccoli—It's easy to end up with a glut of broccoli, so cut the spears, wash, blanch, and tray freeze.

Asparagus—For asparagus to eat into late summer, blanch thin stems for 2 minutes, thick stems for 4 minutes.

Herbs—Finely chop herbs, such as basil and mint, and freeze them into handy cubes in an ice tray.

FREEZING VEGETABLES

Freezing fruit

When you grow your own, summer gluts of fruits such as berries, currants, and plums are unavoidable. The good thing is that fruit is quick and easy to freeze; you'll be able to make enough delicious pies and desserts to see you right through fall, winter, and beyond. Freezing retains the original flavor and texture of most fruits and is also the best way to preserve their valuable nutrient content.

Pan freezing

This simple freezing method suits small soft fruits well. All you need to do is spread the berries out in a single layer on a baking sheet, quickly freeze them, then bag or box it for long-term storage. Putting the fruit on a pan allows it to freeze faster than it would if densely packed into a bag or box. Rapid freezing creates smaller ice crystals than slow freezing, causing less damage to the fruit's cells and preventing everything from collapsing into a juicy mush on thawing. Pan freezing also keeps fruit from freezing into a solid lump, so you can take what you need, rather than having to defrost the whole batch.

Jo's tips

Cherries and plums both freeze well, but you should remove the stones first, otherwise they will give the fruit a bitter taint.

Strawberries are not well suited to freezing whole because they have a high water content, which causes them to become soggy once thawed. Try making sorbet, ice cream, or freezing them as a purée instead.

1 Choose ripe, undamaged fruit and freeze it as soon after harvesting as possible. Pick through it to remove any leaves and stems. Wipe or wash the fruit if necessary and spread it out in a single layer on a baking sheet.

2 Place the pan in the coldest part of the freezer and allow the fruit to freeze until it is completely solid. This should take no longer than 2 hours for small soft fruits such as blueberries or currants.

3 For long-term freezing, transfer the fruit from the baking sheet into freezer bags or boxes. Package it in single portions or larger quantities, as required. After pan freezing, the fruits shouldn't stick together in the bags.

4 Once you have filled the bags, gently squeeze them to remove as much air as possible and then seal them. Label and date each bag. Put them in the freezer, where they will keep for 6 months.

Pan-frozen before being bagged up, blueberries will keep their shape and texture.

TRY THESE

Pan freezing can be used to preserve a wide range of soft fruits. All of those below will freeze well to give you a taste of summer in the depths of winter.

Gooseberries—Top and tail these sharp, green berries before freezing so they can be used from the bag.

Raspberries—Remove the central plugs prior to freezing and wipe clean any dirty fruit rather than washing it.

Cherries—Remove the stalks and stones before freezing. They are worth the work for their gorgeous flavor.

Currants—All currants are easy to freeze. Just pull them gently from their stems directly onto the baking sheet.

FREEZING FRUIT

August: ready to eat

Keep a close eye on crops to pick them perfectly ripe. Beat the birds
to plums and other fruit, and pluck chiles as they turn orange and red.
Garlic, onions, and shallots are delicious now—dry some for storing.

Kohlrabi is best eaten young and tender

Still time for **new potatoes**

It's peak season for **onions** and **shallots** —use them fresh and leave some for drying

Enjoy plentiful salad crops, such as **cucumber**, **lettuce**, **radishes,** and **tomatoes**

Include fresh **broccoli** and **summer cauliflower** with your

Relish new season **eggplant** this month

Make the most of **Chinese cabbage, bok choy,** and **summer cabbage** this month

Pick **sweet peppers**

Eat the last **red-**, **white-,** and **blackcurrants** before they get past their prime

Eat **globe artichokes**

Keep clipping your **cut-and-come-again** salad greens

Use the last of the **fresh garlic**

Harvest **herbs** now and use them fresh or dry them for later in the year
page 161

Broad bean season is nearly over

New season **chiles** are hot this month

Keep eating your spinach and Swiss chard this month

Eat the season's first **melons**

Eat **zucchini** young and they'll continue producing for weeks

High summer brings **peaches**, **nectarines**, and **apricots** to the table

Florence fennel doesn't store well so use it now while it's still good to eat

New season **blueberries**

Enjoy the peas while you still can

Raw or cooked, enjoy **raspberries** and **blackberries**

Serve wilted **spinach** with butter and nutmeg—it's lovely

Cut your first new season **celery**

Feast on new season **plums and damsons**

It's a beanfeast, with **snap** and **runner beans** ready now

Carrots, **turnips**, and **beets** will keep producing for weeks—plan to store some for winter *pages 210–211*

Strawberries are still going strong; eat them fresh and store what you can for later in the year

August can be **fig heaven**

August: what to sow

LATE SEASON CROPS

HARVEST: AUG–DEC

Make one more sowing of these quick crops now for a tasty and bountiful last harvest. They may need cloching in cooler areas.

ARUGULA
Sow in a slightly shaded bed to prevent bolting, ½ in (1 cm) deep in row; thin to 6in (15 cm) apart.

KOHLRABI
Ready to pick in 4–5 weeks, sow in ½ in (1 cm) deep rows, spaced 10 in (25 cm). Thin to 4 in (10 cm).

TURNIP
Sow like kohlrabi, and lift some as baby roots in a few weeks, allowing others to mature fully.

SOW

JAPANESE ONIONS

CARROTS

LATE SEASON CROPS

SPRING BULBS

Certain types of onions, often described as Japanese varieties, can be sown toward the end of late summer, and overwintered for an early crop of bulbs in late spring. Try sowing a variety such as 'Buffalo' or 'Senshyu', in rows 12 in (30 cm) apart and thin to 2–4 in (5–10 cm) apart. This should give you sturdy young plants that will see out the winter and shoot up quickly in spring.

HARVEST: **MAY–JUN**

LAST CARROTS

To make a last sowing of fall carrots, use a faster maturing early-variety, like 'Early Nantes', and cloche the crop at the onset of fall. Sow thinly in rows with 6 in (15 cm) between them, and thin seedlings to 2 in (5 cm) apart. A real advantage of sowing carrots this late is that they shouldn't have any problems with carrot rust fly.

HARVEST: **AUG–DEC**

August: what to plant

HARDY WINTER CROPS

HARVEST: **VARIOUS**

Spring cauliflowers and winter sprouting broccoli, sown in early summer, are now ready to transplant into their winter beds. Space them 2 ft (60 cm) apart each way, firm the soil around plants to keep them from rocking in windy weather, and net to keep off birds.

'CLARET'
A sprouting broccoli, this is a late maturing variety that produces for a long period. Good for cooler regions.

'RUDOLPH'
This early sprouting broccoli produces flavor-rich, dark florets in midwinter. Freeze surpluses.

'WINTER AALSMEER'
For well-formed, smaller curds, try this hardy variety. It ripens over a longer period than most hybrids.

'WALCHEREN WINTER PILGRIM'
Very winter hardy, this robust cauliflower gives a good spring crop of large white heads.

BABY LEAF SALAD

CHICORY

WINTER CAULIFLOWER

PLANT

SALAD LEAVES 24/7

HARVEST: **SEP–FEB**

If you've been sowing salad crops all summer, transplant some seedlings now and bring them under cover for fresh leaves in the lean winter months.

1 PICK YOUR PLANTS
Choose a selection of baby leaf plants, picking the largest, heathiest specimens. Lift them with as much root as possible.

2 POT THEM UP
Fill a large container with potting mix and plant the baby leaf plants, leaving enough space around each one to grow a little.

3 GROW AND HARVEST
Water well and grow the plants on under cover. Harvest regularly, giving the plants time to regrow, especially in cold periods.

WINTER CHICORY

Outdoor chicory crops are prone to rotting in wet winter conditions. To enjoy a reliable harvest of leaves during winter, plant containerized seedlings, sown in early August, under cover in a greenhouse or cold frame. Choose radicchio or sugarloaf varieties and plant out them as soon as they're large enough, spacing the plants 8–10 in (20–25 cm) apart. Water in well.

HARVEST: **OCT–MAR**

August: what to do

LET IN LIGHT
Tomatoes, winter squashes, and pumpkins all need plenty of sunlight to ripen, but the fruit is often shaded by foliage. By late summer, with growth slowing, it's safe to remove a few of their overshadowing leaves. Take off the lower leaves of tomato plants so that the more mature fruit ripen first. In areas that experience hot summers, be cautious: exposed squashes can get sunburned.

POTATO BLIGHT
A fungal disease called late blight commonly occurs in warm, wet summers. The infection causes brown patches on the edges of leaves. Remove affected plant tops as soon as they start to die down. Don't compost them; ideally, burn them.

TEND

TOMATOES & SQUASHES

CORN

RASPBERRIES

POTATOES

READY TO EAT?
Corn tastes good only when perfectly ripe. Wait until the silks at the top of the ear turn dark brown before checking.

1 CHECK THE EAR
Carefully pull back some of the leaves covering the ear. The kernels are ripe when they are a buttery shade of pale yellow.

2 HARVEST LATER
Test several ears, wrapping each one up again if it is not ripe. It's better to wait until next month (p.175) than pick too soon.

CUTTING CANES
As soon as the last berry is picked from summer-fruiting raspberries, cut the fruited canes right down to ground level. The new canes that came up this year will be the ones that bear next year's crop. These need to be spread evenly along the supporting wires and tied in with twine. Cut out any new canes that look weak and spindly, leaving only strong, healthy stems coming from each plant.

BEAT THE SLUGS
In some gardens, small soil-dwelling slugs can cause considerable damage by burrowing into potato crops. The spoiled parts can just be cut out if the potatoes are being eaten right away, but if you plan to store your crop into the winter (pp.210–211), slug damage will allow rot to set in. If you see signs of slug attack on crops destined for storage, lift unmarked tubers as soon as possible to minimize the problem. Make sure the potatoes are dry before storing them in paper bags somewhere cool and dark.

CLEAN UP
Good garden hygiene helps prevent the spread of pests and diseases. When each crop has finished, remove all spent plant material from the bed and compost it, or burn it if disease was present. To help stop diseases from building up in the soil, practice crop rotation: grow groups of closely related plants in a different bed each year.

POTATOES

GARDEN HYGIENE

DISEASES

HEALTH CHECK
Hot, dry conditions in summer cause plants stress and leave them vulnerable to disease (pp.240–245). Feed and water them, and watch for danger signs.

MAGNESIUM DEFICIENCY
Look out for yellowing leaves. Plants affected include fruit trees, potatoes, and tomatoes. Feed magnesium as a foliar spray.

BROWN ROT
This fungus spreads rapidly among tree fruits, causing rot. Cut off all infected fruits, together with their branch tips, and burn them.

BOTRYTIS (GRAY MOLD)
Many plants can be infected by this airborne fungus. Keeping your garden cleared of debris and dead plants is the best defense.

DON'T FORGET

To encourage your hazelnuts to produce more fruit buds and to reduce vigor, snap without breaking off lateral shoots over 12 in (30 cm) long. This is practice is called "brutting."

See STARTING A COMPOST HEAP pages 190–191

August: what to harvest

SUMMER MELONS

If your melons were sown in April (p.74) and planted in the garden in May (p.101), you'll know when they're ripening because of the rich melon scent that fills the air. Melons are ready to pick when, in addition to their sweet aroma, they're slightly softer at the stalk end, and they come away from the stalk when lifted. Pick when fully ripe and eat immediately. Melons don't store well.

READY OR NOT

It can be tricky to tell when eggplants are ripe because not all varieties develop the tell-tale, smooth, shiny skin. Swelling around the middle of the fruit indicates the seeds are forming, and time to harvest. Cut and cook as soon as possible.

HARVEST

PEPPERS & CHILES   **MELONS**   **CELERY**   **EGGPLANT**

PICK YOUR PEPPERS

Both these crops need lots of heat to ripen fully, and during poor summers in cooler regions, the fruits may stay green.

1 PICK GREEN
Cut the first full-sized fruits of peppers and chiles while still green to encourage further fruit to develop on the plants.

2 LEAVE TO RIPEN
Allow later fruit to mature to yellow, orange, or red for a richer, sweeter flavor. Green fruits have a slightly bitter taste.

CRISP CELERY

Self-blanching celery will start to become ready over the next few weeks. You can either cut individual stems at the base to use as you need them, or lift the whole plant at one time with a fork. Sown in spring, celery is best eaten as soon as the stems are crisp and juicy. If you can't eat them all, freeze the surplus (p.148–149), or leave plants in the ground until the first frosts. Don't wait too long—it may become dry and pithy.

LIFT AND DRY BULBS

After a long growing season, spring-sown onions, and garlic planted last fall, are now ready to harvest. Lift garlic bulbs with a fork once their leaves start to yellow, being careful not to bruise the bulbs. The cloves may start to sprout if you leave them too long. Leave onions and shallots until the foliage has died down before gently lifting them. Spread them out on wire mesh or wooden slats outside in the sun to dry for 7–10 days, or do the same in a well ventilated area indoors if it's wet outside.

RIPE TO EAT

Now is peak season for cherry, plum, damson, apricot, and peach trees, but exact ripening times depend on variety and weather. Even on a single tree, the fruit will ripen at different times, so check often. To pick, pull plums and damsons from their stalks, cut cherries with their stems, and lift and twist apricots and peaches in your palm.

ONIONS, GARLIC, & SHALLOTS

TREE FRUIT

BLUEBERRIES

BEAUTIFUL BLUEBERRIES

If planted in fall (p.198), they bear over a few weeks. Pick and eat them as soon as possible. If dry, they will store in the refrigerator for a few days.

'BLUETTA'
A productive variety that bears deep blue berries, roughly ½ in (1 cm) across. It flowers later than many, so is good for cooler regions.

'SPARTAN'
Early-bearing variety with light blue fruit that have a sweet, tangy flavor. Like all blueberries, the taste is more intense when cooked.

'EARLIBLUE'
This variety also bears early, producing a high yield of pale blue fruit, held in conveniently large clusters. Eat fresh or freeze.

HANDY HINT

To help your chiles develop their distinctive fieriness, water them only sparingly as the fruit grows. If you prefer milder chiles, water the plants more.

Try WINE MAKING pages 180–181

Drying fruit and vegetables

Drying is a simple, effective method of preserving fruit and vegetables, for a few weeks to several months. The key to success is ensuring that the produce is totally dehydrated—moisture allows mold to develop. In cooler regions, oven-drying is the most reliable way to dry crops with a high water content, like apples. Those with a low water content, like chiles and herbs, can be easily air-dried indoors.

Oven-drying fruit

An ordinary oven is all you need to dry extra fresh of fruit, such as apples, plums, and tomatoes. Wash and dry the fruit well, and halve or slice larger ones to speed up the drying process. Set the oven at a low temperature and place your produce on wire racks on the lower shelves. How long they take to dry depends on the fruit and how moist it is—the juicier, it is the longer it'll be. Leave them at least 2 hours, then check every 30 minutes. Larger fruit may take several hours.

1 Wash the fruit well. Leave berries whole, but cut plums and tomatoes in half. Strawberries and apples need to be sliced to dry well. Core apples, stone plums, and dip into lemon juice to prevent them from browning.

2 Lay the fruit out evenly on a wire rack, so it doesn't overlap, and so there is plenty of room for air to circulate. If the pieces are too small to sit on a rack, arrange them on a lightly oiled baking sheet instead.

Jo's tips

Try making "fruit leather." Purée the fruit and remove the seeds. Spread it ¼ in (5 mm) thick on a well-oiled baking sheet. Place in the oven on a low heat for several hours until the purée is dehydrated and leathery. Break into pieces and enjoy it as a snack, or add it to cereals.

If you don't have a place to hang crops, you can buy or build a drying box—a large wooden box with ventilation holes and a door for access. This offers an effective way to dry home-grown produce.

3 Switch your oven to the lowest setting and put the fruit inside. The idea is for the food to dehydrate, not cook. To prevent the temperature getting too high, open the oven door periodically. Check the fruit regularly.

4 After several hours, when the fruit feels light and dry to the touch, remove it from the oven. Allow it to cool completely before putting it in airtight jars, sealing, and storing in a cool dark place for 2–4 weeks.

Dried apple rings will keep for a few weeks, but chiles and herbs last for months if kept dry.

Air-drying

One of the best ways to preserve crops that have a low moisture content is to air-dry them. This is a slower process than oven-drying, and is particularly well suited to chiles, bunches of herbs, and shelled beans, which will all keep for months if properly dried and stored. All you need for this technique is somewhere indoors that is warm and well-ventilated, such as a spare room, or even a shed or garage. Avoid kitchens due to the steam caused by cooking, which prevents effective drying.

Chiles and beans—The easiest way to dry chiles and beans is to lay them out on a wire rack and place them in a dry, airy place for a few weeks. Chiles can also be threaded onto a string and hung in bunches to dry.

Herbs—Cut sprigs of woody-stemmed herbs, such as sage, sweet bay, and marjoram, and hang them in bunches somewhere dry and well ventilated. Soft-leaved herbs, such as basil and cilantro, don't dry well—instead freeze them into ice cubes.

Canning fruit in syrup

There's an air of luxury to canned fruit that sets it apart from even the finest jams and frozen berries. Flawless, home-grown fruits, suspended in clear, richly colored syrup, look impressive but are easy to achieve. You don't even have to cook the peaches used in this recipe. The trick to canning is to catch your fruit at perfect ripeness; under-ripe, it'll be hard and lack flavor, over-ripe and it will disintegrate.

RECIPE IDEAS

Canned peaches

Makes 2 cups (2 small jars)
Takes about 15 minutes
Keeps 1 year

Ingredients
4–5 firm, ripe peaches
½ cup granulated sugar
2 ½ cup water

Equipment
Large saucepan
Sharp kitchen knife
2 x preserving jars with lids

1 **Remove skins from** the peaches. If they are difficult to peel, dip the fruit in boiling water for about 30 seconds; the skins should then slip off easily. Cut the peaches in half and carefully remove the stones.

2 **Place the sugar and water** in a large pan, bring to a boil, and continue to boil for about 2 minutes, or until the sugar has dissolved. The quantities given here make a medium-sweet sugar syrup. Add more to taste.

Jo's tips

In addition to peaches, other softer fruits such as berries, cherries, and plums can also be packed into jars raw and covered with sugar syrup to preserve them. Larger, firmer fruits such as apples and pears are usually cooked for a few minutes before canning.

To sterilize your jars, wash them in hot soapy water, place them on a rack in a moderate oven, and leave them to dry thoroughly.

3 **Stand your sterilized jars** in a roasting pan while they are still warm (see Jo's Tips, left). Fill the jars with fruit, leaving a space of about ½ in (1 cm) below the rim. Ladle in the hot sugar syrup until the jars are full.

4 **Seal the jars** with their lids while they are still hot. Allow them to cool, add labels, and store in a dark, cool place. It takes time for the fruit and syrup to fully infuse, so leave for at least 6 weeks before opening.

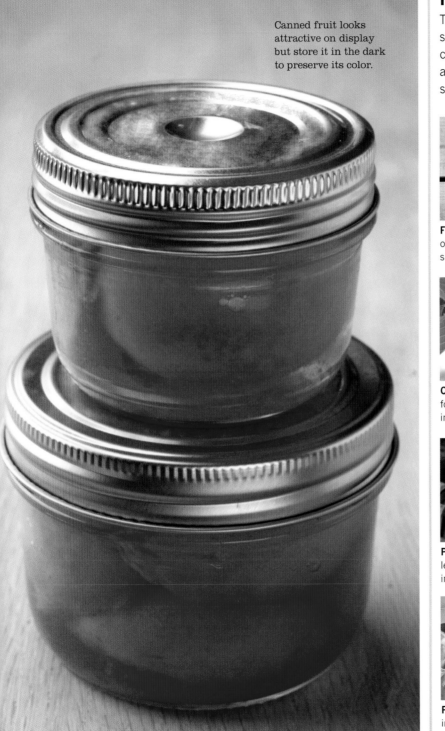

Canned fruit looks attractive on display but store it in the dark to preserve its color.

TRY THESE

Tree fruits often bear heavily, so there are usually plenty for canning. It's a good way of using a glut of fruit that doesn't keep, such as plums and cherries.

Figs—Leave the fruit whole, don't cut off ends and stems, and cook in a light sugar syrup for just a few minutes.

Cherries—Canned cherries are ideal for festive desserts. Pit fruits and bottle in syrup with a splash of kirsch.

Pears—Peel the fruit, cut in half lengthwise, and core before boiling in syrup for about 5 minutes.

Plums—These soft fruits can simmer in spiced syrup, or be packed into jars raw. Remove the stones first.

CANNING FRUIT IN SYRUP

September: ready to eat

Fall is in the air, with early apples ready for harvest, ripe corn, and pumpkins and winter squashes hardening their skins in the sunshine. Parsnips and early leeks are also nearly ready again, too.

New season ears of **corn** are plump and ready to harvest

Collect **seeds** for storing *pages 172–173* from herbs such as fennel, dill, and cilantro

Eat luscious **blackberries**

Globe **artichokes** are at the very end of their season

You may have a final **melon** in the greenhouse

Cauliflowers planted out in early summer should have tight-packed curds now

Pick a head of crunchy fresh **celery**

The last **strawberry** crop will come to an end this month

Figs are ripe and heavy on the tree, so pick and eat them quickly

Enjoy **summer peas** and **beans** while they last

Use some **turnips** now, let others grow larger for storage *pages 210–211*

Pick **spinach** sown in early summer

It may be fall, but **summer salad crops** continue—cucumber, lettuce, tomatoes, and radishes can still be harvested

Crunchy, fresh-picked **carrots** should be keeping you well supplied

This month sees the last of the **peaches**

Let new season **pumpkins** and **winter squashes** harden off for storing

Pick **zucchini** while young, and eat the male flowers, too

Dry **onions** and **shallots** for a week or two before using

Grill some **eggplant**—on the BBQ if the weather is mild

Fall **raspberries** are perfect for special treats

Time to harvest the late-season **potatoes**

Beets sown in the summer are ready to be harvested—pull them while small

Eat early **grapes,** if they're sweet enough, or try making wine
pages 180–181

Use the last **blueberries** to make healthy fruit shakes

Steam or stir-fry versatile **Chinese cabbage**

Early apples are crisp and full of juice

New **leeks** are ready —don't hesitate to try them

Mild-flavored **broccoli** goes well with chicken or pasta dishes

Use **chiles** fresh, or dry or freeze them
pages 148–149
for later

Harvest **Florence fennel** bulbs for cooking and use the leaves for salads

Kohlrabi is tasty when eaten cooked or grated raw in salads

September: what to sow

GROW YOUR OWN SOIL IMPROVERS

Sow green manure crops now to protect and improve empty beds during winter. Dig in the young plants 4 weeks before next year's crops are planted, to improve the soil with nutrients and organic matter.

ALFALFA
This plant has a long taproot that penetrates into heavy soil to help break it up and aid drainage.

RED CLOVER
A legume, this plant absorbs nitrogen from the atmosphere and locks it into the soil for plants.

WINTER RYE
This dense grass helps suppress weeds, while its fine roots improve soil structure. Good on light soil.

SOW

SPINACH & WINTER LETTUCE

GREEN ONIONS & RADISHES

GREEN MANURES

LATE LEAVES

This is an ideal time to sow spinach and winter lettuce to grow on under cover for winter crops. Choose fast-growing spinach varieties, such as 'Triathlon', and winter varieties of butterhead and crisphead lettuce, like 'Valdor' and 'Winter Density'. You may be able to harvest all winter. Sow ½ in (1 cm) deep, and plant out in a cold frame or greenhouse before the end of fall.

HARVEST: **NOV–MAR**

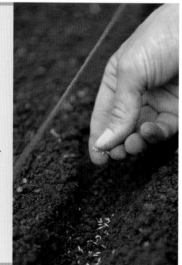

SOW ONIONS

Make a last sowing of green onions and radishes now. Use a hardy spring onion variety, like 'Evergreen Hardy White', for a winter crop, sowing thinly, ½ in (1 cm) deep, in rows 6 in (15 cm) apart. In cold areas, cloche green onions in winter. Also sow summer radishes thinly in rows ½ in (1 cm) deep, thinning to ¾ in (2 cm), to pick in fall.

HARVEST: **OCT–DEC**

September: what to plant

FEELING PEACHY

HARVEST: **AUG–SEPT**

Container-grown trees can be planted at any time, but fall planting is a very good choice. Dig in plenty of compost, especially at the base of walls, and plant at the same depth as the soil mark on the trunk. Water well and stake, or fix fan-trained trees with wires.

PEACH 'DUKE OF YORK'
Grown against a warm wall, this variety will produce a good crop of large, yellow-fleshed fruit.

PEACH 'PEREGRINE'
This is a high-yielding variety, with sweet, red-flushed fruit. Give it a warm, sunny, sheltered site.

NECTARINE 'FANTASIA'
This hardy variety produces large, juicy, yellow-fleshed fruit that ripen throughout July. Suitable for pots.

NECTARINE 'LORD NAPIER'
Late-ripening, this variety has thin-skinned, very juicy fruit that mature red. A reliable producer.

JAPANESE ONIONS

SPRING CABBAGE

PEACHES & NECTARINES

PLANT

ONION SETS

HARVEST: **MAY–JUN**

In mild-winter areas, plant out sets of Japanese over-wintering varieties, such as 'Buffalo', outdoors.

1 PLANT THE SETS
In a sunny, weed-free bed, push each set into the soil so that just the tip is showing.

2 FIRM THEM IN
Space the sets 2–4 in (5–10 cm) apart, and allow about 12 in (30 cm) between rows.

PLANT OUT CABBAGES

Between now and mid-fall, transplant spring cabbages, sown in cell packs or seedbeds (p.132), into their final positions for overwintering. Find a sunny spot, with fertile soil that has not recently been dug over or manured. This will avoid the plants producing soft leafy growth that can be damaged by frosts. Space plants 12 in (30 cm) apart each way to encourage good-sized heads.

HARVEST: **APR–JUN**

See CHOOSING AND PLANTING TREES pages 202–203

September: what to do

CUT DOWN ASPARAGUS

The tall feathery fronds of asparagus will have turned yellow now and may be starting to topple over. Cut them down with a pair of sharp pruners, clipping off the stems as close to the soil as possible. The foliage is prickly, so be careful how you handle it. Once you have cleared the asparagus bed, spread a well-rotted organic mulch over it to help keep the soil in good condition for next year.

FEED LEEKS

A bed of large, healthy leeks should see you through the winter. These tough plants rarely require watering but they do benefit from an occasional feeding with a balanced liquid fertilizer, so give them a boost before the end of the growing season.

TEND

ASPARAGUS

LEEKS

PROTECT

CELERIAC

FROST PROTECTION

Early fall is often mild, but if you live in a cool area where night frosts are likely, then consider covering your late crops.

ROW COVER TUNNEL
Make a protective tunnel cloche by securing lightweight row cover over wire hoops. You can easily remove the fabric in the daytime.

PVC CLOCHE
This type of cloche can be left open during the day for ventilation. For frost protection, close off the ends at night with plastic sheeting.

CELERIAC CARE

To encourage the stems of celeriac to bulk out for a good winter crop, regularly remove any damaged or older leaves. Just pull them away with a firm tug near the base of the plant. The tops of the swollen stems will soon start to appear above the soil. Celeriac plants will benefit from plenty of water during dry weather. The regular application of a balanced liquid fertilizer will also help keep them growing strongly.

EMPTY THE BINS

Fall may see a glut of compostable waste as plants die back and you tidy up for the winter. Make room for this by using up what is already in your compost bin (see pp.190–191). Apply a mulch of home-produced compost around crops that are going to overwinter or add it to recently cleared beds. With your bin empty, you can start again. Plants that have finished producing mix well with fall garden prunings, grass clippings, and fallen leaves to produce more compost for the following year.

RIPEN INDOORS

If frost threatens, take action to salvage the remainder of your outdoor tomatoes. Cut down vining varieties, and either hang them up or lay them out flat, somewhere light to let the fruit finish ripening, in a greenhouse, garage, or sunroom. Container-grown bush varieties can simply be moved under cover to keep growing.

COMPOST

TOMATOES

PERENNIAL HERBS

LIFT AND DIVIDE HERBS

This is the ideal time to lift and divide perennial herbs, such as mint, either to plant in the garden or to pot-up and bring them indoors for a winter crop.

1 LIFT THE PLANT
Large clumps of herbs need splitting. Use a fork or spade to lift the entire plant from the soil. Tip out established pot-grown plants.

2 SPLIT OFF CLUMPS
For larger divisions, use your hands or a hand fork to break off clumps from the original rootball, which you can then replant.

3 TAKE CUTTINGS
Propagate from the spreading stems, or runners, of mint by taking cuttings of small rooted sections and potting up.

DON'T FORGET

As you do your fall tidying, clear up as you go along. Don't leave piles of clippings and other debris lying around to rot and harbor pests. Compost or burn them as soon as possible.

Getting ready for winter

Winter still seems a long way off but around now, nights turn cooler and the days shorten, signaling the end of summer and that it's time to get ready for the season to come. With so much to harvest right now, it's hard to think ahead, but take advantage of September's golden weather to get a few jobs done.

Healthy balance

Tidying up your growing spaces is important to help prevent pests and diseases from lingering in plant debris, ready to attack new growth in spring, and to stop mats of fallen leaves from smothering over-wintering plants, such as perennial herbs. Weeds will still be growing now, so don't allow them to take hold at this late stage, either.

However, it's important to strike a balance. Wildlife relies on food and shelter to survive the cold winter months in the garden. A pile of leaves left in a corner or under a hedge, or a small log pile, is enough to make a winter home for many types of beneficial insects. Birds will flock to fallen fruit during a cold snap, and to any plants you allow to run to seed. Leave your garden neat, but not bare during winter.

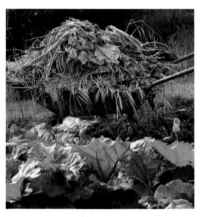

MULCH BARE SOIL
Bare soil and winter weather are not a good combination. Heavy rain leaches nutrients from the soil and ruins its structure. Apply thick mulch to large gaps between plants, and to beds after you have removed spent crops.

GENERAL CLEANING UP
Clear weeds, finished crops, and plant debris from your beds and containers to prevent pests and diseases from overwintering among them. Also rake up fallen leaves to stop them from smothering your winter crops.

Jo's tips

If you have large trees in or near your garden and you have the space, construct a post and chicken wire cage for making leaf mold (p.205). Tree leaves compost more slowly than many other types of garden waste, so it's a good idea to keep them out of the usual heap.

PUT ON STICKY BANDS
To help protect your fruit trees from insect damage, tie sticky bands to the trunks, 2 ft (60 cm) above the ground. This will trap pests making their way up the trunk to lay their eggs.

SUNDRY ROUND UP
Round up pots, labels, wire, watering cans, and other odds and ends that have become scattered during the growing season. Clean and dry them before storing them neatly.

Collect fallen leaves periodically to make leaf mold (see Jo's Tips, opposite), before they pile up, smothering overwintering crops, and harboring pests and diseases.

CLEAN UP

Many essential fall tasks are quick to do but are easily forgotten. Neaten up the shed and clean equipment to keep it in good working ondition.

Clean pruners using steel wool to remove sticky sap and other debris that has adhered to the blades.

Wipe off stakes and plant supports used during summer. Tie them in bundles and store under cover.

Before the first hard frost, make sure you have enough row cover to protect crops and insulate your greenhouse.

Remove greenhouse shade cloth now —any remaining crops will need all of the sun's heat they can get.

GETTING READY FOR WINTER

GROWING FEATURE

Saving your own seeds

Harvesting your own seeds to sow the next year is as easy as growing crops to eat. This not only saves money, it also allows you to select and grow your favorites, and to produce your own seed organically. Saving seed also gives you a good excuse to let vegetables bloom, and enjoy flowers you wouldn't normally see.

Saving seed

Collecting home-grown seed is doubly satisfying because it gives two crops in one. Since you can choose the actual plants you save seed from, you can select those that tasted best or gave the biggest yield. Repeat this process over successive years and you can even develop your own unique strains, just as plant breeders do.

A drawback of saving seeds is that plants must flower, which means leaving them in the ground without harvesting them. This may not be feasible if you have a small crop, or little space to allow plants to mature in. Also, unless you can isolate the plants, natural cross-pollination between varieties means the seed won't be the same as the parents. So, there's little point saving seed from expensive F1 hybrids because their offspring won't be true to type.

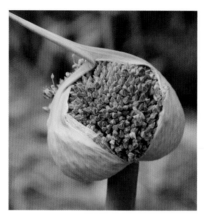

FLOWERS FIRST
To collect seeds, you must first allow the vegetable plants to bloom. Most leaf and root crops are normally harvested before they flower, so to save your own seeds, you need to leave a few plants unharvested.

STORE DRY SEED
Many plants, such as arugula, produce seed in capsules or pods. To harvest these, wait for the pods to turn brown but collect the seeds before they fall to the ground. Empty the seeds out and let them dry before storing them.

Jo's tips

Whatever type of seed you save, make sure it is completely dry before storing it in paper bags or small envelopes. Label the packages with the name of the plant and the date the seed was collected. Always store seed in a cool, dry place, protected from mice.

SEED FROM PODS
Unless the summer is wet, leave fruiting pods, such as beans, on the plants to turn dry and papery. If wet, pick the pods, spread them out to dry indoors, then empty out the seeds.

SEED FROM WET FRUITS
When collecting seeds from moist fruit, such as tomatoes, let the fruit ripen on the plant, pick it, cut it open, and remove the seeds. Spread them on tissue paper to dry, then store.

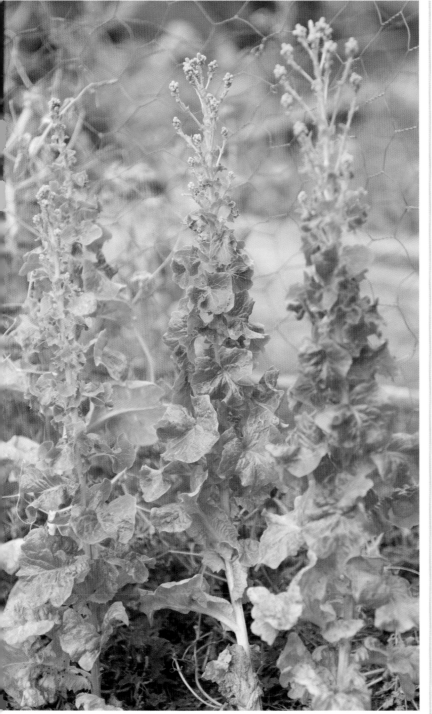

Salad vegetables such as lettuce, readily run to seed. Leave them in the ground and allow them to flower, and collect seeds from the strongest plants.

TRY THESE

The best seeds to collect are those that are expensive to buy, or from crops you plan to grow a lot of next year. You can also share seeds with your friends.

Herbs—Many herbs, such as fennel, caraway, and dill, are grown for their seeds as well as their leaves.

Peas—Leave only the last few pods to mature and dry fully; this will allow the plants to flower and fruit for longer.

Beans—Collect the same way as peas. Dried beans can be used for cooking or sowing. Store them in labeled jars.

Squash and pumpkin—These large fruits are packed with seeds. Collect only those from the best fruits.

SAVING YOUR OWN SEEDS

September: what to harvest

PICK APPLES AND PEARS NOW

As the main season for harvesting apples and pears begins, it's now time to start checking the fruit on your trees for ripeness. To do this, lift apples gently in your hand, and if they come away easily with their stalk intact, they're ready to eat. Pears are trickier. Early-fall ripening varieties should be picked when slightly under-ripe or they will become brown-centered and mealy. Test pears regularly, and if they come away with a lift and a gentle twist, then pick them and leave in a cool place for several days to ripen fully.

CUT CABBAGE, LIFT LEEKS

Red and summer cabbages, sown in March and planted out in May, can be cut as soon as the heads are a usable size. They should do well into fall, but they won't survive very cold weather. Once mature, some varieties stand in the ground longer than others, but watch out for signs of bolting, which spoils them. The first leeks, sown in spring, are ready for lifting. Harvest later-sown crops through winter into spring.

HARVEST

RASPBERRIES

APPLES & PEARS

CABBAGE & LEEKS

FALL TREATS

Fall raspberries, planted in October (p.185), bear ample fruit from now until the first frosts. Less favored by birds than earlier varieties, they shouldn't require netting, although the tough cores make them more difficult to prepare. They are best eaten fresh.

'AUTUMN BLISS'
This variety is shorter than most and can be grown without support. It fruits freely, producing tasty red-pink berries, well into fall.

'JOAN J'
Spine-free and self-supporting, this compact, sweet-tasting variety is suitable for containers. Keep it well watered and fed if pot grown.

'POLKA'
This variety bears especially large fruit that are produced in abundance until November. The berries are noted for their taste and sweetness.

'ALL GOLD'
Similar to 'Autumn Bliss', its fruit matures yellow and doesn't stain clothes or fingers, so it is ideal for gardeners with young children.

GOLDEN CORN

Corn tells you it's ready to pick when the silks at the top of the ears turn brown. To be completely sure it's ripe, pull back the leaves that surround the ear and look for pale, butter-yellow kernels. Early varieties will have been picked already, and now late varieties will be ready. To pick it, twist the ears away from the stems, snapping them at the base. Their sweetness rapidly fades, so use them quickly, but if you can't, blanch and freeze them (pp.148–149). Ears of fresh corn don't keep well in the refrigerator.

LIFT POTATOES

Cut potato plants off to just above ground level in early fall, leaving the tubers in the soil to mature for 2 weeks before lifting with a fork. Lift those for storage on a dry, sunny day, and leave them on the soil surface for up to 2 hours to dry without going green. Store undamaged tubers in large paper bags, in a dark, frost-free place.

CORN

SQUASH & PUMPKINS

FIGS

POTATOES

BUMPER CROPS

Squashes and pumpkins sown in April (p.74) should be cut fresh when required. To store, pick mature fruit with plenty of stem, when they're well colored and the stem has cracked. Before the frosts come, cure the fruit for 10 days in the sun outdoors, or in a greenhouse or indoors in poor weather, to harden the skin so that they keep. Store in a cool, frost-free place.

SWEET FIGS

Figs don't ripen further once picked, so wait until they're hanging heavy from the tree and feel soft. If sap appears at the base of the fruit, it's a good indication of ripeness. Pick the fruit carefully without bruising it and eat quickly. Figs keep fresh for a week or so in a cool place, but are also excellent cooked.

See STORING VEGETABLES pages 210–211

Making cold pickles

Cold pickles can be made using either single crops or a medley of fruit and vegetables for a colorful combination. The method is straightforward and there is no cooking involved. One thing cold pickles need is a good crunch when you bite into them. The best way to ensure a crisp finish is to salt your vegetables for some hours to draw out excess moisture before they are pickled raw in vinegar.

RECIPE IDEAS

Pickled gherkins

Makes 2¼ lb (1 kg) (2 small jars)
Takes about 20 minutes, plus salting time
Keeps 6 months or longer

Ingredients
3 cups small pickling cucumbers
½ cup sea salt
3–4 shallots, peeled
1–2 garlic cloves, peeled (optional)
2–3 dried chiles (optional)
2–3 cloves (optional)
½ tsp cilantro seeds, peppercorns, or dill seeds, or 1 crumbled bay leaf
2 sprigs tarragon, dill, or thyme
1 grape leaf (optional)
3 ½ cups white wine vinegar

1 **Wash and dry the cucumbers,** rubbing each with a cloth to remove the fine down. Snip off the stalks and any dried blossoms. Either leave whole or cut into quarters lengthwise, or into ⅛in (3 mm) slices.

2 **Put a layer of salt** in a bowl, then a layer of cucumbers. Repeat until the cucumbers are used up, ending with a layer of salt. Let stand at room temperature for 24 hours, then rinse the cucumbers to remove the salt.

Jo's tips

Pickle chiles or slices of sweet pepper raw in sweetened white vinegar to eat with cheese or meat, or to use chopped in salsas. Shred red cabbage finely with onions, soak in brine for 6 hours, rinse, and pack in jars with sweetened, spiced vinegar.

To sterilize your preserving jars, wash them in hot soapy water, place them on a rack in a moderate oven, and leave them there to dry thoroughly.

3 **Pack the cucumbers** into sterilized jars (see Jo's Tips, left), leaving about ½ in (1 cm) at the top. Add the shallots, garlic, spices, and herbs, and a grape leaf to keep the pickle crisp. Cover the cucumbers with vinegar.

4 **Seal the jars** with nonmetallic lids, because metal will react with the vinegar and spoil the pickles. Label, and store your pickles in a cool, dark place for at least 3–4 weeks to let the flavors develop before eating.

Sharp and crisp, pickled gherkins are excellent with cheese, cold meats, and sandwiches.

TRY THESE

Choose the firmest fruits and vegetables for making cold pickles. Those shown here all have distinctive flavors that blend well with spices.

Shallots—Pickle these small onions whole, either on their own or mixed with other vegetables.

Garlic—Pickle garlic by itself with some spice, or use it to add extra flavor to mixed vegetable pickles.

Cabbage—Firm red or white cabbage, finely sliced, is delicious pickled. Try adding caraway or cumin seeds.

Cauliflower—Break red or white heads into bite-sized florets. Pickle on its own or mixed with other vegetables.

MAKING COLD PICKLES

Making hot pickles

This time-honored method of preserving fruits and vegetables using vinegar is an effective and delicious way of keeping produce for many months without it spoiling. Hot pickling enables you to create a whole range of new flavors by using different vinegars and spices or combining crops. Fruit pickles are all made following the same basic steps, as illustrated in the recipe below.

Spiced pear pickle

Makes 1½ pints (900 ml) (2 medium jars)
Takes 40 minutes
Keeps 9 months

Ingredients
2¼ lb (1 kg) firm pears, peeled, cored, and quartered

To make the syrup
1¾ cup granulated sugar
¾ cup cider vinegar
Zest of ½ lemon
1 in (2.5 cm) piece fresh ginger root, chopped
Seeds from 6 cardamom pods

Jo's tips

The hot pickling method produces soft-textured condiments. If you enjoy eating something with a crunch, try the cold pickling technique (see pages 176–177).

Once you have opened a jar of pickles, make sure the remaining contents stay covered by their liquid and keep them refrigerated.

To sterilize your preserving jars, wash them in hot soapy water, place them on a rack in a moderate oven, and leave them there to dry thoroughly.

1 Put all the syrup ingredients into a large preserving pan or heavy-based, stainless steel saucepan and bring to a boil, stirring until the sugar dissolves. Simmer for 5 minutes then remove from the heat.

2 Put the pear quarters into the syrup, making sure they are covered. Poach for 5–10 minutes, until just soft. Test each piece with a skewer and remove it from the pan as soon as it reaches the right consistency.

3 Pack the cooked pears into warm, sterilized preserving jars (see Jo's Tips, left). Return the syrup to the heat, bring back to a boil and cook for a further 5 minutes, or until the liquid has reduced by about a third.

4 Carefully pour the boiling syrup over the pears, completely covering them. Top with waxed paper disks and seal the jars with nonmetallic lids. Label, and store in a cool, dark place for 1 month before using.

Spicy fruit pickles keep well in a pantry cabinet. They are especially good with rice dishes.

TRY PICCALILLI

This is a classic hot pickle that combines summer vegetables with spices. Try varying the vegetables you use according to the crops you've grown.

Makes 5 lb (2.25 kg) (3 medium jars)
Takes 35 minutes
Keeps 6 months

Ingredients

3 tbsp sea salt
1 large cauliflower
2 large onions, peeled and diced
6 cups mixed vegetables
2 tbsp flour
1 cup granulated sugar
1 tbsp turmeric
2 tbsp dry mustard
4 cups pickling vinegar

1 Dissolve the salt in 2 pints (1.2 liters) of water and soak the vegetables thoroughly for 24 hours. Drain, rinse, and blanch in hot water.
2 Mix the dry ingredients in a bowl with a little vinegar to make a paste. Put in a pan, add the rest of the vinegar, bring to a boil, then simmer, stirring, for 15 minutes.
3 Add vegetables, coat well with sauce, then spoon into sterilized jars, leaving no air pockets. Cover with vinegar-proof lids. Store in the dark; start using after 1 month.

MAKING HOT PICKLES

Making plum wine

You don't need a vineyard to make your own wine, in fact you don't need grapes at all. With the right technique, many different fruits and vegetables can be turned into a delicious alcoholic cocktail.

Plum (and greengage) trees fruit heavily in late summer, and with basic equipment you can turn this bounty into glorious homemade wine. Once you feel confident, you can go on to more complicated wines.

Plum wine

Makes 1 gallon (4.5 liters)
Takes 2 hours, plus time to freeze the fruit, ferment, and stabilize

Ingredients
14 cups plums or greengages, washed
Juice of one lemon
1 tsp pectolase
1 tsp wine yeast
8 cups sugar

Equipment
Large fermentation bucket with lid
Potato masher
Demijohn with cork and airlock
Plastic funnel and sieve
Plastic measuring jug
Plastic tubing for siphoning

1 **Stone the fruit,** freeze, thaw, and mash it, and add the lemon juice. Put into a bucket with 6 pints of boiling water. Let cool and add the pectolase. Leave at room temperature for 24 hours, add yeast, and cover.

2 **After 4–5 days, strain the pulped fruit** into a sterilized container to remove any large solids. Dissolve the sugar fully in about 2 pints hot water and add this to the mashed fruit. Stir the mixture thoroughly.

Jo's tips

Plums, gages, and certain other fruit ssuch as apples, are naturally high in pectin, which can cause your wine to become cloudy. Adding the enzyme pectolase breaks down the pectin, but as a further precaution, freeze and thaw the fruit before mashing. This also helps destroy the pectin.

Always use sterilized equipment for wine-making, or you run the risk of producing vinegar.

3 **Using a sterilized funnel**, carefully pour the liquid into a sterilized demijohn. The liquid still contains fruit solids at this stage, which are essential to fermentation. These will settle and can be filtered out later.

4 **Fit and fill the airlock,** and leave the liquid to ferment at room temperature for 2 months. When no more bubbles appear in the airlock, siphon the wine into bottles, seal, and store them in the dark for 6 months.

Homemade wines are ready to drink after 6 months and keep well for about 2 years.

TRY THESE

Variations on this basic technique can be used to make wine from many different fruits and vegetables. Look for a specific recipe before you start.

Parsnip—These, and most other root vegetables, are high in natural sugars, and make excellent, potent wine.

Cherry—Fresh cherries don't keep well, so if you have plenty of them, the fruits make a gloriously dark-red wine.

Rhubarb—An established rhubarb plant can provide a mountain of stems, so use spare ones for wine-making.

Blackberry—All summer berries can be used for wine. Mix the last of your crops together for a mixed berry wine.

MAKING PLUM WINE

October: ready to eat

Before the first frosts, lift potatoes, carrots, and beets for storage.
To enjoy now, new fall crops, including celeriac and rutabagas,
are coming in; their rich, earthy flavors suit the season perfectly.

Fresh greens are guaranteed with cut-and-come-again **arugula**

Spinach and **Swiss chard** are useful, whatever the season

End-of-season **Potatoes** *should see you through the month*

Enjoy the last of the **summer cauliflower** and **broccoli**

Leeks are still new, tender, and full of flavor

Roast the last of the **corn** and serve with melted butter

Pears are best picked while still slightly hard

Taste **grapes** for ripeness before cutting a whole bunch

Gather the last **eggplant, peppers, zucchini,** and **tomatoes** to make a tasty ratatouille that will freeze well

Cut the last sprigs from summer **annual herbs**

It's the end of the summer **onions**, unless you plan to dry some for winter use

Have a sweet feast with the last **cane fruits**

Keep some **beets** for storage
pages 210–211

Late **plums** make great pies and crumbles

Harvest **hazelnuts** —unless the squirrels have beaten you to it

Steam **bok choy** as a delicious and healthy side dish

Winter squashes make delicious, filling soups

Pick the remaining **sweet peppers**

Use the last fresh **chiles** and dry any surplus

Harvest new season **celery**—it's deliciously crisp and tasty

Dig your **turnips** before they grow too large— the little ones have the best flavor and texture

Florence fennel won't be around during the winter—so make the most of it now

Say goodbye to summer with the final harvest of **peas** and **runner** and **snap beans**

Even windfall **apples** taste good

Not too late in the year for a summer salad of **lettuce, tomato,** and **cucumber**

Sugarloaf chicory adds a distinctive tang to salads and soups

Celeriac is ready this month to replace some of your summer favorites

Summer and **winter radishes** are both available this month

The new **rutabaga** crop is ready for lifting and eating mashed or in soup

New season **kale** tastes wonderful

Monster **pumpkins** are better for ornament than eating

October: what to sow

SOW CAULIFLOWER

For an extra early crop of summer cauliflowers, sow them now under cover into pots or rows ½ in (1 cm) deep. Thin rows of seedlings as they grow to 4 in (10 cm) apart, ready for transplanting in spring (p.62). Keep the seedlings protected but not heated until then. Water as required, and protect them against slugs.

HARVEST: **MAY–JUN**

EXTRA EARLY BEANS

HARVEST: **APR–JUN**

If you have mild winters, and want extra-early broad beans, sow hardy varieties now, 2 in (5 cm) deep, and protect the plants with cloches.

'STEREO'
This variety is like snap beans in that you can eat the entire pods. They can also be eaten skinned.

'SUPER AQUADULCE'
This is one of the hardiest bean varieties, and is suitable for growing in colder areas.

'THE SUTTON'
A dwarf variety, suitable for smaller gardens, it produces large pods with five beans apiece.

SOW

GARLIC

SUMMER CAULIFLOWER

PEAS

BROAD BEANS

GROW GARLIC

HARVEST: **JUN–AUG**

Garlic needs a winter chilling operod in order to produce sizeable bulbs. This is a perfect time to plant garlic in many regions.

1 BREAK UP BULB
Buy certified disease-free garlic bulbs and break them into individual cloves, removing most of the outer papery layers of the bulb.

2 PREPARE SITE
Choose fertile soil that has not been recently manured, dig it over lightly, and rake it to remove any large clods and stones.

3 PLANT OUT
Push cloves into the soil, ¾ in (2 cm) deep, 8 in (20 cm) apart each way. Plant flat-end down. Use a dibble to make holes if it helps.

SUPER EARLY PEAS

Even tough pea seeds will rot in wet winter soils. But if you live in a mild-winter area and you have a raised bed that drains freely (p.33), you can sow now for an extra early crop. Choose early varieties, like 'Canoe', and sow thinly, 1½ in (4 cm) deep in drills, about 6 in (15 cm) wide. Insert pea sticks or taut plastic netting for support, and tie in the young plants as they grow. Cover plants in extreme weather.

HARVEST: **MAY–JUN**

October: what to plant

BLACKBERRIES, RASPBERRIES & FAMILY

HARVEST: **JUL–OCT**

Bare-rooted blackberries, raspberries, and their hybrids, can be planted now. Plant raspberries 18 in (45 cm) apart, 3–4 in (8–10 cm) deep, with 5 ft (1.5 m) between rows. Plant blackberries and hybrids 6 ft (2 m) apart. Cut canes to a bud 10 in (25 cm) above the soil.

BOYSENBERRY
A cross between a blackberry, loganberry, and raspberry, its dark red fruit have a rich bramble taste.

LOGANBERRY
Best grown like a blackberry, the fruit tastes like a sharp raspberry, and is best cooked with lots of sugar.

TAYBERRY
Ripening dark red, this vigorous hybrid produces sweet-tasting fruit over a very long period.

JAPANESE WINEBERRY
This distinct species has small, soft, orange-red berries with an unusual winelike flavor.

SUMMER BERRIES

PLANT

GOOSEBERRIES & CURRANTS

BELGIAN ENDIVE

PLANT BARE ROOTED

Plant bare-root gooseberries and currants now in a sunny, sheltered site, in fertile, well-drained soil. Soak first, setting gooseberries, red- and whitecurrants 5 ft (1.5 m) apart, and blackcurrants 6 ft (1.8 m) apart. Plant to the same depth as the soil mark on the stems, then prune (pp.206–207). When possible, choose certified disease-free, two-year-old blackcurrant plants.

HARVEST: **VARIOUS**

FORCED ENDIVE

If you want Belgian endive roots to force indoors for winter, lift plants sown in May, from now until early winter. Leave the roots in a shed for a week, cut off all the leaves ¾ in (2 cm) above the root, and store them flat in sand-filled boxes. To force, plant several roots in a large pot with their tops at the soil surface (p.216).

HARVEST: **NOV–MAR**

See PRUNING FRUIT IN FALL pages 206–207

TAKE YOUR PICK

Raspberries

Summer raspberries are one of the season's great joys, and given support and protection from birds, they are easy to grow. Also try fall varieties (p.174).

1 'Glen Fyne' produces a heavy crop of rich red berries with an excellent flavor, mid-June to mid-August. Spine-free, it is a rewarding and easy variety to grow; good for beginners.

2 'Malling Jewel' is a traditional, compact, virus-resistant variety that is good for smaller gardens. It gives a reasonable crop of flavorful berries from early July to mid-August.

3 'Glen Prosen' is a spinefree variety that produces a large, crop of tasty berries, mid-July to mid-August. The berries are particularly firm, making them ideal for freezing (pp.150–151).

4 'Cascade Delight' is a heavy-cropping raspberry that tolerates wet conditions better than many varieties, making it ideal for cool, damp regions. The rich-tasting fruit is large and firm.

5 'Tulameen' is a very hardy variety that gives an excellent crop of large, tasty fruit, mid-July to mid-August. The canes are tall, 6 ft (2 m), but have few spines. Don't cut back after planting.

Other varieties to try:
'Allen'
'Jewel'
'Latham'
'Meeker'
'Taylor'

Blackberries

Most gardens only have room for one or two of these large, productive plants, which require only simple pruning and training for a bumper crop (p.118).

1 'Waldo' is a compact variety that gives a good-sized crop in midsummer, but takes up little space. It is also thornless, making it easier to pick from and safer to grow near children.

2 'Black Butte' produces exceptionally large fruit, twice the normal size at 2 in (5 cm) long, which are good for cooking and eating raw. It is also an early variety, ready for picking in mid-July.

3 'Loch Ness' is a bushy, compact variety, and a good choice for where space is limited. Thornless and high-yielding, it can also be grown in containers. It bears in late summer.

4 'Silvan' is a thorned variety that produces a heavy, early crop of large, richly flavored berries. It is a full-sized variety, and requires about 12 ft (4 m) of wall or fence space.

5 'Oregon Thornless' is a vigorous variety that fruits into fall. It has attractive, dissected foliage, and can also be grown as an ornamental, making it easy to accommodate in smaller plots.

Other varieties to try:
'Apache'
'Fantasia'
'Helen'
'Karaka Black'
'Veronique'

October: what to do

STORE IN THE SOIL

As the foliage on tall Jerusalem artichoke stems dies back, its goodness is taken up by the underground tubers. Once the leaves are brown, cut the stems down to 3–4 in (8–10 cm) above the soil and chop them into small pieces for composting. Leave the tubers where they are because they keep best in the soil.

GREENHOUSE MAINTENANCE

Keep your greenhouse free from pests and diseases and insulated from the winter cold. Mid-fall is a good time for these maintenance jobs.

1 CLEAN
Clear plant debris, wipe away shading paint with a dry cloth, and clean the glass inside and out.

2 DISINFECT
Scrub glazing bars, hard paths, and shelves or benches with a diluted disinfectant solution.

3 INSULATE
Cut sheets of bubble wrap to fit the framework of the glazing. Do not block the vents.

TEND

ARTICHOKES

GREENHOUSES

CELERIAC

CONTAINER-GROWN FRUIT

WARM BEDDING

With the right preparation, both parsnips and celeriac can be left in the soil during the winter. To protect their roots from extremely cold weather, or to prevent soil from freezing and enable lifting during winter, mulch them with a thick layer of straw. Celeriac keeps its leaves throughout the winter, so tuck the straw under the leaves to make sure that the roots have maximum protection from frosts.

REPOT FRUIT

For good yields you must repot fruit trees and bushes every year until they are full sized. Knock the plant out of its pot in mid- to late fall and tease the roots out of the edge of the rootball. Repot into a container about 4 in (10 cm) wider at the top than the last. Use a well-drained soilless potting mix with some rich compost added.

PROTECT SALAD CROPS

Many leafy vegetable crops, such as winter lettuce, chard, and spinach, are resistant to cold and can be kept going well into the winter. However, they need some protection because their foliage can quickly be ruined by harsh and wet weather. Cloching your crops at this stage in the season will protect the plants from the worst of the weather, allowing them to keep producing fresh leaves for longer. If you take precautions now, you will have top-quality leaves available for picking into winter.

BRING INDOORS

Citrus trees in containers that have enjoyed a sheltered, sunny spot outside all summer should now be brought back indoors. Find them a well-ventilated place, with plenty of light and a minimum temperature of 45º F (7º C). Keep them away from radiators and cold drafts. They will not need further feeding until spring.

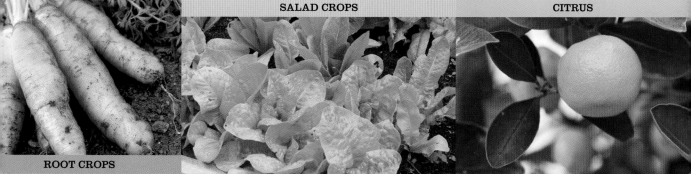

SALAD CROPS

CITRUS

ROOT CROPS

LIFTING AND STORING ROOTS

Root crops, such as Jerusalem artichoke, can be left in the ground during winter and actually store better in the soil. However, if your soil is heavy or you live in a cold area, it's worth being cautious and lifting what you can now to store under cover (pp.210–211).

CARROTS
Dig up before the frosts and cut off the foliage to within ½ in (1 cm) of the root. Store in layers in soil or sand-filled boxes. Keep frost free.

POTATOES
Lift potatoes on a dry day and leave them on the soil surface to dry for a few hours. Store in paper bags or in a clamp if you have a large crop.

BEETS
As with carrots, lift the roots before the first frost, and snap off the leaves. Store in layers in sand-filled boxes kept somewhere frost free.

TURNIPS
These can be harvested until winter, but if the weather allows, lift them now and store the roots in boxes of dry soil or sand. Keep frost free.

See CITRUS pages 222–223

Starting a compost heap

Every garden, however small, should have at least one compost heap to provide a free and fabulous soil improver. The process could not be simpler—in goes green and twiggy garden debris, and kitchen peelings that would otherwise go in the garbage, and in 6–12 months, out comes amazing, crumbly garden compost.

Making compost

To make good compost, mix waste material together as you build the heap, to allow moisture and air to penetrate into the center. This creates ideal conditions for the correct bacteria, fungi, and insects to flourish, and quickly break down the waste, without any nasty smells. A good mix of about half carbon-rich woody material and half nitrogen-rich green material helps keep composting organisms working well.

Check your heap regularly, and if it is wet and slimy and smells bad, then too much nitrogen-rich waste, such as vegetable peelings, has been added. To remedy this, mix in small or shredded woody material. Similarly, a dry heap won't break down quickly, so mix in moist green waste, add water, and turn the heap if the edges dry out (p.47).

MIX IT UP
Avoid adding material in thick layers, which will prevent air and moisture from circulating. When adding lots of one type, mix it in using a fork.

TURN REGULARLY
You need to turn your heap at least once to make good compost. The easiest way is to have a separate bin and swap material across.

To achieve finished compost, stop adding fresh waste material when your bin is full, and cover the top with old carpet or the lid. Wait for the level in the bin to stop going down and turn the contents to make sure all material is fully broken down. The compost should then be ready in a month or two, so have a second bin to fill in the meantime. Once the first bin is finished, empty it and start again.

Types of compost bins

Choose to make or buy a bin that suits your garden. Site it in sun or part shade, directly on the soil rather than on paving, to help attract beneficial organisms. Work out how much waste you will have to put on the heap, and try to match this to the size of your bin. Also consider access, and pick a design you can reach into easily when filling or emptying the bin.

(left to right) **Build your own bin** to look attractive or blend into the background, with sliding slats at the front for hassle-free turning. **Plastic bins** are compact and cheap, and offer a quick way to get started, but aren't always easy to turn. **Construction bags** are large and often free, and are a good option for gardens of any size.

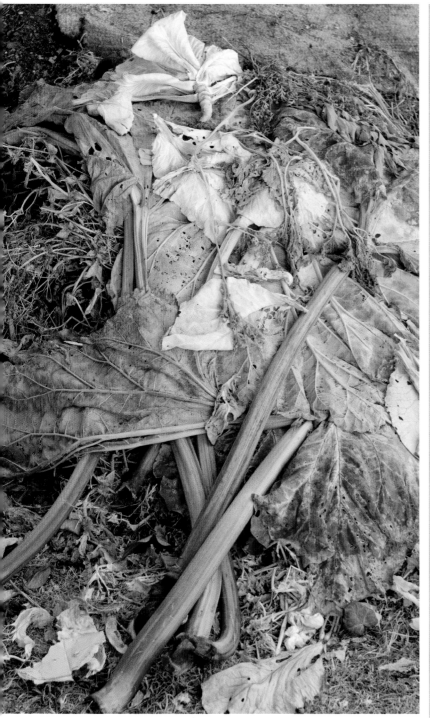

Compost heaps can be just that, a straightforward heap. If you have space, and somewhere to keep it out of sight, simply pile up your garden waste into a heap and it will slowly compost.

TRY THESE

Compost heaps need a mixture of moist and dry material. Avoid adding perennial weeds, cooked food, diseased growth, and thick branches.

Vegetable peelings contain nitrogen and moisture; collect them along with tea bags and coffee grounds.

Shredded paper and cardboard add carbon to wet, nitrogen-rich compost. Avoid plastic-coated paper.

Prunings and annual weeds make up the bulk of a compost heap. Avoid composting any diseased material.

Thin woody prunings, less than a pencil thickness, help aerate larger compost heaps, and also add bulk.

October: what to harvest

LAST SUMMER HARVEST
For a final taste of fresh summer vegetables, go out picking now while the weather allows, and harvest the last of your peas, corn, squash, zucchinis, carrots, cucumbers, and Florence fennel, before they're spoiled by the frost. Many of these plants will already be winding down for winter, so harvest and enjoy what is there, then remove and compost any remaining plant material.

CELERY STICKS
Don't delay in lifting the last of your celery plants, sown in February (p.40), because they won't survive in the soil through frost. Stems deteriorate in quality anyway through fall. The small, inner stems keep well if stored in a plastic bag in a cool place after harvest.

HARVEST

LATE SUMMER CROPS

CELERY

NUTS

APPLES & PEARS

HARVEST NUTS NOW
Nuts are a real mid-fall treat that should not be overlooked. Pick hazelnuts from among the branches when their shells have hardened and turned brown. If you're lucky enough to have a walnut tree, gather the nuts from the ground as soon as they have fallen, remove their husks right away, and scrub the shells to remove husk fibers before drying. Both types of nuts can be eaten fresh now, or spread out in a warm place and allowed to dry for storage in a cool, airy place. They will keep well for weeks; check occasionally for pest damage.

LATE APPLES AND PEARS
Late varieties of apples and pears should be left on the tree to ripen for as long as possible. Even then, most pears will stay hard and need a period of storage to bring them to perfection (pp.194–195). The trick is to leave the fruit on the tree for as long as you can, hoping that it won't be knocked off and damaged by fall weather, making it useless for storing. Of course, any windfall apples and pears will still be delicious, although they cannot be stored because of their impact bruises. If you have a glut, juice them or make them into wine (pp.180–181).

PICK YOUR OWN GRAPES

Grapes require patience, because even though they may look ripe, they need time on the vine to allow the fruit sugars to develop. Mid-fall grapes need 4 weeks, late varieties want 10 weeks. When picking, use pruners to avoid spoiling the fruits' white bloom.

'BOSKOOP GLORY'
This is a good dessert variety for cooler areas, and gives a reliable harvest of delicious dark grapes that can be eaten straight from the vine.

'REGENT'
A vigorous variety, it bears large, sweet blue-black fruit. Its foliage also develops rich coloring, so it doubles as an ornamental climber.

'SIEGERREBE'
Dessert grape, its sweet, juicy fruit ripen with a rich brown tint, and can be eaten fresh or used to make wine. It is suitable for cooler regions.

'MÜLLER-THURGAU'
This variety is widely grown for wine-making, and is a good choice for cooler areas. The grapes are also sweet enough to eat fresh.

BEANS · **GRAPES** · **TOMATOES, PEPPERS, & CHILES**

LAST BEANS

This brings the last crops of snap and runner beans that have been growing all summer. Pick bright and tender pods whole. This is also the time to harvest dry bean varieties, after the pods have turned dry and brown on the plants. Alternatively, you can pull whole plants to finish drying indoors. Runner beans are not as palatable dried in this way.

RIPEN INDOORS

If your last harvested tomatoes are refusing to ripen, put them in a paper bag or fruit bowl with some bananas, which give off natural fruit-ripening vapors. Peppers and chiles won't ripen further once picked. Green peppers don't keep well, but freeze your chiles whole and use them when needed.

Try DRYING FRUIT & VEGETABLES pages 160–161

Storing apples and pears

Old-fashioned methods are often the best, and if you are lucky enough to get a good crop of apples and pears every year, the easiest way to keep them is the traditional method of wrapping them up for storage in a cool room. Some late varieties need storage of this kind to ripen properly, and it's a pleasure to have fruit stored in its natural state, to take out and use throughout the winter, when you please.

HARVESTING IDEAS

How to store fruit

Finding a place with suitable conditions is vital for the success of this storage method. The temperature needs to be fairly stable, below 50°F (10°C), but frost-free. There should be good air circulation to reduce the risk of rotting, and measures must be taken to exclude pests such as mice and birds. A cool attic, cellar, or insulated shed can all work well, but anywhere in a centrally heated house generally won't. Also ensure that fruit is kept away from chemicals such as pesticides, paint, and wood preservative.

1 **Pick your fruit carefully** (see Jo's Tips, left) and the majority should be suitable for storing. Discard or use immediately any with damage and signs of disease. Dry off wet fruit to help prevent decay during storage.

2 **Wrap up apples** individually to keep them from shriveling during storage. Use wax paper, such as baking paper. Cooking apples can be wrapped in old newspaper. Leave stored pears unwrapped.

Jo's tips

The stage at which fruit is picked makes a big difference to how it tastes after storage. Pick all but the latest apples when they're ripe and come away with their stalks when lifted. Pick pears before they're fully ripe, when they still require a twist and tug to pull them away with their stalk. Organize your storage so that different fruits and their varieties are stored separately. Never store bruised or damaged fruit, because rot will set in rapidly.

3 **To arrange your fruit**, wrapped apples can be stored touching and piled up in layers. Leave small spaces between unwrapped pears, and keep them in a single layer to allow air circulation and to prevent bruising.

4 **Stack boxes or trays** of fruit, or leave them on shelves, making sure there is ventilation between them. Check stores regularly to catch fruit at the peak of ripeness, and also check for signs of deterioration.

Unwrapped apples are easier to inspect, although are more at risk of drying out.

TRY THESE

Some varieties suit storage better than others. Culinary types are often successful, but meltingly ripe dessert fruit is always a winter highlight.

Apple 'Egremont Russet'—This mid-season variety retains its nutty flavor when picked in mid fall.

Apple 'Idared'—One of the best keepers, picked mid-fall, this late variety holds on to its sweet flavor.

Pear 'Doyenne du Comice' —This fine dessert pear is picked and stored mid-fall and eaten to early winter.

Pear 'Concorde'—A reliable, heavy cropper, this mid-season dessert variety keeps well through winter.

STORING APPLES AND PEARS

November: ready to eat

Add late apples and pears to your storage shelves and harvest hardy celeriac roots and winter cabbages as needed. Salad greens grown under cover, such as endive and chicory, lettuce, and arugula, are a fresh touch of green.

Stir-fry late-season **bok choy**

Cut-and-come-again salads give a fresh taste of summer all year long

Enjoy tasty **rutabaga**

Radicchio has a rich, bitter taste that goes well with bread and cheese

Use dried bunches of **herbs** and **chiles**—they don't last long
page 161

Harvest new season **brussels sprouts**

Slice fresh **green onions** directly into your dishes

Use late root veggies in rich and spicy chutneys

Use fresh, crisp **Swiss chard** as an alternative to spinach in your pasta dishes

Start using stored **apples** and **pears**

If they're too sour to eat, use the last **indoor grapes** to make your own **homemade wine**
pages 180–181

Eat the last of this year's lettuce crop, grown under cover

Serve new season **kale,** lightly steamed, with your roast

Harvest the last crisp **Chinese cabbage**

Eat late fresh **apples** and **pears**

Make a spicy curry with the last of your **autumn cauliflower**

Pick the last of the **kohlrabi**

Use oven-dried **tomatoes** to add Mediterranean flavor *page 160*

Cut the last of the **fall cabbage**, with its strong, rich taste

Give a mild onion flavor to your soups and stews with fresh **leeks** *pages 226–227*

Relish the last of your **summer radishes**, and the first of the **winter varieties**

Slice and fry delicious **mushrooms** grown indoors

Defrost frozen **pesto** made in summer *page 147*

Eat the last of your **spinach**

Fresh **parsnips** and **celeriac** are the route to a good meal

Savour the nutty flavor of new season **salsify**

Roast freshly pulled **turnips** and **carrots**

Mash new season **Jerusalem artichokes** for a culinary treat

Add tasty, vitamin-rich **sprouting seeds** to your sandwiches, salads, and stir-fries

Pick evergreen herbs, including **rosemary**, **thyme**, **sage**, and **bay leaf**

November: what to plant

THRIVING GRAPES

Grape vines thrive in sunshine and a well-drained, enriched soil. Before planting, put up horizontal wires, spaced 12 in (30 cm) apart. Plant the vines 4–5 ft (1.2–1.5 m) apart. Between now and early spring, prune the stems to two buds above the soil or graft union.

HARVEST: **AUG–NOV**

TIME FOR TREES

In milder-winter areas, plant fruit trees now, while the soil is still warm. Choose a well-drained, sunny site away from frost pockets. Allow each tree ample space, dig in compost, and drive in a stake for free-standing trees or put up horizontal wires for wall-trained trees. Dig a hole, spread out the roots, backfill, and firm the soil gently. Keep the trunk 2 in (5 cm) from the stake.

HARVEST: **VARIOUS**

PLANT

BLUEBERRIES   RHUBARB   GRAPE VINES   FRUIT TREES

POTTED BLUEBERRIES

Blueberries are easy to grow if you can get the soil right. They need a moist, acid soil with a pH of 4–5.5, so unless your garden naturally has these conditions grow them in pots filled with ericaceous potting mix. Knock plants from their pots and plant 5 ft (1.5 m) apart in the soil, or in containers a little larger than their root ball. Firm the soil lightly and water thoroughly. Keep moist until established.

HARVEST: **AUG–SEPT**

RHUBARB SETS

Well-fed rhubarb plants will produce prolifically for many years. Choose an unshaded patch and improve the soil with a generous amount of well-rotted manure before planting. Space the sets (young plants) at least 36 in (90 cm) apart and plant them with their crowns just above soil level to stop the new buds rotting in winter.

HARVEST: **MAR–JUL**

HARDY HERBS

Many tough perennial herbs, such as mint and fennel, are happy to be planted out in late fall. Unless in a sheltered position, Mediterranean herbs, such sage, thyme, and rosemary, may struggle through cold winters when newly planted. Protect them with row cover fabric.

BAY
This tolerant shrubby herb will grow in full sun or partial shade, in moist or dry soil. It is best in milder areas.

CHIVES
Plant this bulb-forming herb in full sun and well-drained soil. It will tolerate shade but becomes leggy.

LEMON BALM
This is a hardy, highly aromatic herb that grows best in a sunny site with free-draining soil. Good in pots.

ROSEMARY
Grow this woody herb in a sheltered, sunny site, with well-drained soil. It is best in milder regions.

FIGS

PATIO FRUIT

PERENNIAL HERBS

MAKE A FIG PIT

HARVEST: AUG–SEP

Figs are vigorous plants that are often planted in a restricted area to keep them from growing too large.

1 DIG THE PIT
Dig a hole 24 in (60 cm) square and deep. Line the sides with paving slabs and put in a layer of rubble, allowing good drainage.

2 PLANT AND SUPPORT
Fill the hole with good topsoil, attach strong horizontal supporting wires to the wall, 12 in (30 cm) apart, then plant and tie in the fig.

PATIO FRUIT

The full range of fruit trees will flourish in containers, which restrict the size that trees can grow to. This is the ideal way to grow fruit in small gardens. Choose a pot a little bigger than the root system and layer the base with stones. Plant the tree in the soil at the same level as the original soil mark on the stem, and fill firmly with well-drained potting mix. Water in well and keep the tree moist.

HARVEST: **VARIOUS**

See DRYING FRUIT AND VEGETABLES pages 160–161

Apples

Select the right varieties and you be could harvesting apples from early fall onward, and still enjoying stored fruit throughout the long winter months.

1 'James Grieve' is a versatile, soft-fleshed variety that ripens in September. It can be enjoyed as a dessert apple although, because of its sharp flavor, some prefer to use it as a cooking variety.

2 'Egremont Russet' is a long-established and popular variety of dessert apple with a crisp flesh. Pick these sweet, nutty-tasting russets in October.

3 'Greensleeves' has sweet-tasting, golden-yellow flesh. This dessert apple produces heavy crops that are ready to harvest in October. It is probably best eaten freshly picked rather than stored.

4 'Ashmead's Kernel' is a firm-fleshed dessert apple with an outstanding flavor, both sharp and sweet. It is ready for picking in mid October and develops its full flavor in storage.

5 'Falstaff' has been highly praised for its excellent flavor and resistance to disease. The crisp-fleshed fruits of this dessert variety are bright red when fully ripened in October.

6 'Golden Noble' is regarded as one of the best cooking apples. It has a tangy, but not acid, flavor. This variety, which is well suited to cooler areas, is ready for harvest in early October.

Other varieties to try:
'Ellison's Orange'—dessert
'Golden Delicious'—dessert
'Jonagold'—dessert
'Stayman Winesap'—cooking

TAKE YOUR PICK

Pears

Beautiful blossoms and aromatic fruit make a pear tree welcome in any garden. If a large tree isn't an option, train an espalier or a cordon on a sunny fence.

1 'Doyenne du Comice' is regarded as an outstanding dessert variety for flavor and texture. This pear needs plenty of warmth and should be placed in a sheltered spot. The fruit is ripe for picking around mid October.

2 'Packham's Triumph' produces good crops of sweet, juicy fruit that ripens in mid October. This dessert pear keeps well and if the fruit is stored with care it should last until the end of the year.

3 'Concorde' is a late-ripening dessert variety that is ready for picking around late October. The fruit has juicy flesh with a delicate flavor, and will store well until after Christmas.

4 'Beurre Superfin' is a large pear with a well-rounded shape and fine-textured, juicy flesh. It is an excellent dessert and cooking variety. Start picking the fruit in late September or early October.

5 'Williams' bon Chrétien' is one of the best-known varieties of pear in the world, and has been popular for over two centuries. It has fine, white flesh that is suitable for both eating raw and cooking. This pear ripens in September. Use it right from the tree because this fruit does not store well.

Other varieties to try:
'Bartlett'—cooking
'Beth'—dessert
'Conference'—dessert/cooking
'Glou Morceau'—dessert
'Onward'—dessert

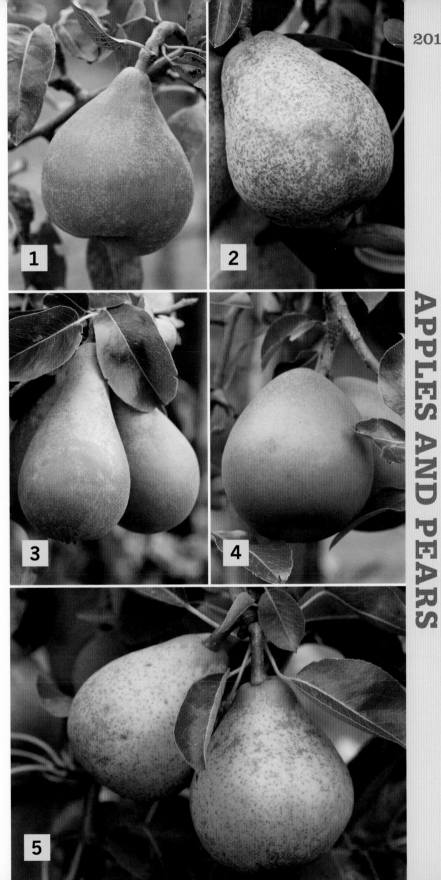

Choosing and planting fruit trees

Fruit trees will be with you for years to come, so consider your choices carefully, and if planting more than one, select early, mid- and late varieties for a longer harvest. Some fruit trees need a pollinator to grow alongside, while others are self-fertile and can be planted singly. Many trees are also grafted to control their size. Seek advice from a fruit nursery to help decide what best suits you and your yard.

Choosing a tree

Once you have decided which fruit to grow there are still other considerations, too. For instance, would you prefer sweet dessert fruit or a culinary variety suited to cooking and preserving?

Fruit trees are grafted onto a rootstock, which determines their final size. Dwarfing rootstocks are ideal for smaller yards, but need good soil to thrive, whereas semidwarfing rootstocks tolerate a wider range of conditions.

Many trees need a partner with an overlapping flowering period for pollination to occur and fruit to set. Varieties that flower at the same time are classed in the same pollination group, and for a good crop, plant two from the same group. If you lack space for two trees, look for possible pollinators growing in neighboring yards.

Planting in pots

Growing fruit trees in pots limits their size, which is ideal for smaller yards. Select a container 3 in (8 cm) wider than the root system, and make sure that it has adequate drainage holes. Be sure to use a well-drained potting mix, and fill around the roots to the soil mark on the stem. Stake, firm in, and water the new tree well.

CONTAINER GROWN
Container-grown trees are available year-round. They can be planted at any time of year, but preferably not during hot summer weather. They can be expensive to buy.

BARE-ROOT
Field-grown, bare-root trees are lifted and sold dormant, mainly by specialist nurseries, in fall and winter. Plant immediately, soaking the roots. Only buy well-rooted, undamaged plants.

PLANTING IN POTS
The best fruit trees to grow in containers are compact varieties grafted onto semi-dwarfing rootstocks. Ask your fruit supplier to recommend suitable varieties.

Planting new trees

The basic approach to planting container-grown and bare-root trees is similar, although there are important differences.

When planting container-grown trees, tease some of the outer roots away from the rootball first, to help them establish properly in the surrounding soil. A good bare-root tree has plenty of spreading roots, which should be soaked before planting if they look dry. Trim any that are damaged.

Always stake new trees to steady them in the wind, and to allow new roots to establish in the soil without being broken.

1 DIG A HOLE
Choose a sunny site, sheltered from wind and any frost pockets. Dig a hole large enough for the roots. If planting bare-root trees, mound the soil in the center. Hammer in a stake.

2 POSITION THE TREE
Place the tree in the hole, level with the soil mark on the stem. Spread out the roots and ease soil around them, firming well. Attach the tree to the stake using a cushioned tie.

3 WATER AND FIRM IN WELL
Firm the tree in, ensuring that the trunk is upright. Water it in well and apply a thick mulch of organic matter to help conserve moisture and gradually nourish the establishing tree.

4 STAKING AND AFTERCARE
Attach the tree tie to the stake using a nail. Check a few weeks later to ensure the tie is still in place, and is not rubbing against the tree. Adjust if necessary. Keep the tree watered.

Trained trees

Espaliers and vines take up little space trained against a wall or fence, making them ideal for urban gardens. Vines are single stems, usually trained at a 45° angle, with lots of short, fruiting sideshoots; while espaliers have long arms branching from a central stem, and need more room. These tree forms are controlled by summer pruning (p.137). Buy ready-trained trees from specialty nurseries to avoid much of the formative, fall pruning of young trees (pp.206–207).

Espalier—The orderly tiers of a well-trained espalier look magnificent, but need plenty of space to spread; allow 10ft (3m) for trees grafted on dwarfing rootstocks. Espalier trees are usually limited to two or three tiers.

Vines—This single-stemmed form suits apples and pears. It requires only 30in (75cm) between each tree, which means several varieties can be trained along an average-sized garden fence. Avoid tip-bearing varieties, which won't fruit well when Ωpruned in this way.

November: what to do

MARK PARSNIPS

These hardy roots will happily sit in the soil over winter, so if you are short of storage space, they can stay in the ground until you need them. But finding them once their leaves have died down, or if there is snow on the ground, can involve a bit of guesswork. Take a moment to mark the rows with stakes that are easy to spot, to make it easier to earth up your parsnip crop later on.

WORK SOIL

Late fall is the ideal time to cultivate heavy, clay soils, working in organic matter to improve the structure. Digging sticky soils is hard work but allows frosts to help break the clods into crumbs by repeated freezing and thawing. Light, sandy soils are best protected with mulch now and dug over in early spring.

TEND

WINTER POTS

PARSNIPS

DIG BEDS

PREPARING POTS FOR WINTER

Planted or empty, pots and pot-grown plants can be damaged in winter, particularly by frosts (above). Take time now to protect them.

Smaller pots and those made from terracotta and thin materials are most at risk. Heavy concrete pots are usually winter-proof.

CLEAN EMPTY POTS
Pots made of porous materials may become stained by algae or lime scale. Although these are harmless, clean your pots now.

LINE CLAY POTS
In colder areas, line pots with bubble plastic before planting trees in them, to help protect the roots from hard frosts. Don't block drainage holes.

RAISE POTS OFF GROUND
To help keep terracotta pots dry in winter, and protect them against frost damage, raise them off the ground to ensure they drain freely.

WRAP TENDER POTS
In colder areas, protect your pots, and any plant roots inside, from hard frost by wrapping them in bubble plastic, fleece, or hessian sacking.

PROTECT TALL POTS

Safeguard larger container-grown plants, such as fruit trees and bushes, and shrubby herbs, from winter damage by moving them to a sheltered spot. Strong winds can blow plants over and break containers. Pot-grown plants are also at risk of frosted roots, so move tender plants nearer to the house for warmth.

PRUNE OUTDOOR VINES

Now is the time to prune outdoor vines trained using the double guyot system (p.141), where two arms are tied horizontally to bear vertical, fruiting shoots.

1 REMOVE SPENT STEMS
Using sharp pruners or loppers, cut out the two horizontal arms that fruited last summer. Cut them close to the main stem.

2 PLAN AHEAD
Cut back the middle shoot to three healthy buds. This will grow and bear the three new shoots to train the following season (p.141).

3 TRAIN NEW SHOOTS
Tie down the two outer shoots, trained in summer (p.141), onto the wire; one to the left, one to the right. Fruiting stems will soon grow.

TALL POT PLANTS

GRAPES

WINTER PROTECTION

FALLEN LEAVES

COLD COMFORT

Most crops that grow through winter are fully hardy but can still be damaged by harsh winter winds and rain. If you live in an exposed area, it's well worth providing extra support for taller crops, such as brussels sprouts and kale, by staking them. Short wooden stakes are best, hammered in close to each plant. If you have a small bed of crops, consider screening right around it with windbreak fabric.

LEAF MOLD

Rather than burning fallen leaves, pile them into their own composting bay to slowly break down into leaf mold. Construct a simple bin using posts and wire mesh, fill with leaves, and in a year or two you'll have crumbly compost for potting and mulching. If space is limited, and you have few leaves, compost them in damp plastic bags.

See PRUNING FRUIT IN FALL pages 206–207

Pruning fruit in fall

The exact time to prune in fall depends on your regional climate—get advice from your nursery before you start. Removing old, unproductive growth encourages a good supply of new shoots to bear bumper future crops. The pruning methods used for each type of fruit are straightforward, made easier by the leafless branches that allow you to see the shape of the plant, and to identify diseased or weak growth.

Pruning fruit bushes

In addition to established plants, you should also prune newly planted fruit bushes now (p.31).

To prune, make the cuts just above the buds at a 45° angle sloping away from the shoot, so rainwater drains off the wound. Use clean, sharp tools, and remember to clean the blades between one plant and the next, to prevent the spread of disease.

When pruning in fall, use currant and gooseberry prunings for hardwood cuttings. Insert them into the soil, 6 in (15 cm) deep, buds pointing upward, and they will soon take root.

REDCURRANTS
These fruit at the base of one-year-old shoots and on older wood, so leave a permanent framework of branches. Cut branch leaders by half and side-shoots pruned in summer to one bud.

GOOSEBERRIES
Remove stems crowding the center, and any dead or diseased wood. Cut back sideshoots pruned in summer to two buds, and prune half of this year's growth from leading shoots.

SINGLE CORDON GRAPEVINES
Prune established greenhouse vines only now. Cut back the top growing point so about 1 in (2.5 cm) of new growth remains, and prune summer sideshoots back to a single bud.

BLACKBERRIES AND HYBRIDS
Now that the old canes have finished fruiting, untie them from the supports and cut them at the base. Train the new canes that will fruit next year onto the wires and tie them in securely.

BLACKCURRANTS
These fruit best on new wood from the previous summer. Prune a third of the oldest shoots to the base to encourage plenty of strong new growth that will bear fruit next year.

Pruning fruit trees

Tackling a large, established tree can be daunting, but only moderate pruning is required to keep an open shape, letting in light and air, and to encourage new growth to fruit next year. Over-pruning causes vigorous, vertical, unfruitful growth, while under-pruning leaves trees congested and prone to disease, so try to get the balance right. Fruit trees are either spur-bearers (producing fruit along their shoots on short, dumpy stems) or tip-bearers, which fruit at the shoot tips. Check your variety and prune accordingly.

PRUNING SPUR-BEARERS
Cut back long sideshoots to about six buds to encourage new fruiting-spur formation. Prune back branch leaders by a third of last season's growth. Thin out congested or shaded spurs.

PRUNING TIP-BEARERS
Prune lightly, removing older shoots that have already fruited to their base. This should give rise to new, young wood that will fruit next year at the tips. Always prune the weakest growth.

REMOVE POOR GROWTH
Cut back to healthy growth any branches that show signs of disease, such as canker (p.241) and coral spot (shown). Remove thick material with a pruning saw and burn infected growth.

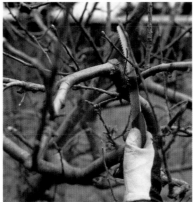

IMPROVE THE SHAPE
Look at the overall tree, and thin out any branches that crowd the middle of the framework, plus any that cross over each other, or rub together. Cut to outward-facing shoots.

CUTTING BRANCHES

When pruning large branches from fruit trees, first reduce their length and weight to prevent causing unnecessary damage and ripped bark.

1 **Part undercut the branch** midway along, then saw through from the top, slightly farther from the trunk.

2 **Remove the short stump**, sawing it off just beyond the crotch where the branch and trunk meet.

3 **Allow wound to heal** naturally, don't apply pruning paint. It will eventually form a weather-tight scar.

4 **Clean the saw after use** with detergent to reduce the spread of diseases, then apply oil to prevent rust.

PRUNING FRUIT

November: what to harvest

ROOT THEM OUT

Having grown all summer, Jerusalem artichokes have now died back until spring, so you can start lifting the strange-looking, knobbly tubers, with their delicious, nutty flavor. Dig them out using a fork only when needed in the kitchen because they soon dry out and spoil. The roots keep very well in the soil and can be dug up all through winter, providing the ground isn't frozen. When lifting the tubers, be sure to get even the tiny ones because they will regrow and spread next year if left in the soil. This perennial crop can be invasive.

FROSTED FIRST

From a spring sowing, parsnips can be lifted now, although they develop the sweetest flavor after a few frosts, so leave some to lift through winter. In light soils the roots can reach a good length. Loosen the earth around them with a fork, and lift them carefully to avoid damage. They're best harvested as required because they keep better in the ground. If you must store them to make space outside, see pages 210–211.

JERUSALEM ARTICHOKES

PARSNIPS

KOHLRABI

KOHL SHORTAGE

Late-growing kohlrabi (p.154) plants endure cold weather, but will be spoiled by frost. Either pull them up and use the swollen stems before winter arrives, cloche the remaining plants, or lift them, remove the outer leaves and store in boxes of sand in a cool, frost-free place.

'PURPLE DANUBE'
Dark on the outside, its tasty flesh is pure white, and most tender when harvested young. Older, larger plants can become slightly bitter tasting.

'KOLIBRI'
Best eaten golf-ball sized, and ready in as little as 8 weeks, this variety is good in smaller gardens where it will give several crops during summer.

'LANRO'
Harvest when the swollen green stems reach 2 in (5 cm) across. They can be eaten diced and boiled, but are delicious grated in salads.

'SUPERSCHMELZ'
Gradually reaching 10 in (25 cm) across, this is a larger variety that can also be harvested small. It has a mild, sweet, turniplike flavor.

HARVEST SALSIFY ROOTS
Salsify, sown directly outside in May (p.94), is ready to harvest, allowing you the chance to enjoy the unusual, nutty-tasting roots that have become a "must have" among top chefs. Dig deeply with a fork to lift the roots as required, from now until spring. Roots left in the soil have a superior flavor to those lifted and stored in sand-filled boxes (pp.210–211), but storing is useful in areas with cold winters, where the ground may freeze. The skins must be removed; smaller roots are easier to peel after cooking.

ROOT SUCCESS
Rutabagas, sown in May (p.94), will be full of flavor, and should be harvested as required until midwinter. If the weather allows, dig them up and store them in dry boxes, covered with sand. If the weather is poor, wait until spring, although the roots will be woody and tougher to eat by then.

SALSIFY

RUTABAGA

CELERIAC

WINTER SALAD

WINTER CELERIAC
Celeriac can be harvested this month, right through until spring, making it a really useful crop. The roots are tough enough to be left in the ground all winter in most places, and lifted as required. If you live in a very cold area, where the ground may freeze, lift the entire crop now, trim off the outer leaves, and store the roots in boxes of dry sand, (pp.210–211).

TAKE A LEAF
Winter salad leaves, grown under cover since late summer, are ready to crop. Mizuna, mibuna, oriental mustard, arugula, lettuce, perpetual spinach, and corn salad are all plants to take baby leaves from throughout winter. Even under cover, growth will be slow at this time, so these cut-and-come-again crops will take time to resprout.

Try MAKING SOUPS
pages 226–228

Storing vegetables

By using traditional storage techniques, you can look forward to home-grown vegetables throughout winter, anything from stacks of potatoes to a few prized squash. Some root crops can be left in the soil in mild areas, but most other vegetables should be harvested and stored. The important point is to keep them fresh, and to protect them from frosts, weather damage, and hungry insects and animals.

HARVESTING IDEAS

Roots in boxes

If you have space available in a cool, frost-free place, such as a shed, cellar, or garage, then try storing smaller root vegetables in boxes filled with light soil or sand. The method is simple and it keeps roots firm and fresh right through winter. Carrots, beets, turnips, and parsnips can all be stored like this. You can fit several layers into a single box, which is ideal if you have only limited space indoors.

Whichever roots you store, lift them carefully, if possible when the soil is reasonably dry. If the roots are wet, lay them out on newspaper to dry fully and then brush off loose soil. Check each one, and store only crops that are disease-free and undamaged.

Jo's tips

The larger the root, the longer it will keep, so when storing in sand-filled boxes, pack the biggest specimens in the bottom layers and the smallest ones at the top.

Not all root crops keep well when lifted. Jerusalem artichokes and salsify lose their flavor and dry out once harvested.

1 REMOVE LEAVES
Remove all foliage before storing. Cut off carrot leaves ½ in (1 cm) above the roots and twist off the leaves of other vegetables with your hands, leaving a short tuft of stems at the top.

2 PREPARE YOUR BOX
Find a cardboard or wooden box that is wide and fairly shallow. Line it with newspaper if there are any gaps. Cover the base with a layer of light soil or sand about 1 in (2.5 cm) thick.

3 ARRANGE THE ROOTS
Place the first layer of roots with care to make maximum use of the space without one root touching another. Contact between them could allow rot to spread through the box.

4 LAYER THEM UP
Once the first layer is complete, cover it with at least 1 in (2.5 cm) of light soil or sand. Repeat the whole process until the box is full. Store in a dry, frost- and rodent-free place.

Clamping

This traditional method is ideal for storing large quantities of root crops, and involves piling them in a heap and insulating them with layers of straw. Providing the clamp can be kept dry, crops can be stored this way indoors or out. Stored vegetables must be dry, clean, and undamaged, so check them thoroughly first. Outdoor clamps are prone to rodent attack, so watch for signs of disturbance and set traps if need be. When emptying the clamp, take roots from one end only and carefully replace the layers once you have removed what you need.

1 LAY THE BASE
Spread a 8 in (20 cm) deep bed of straw on the soil in a sheltered spot, ideally against a wall. Arrange the roots on top to make a tapering heap that is a maximum 2 ft (60 cm) high.

2 PROVIDE INSULATION
Pack the same thickness of dry straw over the entire heap. If your clamp is indoors you can just cover it with burlap or row cover fabric weighed down at the edges.

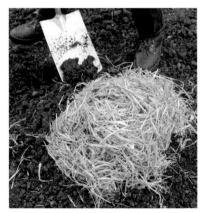

3 ALL-WEATHER PROTECTION
Cover your outdoor clamp with a further layer of soil, about 6 in (15 cm) thick, to provide extra protection against cold and wet. Pack soil onto the straw from the base upward.

4 ENSURE GOOD DRAINAGE
Soggy soil will rot stored roots from the base, so improve drainage by digging a shallow ditch around the edge of the clamp, using the soil to finish covering the top of the heap.

TRY THESE

Traditional methods can be used to store a wide range of crops, keeping them fresh to use without taking up space in your refrigerator or freezer.

Potatoes—Store late-season varieties somewhere dry and frost-free in paper bags, folded over to exclude light.

Bulbs—When dried (p.159), hang onions, shallots, and garlic in bunches somewhere cool, dry, and frost-free.

Squash—Once cured (p.175), store squash and pumpkins under cover, on straw or shredded paper.

Beans—When the pods are dry and brittle, store the beans in screw-top jars indoors. Check them occasionally.

STORING VEGETABLES

Making simple chutney

Chutneys are a gift to gardeners reluctant to waste the mountain of leftover fruit and vegetables as summer turns to fall. The joy of these preserves, apart from the fact that they are child's play to make, is that you can create your own recipe with almost any produce. The only rules are that a chutney should contain good quality vinegar to prevent spoiling, and sugar and spices for a rich, punchy flavor.

Spicy plum and apple chutney

Makes approx 3 lb (1.35 kg)
(3 large jars)
Takes 2 hours
Keeps 1 year

Ingredients

12 oz (350 g) cooking apples
2¼ lb (1 kg) plums
2 onions
3 oz (75 g) fresh ginger root
4½ oz (125 g) raisins
10 oz (300 g) light brown sugar
1 tsp salt
1 tsp allspice
1 tsp ground cloves
1 tsp ground cinnamon
1 pint (600 ml) cider vinegar

Jo's tips

Chutneys should have a thick consistency, so they spread well in sandwiches and sit in appetizing mounds on plates of cold meat. If a watery layer develops on chutney in the jar, it needs to be cooked longer, so pour it back into a pan and simmer until thickened.

To sterilize your jars, wash them in hot soapy water, place them on a rack in a moderate oven, and let them dry thoroughly.

1 Start by peeling, coring, and cutting up the apples. Wash the plums and chop them roughly, taking care to remove all the stones. Take the skins off the onions before slicing them, and grate the ginger.

2 Put all the fresh ingredients into a preserving pan or large saucepan, and add the raisins, sugar, salt, spices, and cider vinegar. Bring to a boil slowly, stirring regularly until the sugar has dissolved.

3 Reduce the heat and simmer gently for about 1½ hours, until the mixture is thick, excess liquid has evaporated, and some of the fruit and vegetables have cooked to a pulp. Stir frequently to avoid sticking.

4 Pour or ladle the chutney into sterilized jars while they are still warm (see Jo's Tips, left). Seal the jars while the chutney is hot. Use nonmetallic lids because vinegar will react with metal and taint the chutney.

Chutney improves with keeping, so leave it unopened for at least 4 weeks before eating.

TRY THESE

This technique for making chutney can be used with an array of vegetables, fruit, and spices, such as those suggested below. There are others to try.

Gooseberry and ginger—Deliciously fruity and spicy, this combination makes the perfect partner for cheese.

Beets—Rich red, sweet, and flavored with cloves and allspice, what could be better with cold meats?

Zucchini—Beef up the flavor with onions, garlic, and tomatoes, and maybe add some fire with a chile.

Runner beans—This chutney has a chunky texture. Add tomatoes, turmeric, and mustard for flavor.

December: ready to eat

It's time for fresh brussels sprouts, kale, and cabbage, along with sweet roasted root vegetables. Bring out the homemade chutney as a tangy accompaniment, and enjoy desserts made from stored summer fruit.

Eat **winter radishes**, pulled fresh from the soil and grated into salads

Harvest the last of your **celery**

Keep harvesting fresh **cut-and-come-again** greens

New season **winter cabbages** are a high point this month

Add the last newly dug **turnips** to stews and stir-fries

Use up stored **hazelnuts**

Add **endive**, grown under cover, to give your salads a bitter twist

Enjoy fresh **sprouting seeds** every few days
pages 36–37

Try mashed **rutabaga,** using newly dug or stored roots

Pull fresh **parsnips** or use them from your storage

Enjoy **cauliflower** florets from the freezer or in punchy fall pickles

Eat under cover crops of **Swiss chard** and **spinach**

Tasty **kale** will crop for months; try it shredded and stir-fried

Bake stored **winter squash** —eat with a pat of butter

Continue to eat fresh **salsify**—it tastes much better than it looks!

Remember to use your frozen **beans** and **peas** *pages 148–149*

Tis the season... to enjoy your homemade wine pages 180–181

Use dried, **home-grown herbs** *page 161* in seasonal stuffing

Keep on picking and enjoying your brussels sprouts

Leeks, lightly fried in butter, have a wonderfully sweet, onion flavor

Use **dried chiles** *page 161* to give your meals some bite

Put a bowl of homemade **chutney** on the table *pages 212–213*

Celeriac—looks weird, tastes terrific

Roast stored **potatoes** and root vegetables

Make tastier winter salads using **radicchio** grown under cover

Jerusalem artichokes are costly to buy, so dig your own, fresh, nutty tubers

Make hot puddings from stored **apples** and **pears** *pages 194–195*

Homemade **pickles** will keep you going *pages 176–179*

Carry on using **onions**, **shallots**, and **garlic** from your storage

Eat the last freshly dug **carrots**

December: what to sow

FORCING BELGIAN ENDIVE

HARVEST: **JAN–MAR**

Having lifted and stored your Belgian endive roots (see p.185), they're now ready for the next stage of the forcing process. Act now, and in less than a month, you can be enjoying a leafy luxury that's normally expensive to buy. You might even get a second harvest.

1 POT UP THE ROOTS
Plant several stored roots into a large pot, leaving the trimmed tops above the surface of the soil.

2 BLOCK OUT THE LIGHT
Cover the pot with another the same size, but block the drainage holes to exclude light from the roots.

3 GROW ON INDOORS
Grow the roots indoors at a temperature of 50° F (10° C) for 3–4 weeks. Water only in the dark.

4 HARVEST
After harvesting the leaves, water and re-cover the roots with the pot. They may regrow again.

SOW

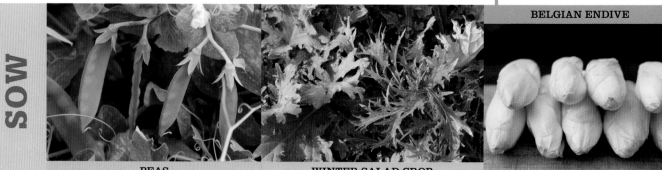

PEAS

WINTER SALAD CROP

BELGIAN ENDIVE

NEW YEAR PEAS

HARVEST: **MAY–JUN**

If you live in a mild area, hardy peas can still be sown directly outside (p.184). In colder regions, sow them under cover for planting out in spring.

'DOUCE PROVENCE'
This is a high-yield, dwarf variety that produces masses of sweet-tasting peas. It only requires support in exposed sites.

'FELTHAM FIRST'
Very hardy, this dwarf variety gives an early crop of 4 in (10 cm) long green pods, packed with large peas. It is suitable for containers.

'METEOR'
Dwarf but highly productive, this variety produces abundant small pods, filled with fine-tasting peas. Grows well on exposed sites.

WINTER SALAD

If you have space in an unheated greenhouse or beneath a cold frame, you still have time to sow hardy oriental salad leaves, such as mizuna and mustard, for an early cut-and-come-again crop. Sow ½ in (1 cm) deep, in trenches 4–6 in (10–15 cm) wide, directly in the soil. You can also sow into large pots and bring them under cover. Harvest young plants after a few weeks, although they may take some time to re-grow.

HARVEST: **ALL YEAR**

December: what to plant

PICK GARDEN NUTS

HARVEST: **SEP–OCT**

If you have space in your garden for a small apple tree, you could plant a hazelnut instead. Depending on variety, you may need two for pollination.

'COSFORD'
This variety produces a heavy crop of thin-shelled, sweet-tasting nuts that are easy to crack open.

'KENTISH COB'
A self-fertile variety, so you only need one plant. It bears delicious, large nuts in late summer.

'RED FILBERT'
This red-leaved variety produces masses of tasty, red-shelled nuts. It is an attractive garden shrub.

HAZELNUTS

PLANT

CARE FOR TOOLS

APRICOTS

TIMELY TOOL CARE
Finding time to maintain your gardening tools is difficult in the growing season, so make use of the relative lull now to lavish some care on them. Use a wire brush to remove mud from metal tools, and rub them with an oily cloth to prevent rust. Clean the blades of cutting tools, such as pruners and loppers, with steel wool and sharpen them. Replace any blades that are damaged.

TREE PLANTING
Despite seeming tender, apricots can be planted from now until March, if the soil isn't frozen. To help protect the early blossoms from frost and to ripen the fruit, pick a warm position against a south-facing wall. Add compost to the soil, and plant the tree to the same depth as it was in the nursery. Firm the soil and water-in well.

HARVEST: **JUL–AUG**

See CHOOSING & PLANTING FRUIT TREES pages 202–203

Plums

Plums are easy to grow and often bear heavily. They are vigorous, so for smaller plots choose a tree on a dwarfing rootstock or train it as a fan against a wall.

1 'Early Laxton' is one of the first plums to ripen in summer, although not one of the tastiest. It is partially self-fertile, but gives a better crop with a suitable pollination partner nearby.

2 'Opal' is an early variety that gives a heavy crop of tasty red fruit in early August. It is self-fertile, so you'll only need one tree for a crop, making it a good choice for smaller gardens.

3 'Victoria' gives an excellent crop of dark red fruit during late summer, which are deliciously sweet when eaten raw or cooked. Use surplus fruit for jam (pp.128–129) or wine (pp.180–181).

4 'Shiro' is a golden-fruited variety, with pale yellow skin and transparent flesh. It flowers in early spring, and its blossoms can be damaged by frost, so it's best suited to milder regions.

5 'Giant Prune' gives a heavy crop of large dark red fruit in late summer that are particularly good for storing. It is self-fertile, hardy, and disease-resistant, making it a good choice for beginners.

Other varieties to try:
'Blue Tit'
'Czar'
'Majorie's Seedling'
'Methley'
'Warwickshire Drooper'

Damsons and gages

Small and dark, with a sharp taste, damsons are best used for cooking and preserving. Gages are sweeter, and delicious in desserts, jams, and cordials.

1 'Merryweather Damson' is a high-yielding variety that produces large, blue-black fruit with yellow flesh, which can be eaten raw or cooked. Self-fertile, it sets fruit without a pollinator variety.

2 'Prune Damson' is a traditional variety that bears small, dark, rich-tasting fruit in late summer, which are excellent cooked. The harvest isn't large, but it grows well in cold regions.

3 'Cambridge Gage' is a reliable, high-yielding variety that gives an ample harvest of sweet, green fruit that are good to eat cooked or raw. Partially self-fertile; it is best with a pollinator.

4 'Old Green Gage' is an old variety that produces rich, sweet-tasting, yellow-green fruit in early fall. Self-sterile, it must be grown with a pollinating variety for a good crop.

5 'Oullins Golden Gage' produces large, sweet, yellow fruit, with clear flesh. It is self-fertile and a reliable producer, giving a reasonable harvest in late summer. Eat the fruit raw or cooked.

Other varieties to try:
'Bradley's King Damson'
'Denniston's Superb'—gage
'Farleigh Damson'
'Laxton's Gage'

PLUMS, DAMSONS AND GAGES

Cherries

Choose dwarfing rootstock for cherry trees that are suitable for any size garden. Eat sweet cherries straight from the tree; sour varieties are better cooked.

1 'Stella' produces abundant crops of sweet, dark-red fruit that are ready to harvest from around mid-July to August. This self-fertile variety is easy to grow.

2 'Lapins' has very large, almost black fruit with a superb flavor. These sweet cherries are ready to pick in late June. The self-fertile tree needs little pruning.

3 'May Duke' is a long-established variety used mainly for cooking. This cherry has a tangy flavor midway between sweet and acid. The bright red fruits are ripe for picking in mid-July.

4 'Morello' is a sour cooking cherry, with large juicy fruits that are excellent for pies and jam-making. It bears abundantly and the first cherries are ready for picking in late August.

5 'Sweetheart' has a long picking season because the sweet, dark red fruit ripens in stages over an extended period. The first crop can be picked from late August onward.

Other varieties to try:
'Celeste'—sweet
'Nabella'—sour
'Summer Sun'—sweet
'Vega'—sweet

TAKE YOUR PICK

Currants

Draped in their heavy crops of berries, these bushes look beautiful and will fruit for years in a bed, large patio pots, or trained as space-saving cordons on a fence.

1 'Ben Sarek' is a compact bush that makes a good choice for the smaller garden. This variety is resistant to mildew. The abundant fruit, which freezes well, is ready for picking from around mid-July.

2 'Ben Connan' produces large fruit with an exceptional flavor. Once a bush is well established, you should expect heavy crops in mid-July. This variety is good eaten as a dessert fruit and can also be used for jams and jellies.

3 'White Versailles' has delicate, creamy white fruit that hangs heavily in long trusses. These currants have a sweet flavor and can be eaten fresh or used for cooking. The crop ripens from midsummer onward.

4 'Blanca' ripens slightly later than most currants. Its large, yellowish white berries are not fully ripe until the end of July. Pick and eat the fruit fresh from the bush or use it for making preserves.

5 'Red Lake' is a popular redcurrant often recommended for its abundant crops. The fruit, sweet, and well flavored, ripens by mid-July.

6 'Jonkheer van Tets' has plump, juicy, glowing red fruits. This hardy variety is easy to grow and ripens early, usually producing a heavy crop that is ready to pick in early July.

Other varieties to try:
'Ben Lomond'—blackcurrant
'Ebony' –blackcurrant
'Stanza'—redcurrant

CHERRIES AND CURRANTS

TAKE YOUR PICK

Citrus

Citrus trees are handsome evergreen plants that produce gloriously scented white flowers, usually in spring but also sporadically throughout the year. They look attractive in containers and can be grown singly; being self-fertile, they don't need a partner for pollination. Consistent warmth is the secret of success.

The right climate

These exotic plants have been grown in temperate regions for centuries, although almost always sheltered under glass during winter. To successfully produce fruit, citrus trees need periods of several months where the temperature doesn't fall below 59°F (15°C). Where frosts are mild and summers hot, citrus trees can be a permanent outdoor feature. However, most gardeners prefer to grow them in containers in a cool, bright indoor room, sunroom, or heated greenhouse during winter and move them outside to grace a sunny patio in summer.

Winter indoors

Although most citrus trees can survive temperatures near the freezing point for short periods, it is best not to test them too severely. Move your container-grown trees under cover as soon as nights become cool at the beginning of fall.

Citrus trees need high humidity and centrally heated houses tend to have a dry atmosphere, so stand the pot on a tray of wet gravel to keep the air moist. Don't place the container near radiators or in cold drafts. Water the tree sparingly during winter and watch for pests. Indoor citrus plants are prone to attack by aphids, mealy bugs, red spider mites, and scale insects. Squash any pests as soon as you spot them and treat infestations with insecticidal soap or suitable biological controls.

In early spring, repot into a slightly larger container, ideally using a well-drained potting mix with compost added. Spring is also the time for light pruning to remove crossing or dead branches.

Summer outdoors

Once the last frosts have passed, move citrus trees outside to a warm, sheltered spot for the summer. Do this gradually, hardening them off over a few weeks, and be prepared to protect them with row cover if temperatures drop unexpectedly.

Plants in containers need feeding every 2 weeks during the growing season with a special citrus fertilizer. Citrus trees are sensitive to waterlogging, so make sure that pots are well drained. Small trees can produce only a few fruits without becoming stressed, so limit the crop to about four fruits on the tree at any given time. These will take 6 months or more to ripen, so be patient.

1

4

7

CITRUS

1 Kumquat—Although a close relative of other citrus fruits, the kumquat is not a member of the *Citrus* genus. It can tolerate temperatures down to 23°F (-5°C). Eat the small oval fruit whole.

2 Lime—One of the tenderest citrus fruits, limes will fruit under cover if given adequate heat. The variety 'Bearss' is more tolerant of cold than most.

3 Makrut—This citrus, sometimes known as kaffir lime, is grown for its aromatic, double-lobed leaves, which are well known as a key ingredient in Thai cuisine. The knobbly fruit is inedible.

4 Lemon—A fast-growing plant that can flower and fruit throughout the year, this is a good choice for beginners. 'Meyer' and 'Ponderosa' are excellent varieties.

5 Orange—Attractive trees with beautiful flowers, sweet oranges need reliably high temperatures for the fruit to ripen. Try 'Valencia' or the variegated 'Tiger Navel'.

6 Mandarin—Easy for beginners, the mandarin is more resilient to cold than most other citrus. The thin-skinned, flattened fruits are easy to peel.

7 Calamondin—Popular as an indoor ornamental, this dwarf citrus produces small round fruits. The flesh is sweet but acidic when fully ripe. It is mostly used for making drinks or marmalades.

8 Grapefruit—Only a large tree can carry the heavy fruits, which take many months to ripen fully. Grapefruit needs high temperatures and presents a challenge for any grower.

Other varieties to try:
Blood orange—sweet pink or red flesh
Clementine—mandarin/orange hybrid
Limequat—lime/kumquat hybrid
Satsuma—mandarin/orange hybrid
Sour orange—for marmalades

December: what to harvest

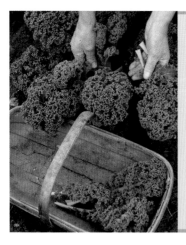

WINTER KALE

Kale is a useful ally among winter vegetables, and can be relied upon to tough-out almost any winter weather. It's a particularly good crop for smaller gardens because, although the plants are quite large and grow all summer, the leaves can be picked a few at a time, all the way through winter. If the weather turns really bad, such as heavy snowfall, harvest the best leaves and freeze them until needed (pp.148–149). Even if your plants are damaged, leave them to recover and they may produce new leaves and shoots.

LAST OF THE CELERY

Able to withstand light frosts, celery is a good choice for mild-winter areas, where it can be harvested through winter. As an extra precaution, give it a protective mulch of straw to keep it at its best. Lift earthed-up plants with a fork, or cut those blanched using collars right at the base, as required. Cut stems can be kept somewhere cool, stored in plastic bags, but whole plants are best left growing in the ground until needed.

HARVEST

KALE

CELERY

POTATOES

PAK CHOI

LATE POTATOES

If you planted maincrop potatoes in midsummer (p.132), either in the ground or containers, you could well have tubers still to harvest. If the weather is cold, protect the remaining crop from frost by mulching with a thick layer of straw, or by moving containers under cover. Simply unearth the potatoes with a fork as required, and enjoy new potatoes at Christmas.

BOK CHOY NOW

Any late-summer sown bok choy, that were cloched or transplanted under cover in early fall, should now be ready to harvest. Their fresh, mild leaves make a welcome contrast to the strong-flavored, hardy winter brassicas. Pull up the plants whole or cut them off just above the soil, and they may well resprout.

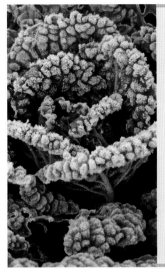

SWEET WINTER GREENS

The first winter cabbages and endive, planted out in July (p.133), are ready to cut. If you have other vegetables to pick as well, leave a few cabbages growing for later. After a few hard frosts, their leaves become deliciously sweet, and are a real highlight of the season. To harvest, pull up the whole plant, and cut away the stem and any damaged outer foliage, leaving the firm green heart. While growing, these cabbages make handsome garden features, especially when they're dusted with crisp winter frost.

TASTY SPROUTS

Love or hate them, there's no denying that brussels sprouts give a good winter crop. If you began sowing a succession of sprout varieties in February (p.41), then you'll be picking them from now until spring. Harvest the lower sprouts first, twisting them with your fingers, and work your way up the stem. Don't miss the leafy tops.

LEEKS

WINTER CABBAGE & ENDIVE

BRUSSELS SPROUTS

LIFT YOUR LEEKS

Mid- and late-season leeks, sown in spring, are ready to lift. Unearth them using a fork to prevent damaging the stems; the small roots hold on tight.

'KING RICHARD'
Although this is an early variety, it will stand until December in milder areas. It doesn't need earthing-up and is suitable for growing in pots.

'MUSSELBURGH'
This is a reliable, tasty variety that produces a heavy crop of strong, thick stems. It tolerates cold very well, and is good for exposed sites.

'TOLEDO'
A very hardy, late-season variety, it produces long tasty stems and resists bolting. The harvested leeks also store well if heeled in.

DON'T FORGET

If a spell of very cold weather is forecast, mulch any root crops still in the ground with thick straw. This stops the soil from freezing, so they can still be dug up.

Try FREEZING VEGETABLES pages 148–149

Making soups

Everyone who grows vegetables needs a collection of favorite soup recipes to use throughout the year. Chunky or smooth, rustic and hearty, sophisticated and light, there is a soup for all tastes.

You can make soups with in-season crops or use vegetables from your freezer or winter stores. Soups are also a good way of using gluts, because it's easy to cook large quantities and freeze the surplus.

Leek and potato soup

Serves 4
Preparation 15 minutes
Cook 20 minutes
Keeps 3 months in freezer

Ingredients

1⅓ cups leeks
1 cup potatoes
1 large onion
1 tbsp olive oil
1 tsp ground cumin
4 cups hot chicken stock
salt and freshly ground black pepper
2 tbsp dry white wine
2 tbsp double cream
1 tbsp lemon juice
chives, to garnish

Jo's **tips**

For great soup, make your own stock or buy the best you can find. Vegetable or chicken stocks let the produce dominate, but sometimes only heavier stock, such as beef in French onion soup, will do.

For richer, sweeter soups, try roasting vegetables, such as squashes, tomatoes, and parsnips, in the oven for about 40 minutes to intensify their flavor, before adding to the other ingredients.

1 Wash the leeks thoroughly, taking care to remove all grit between the leaves. Using a sharp knife, slice them lengthwise and then into 1 in (2.5 cm) lengths. Dice the potatoes and thinly slice the onions.

2 Heat the olive oil in a heavy saucepan. Add the leeks, onions, potatoes, cumin, stock, salt, and freshly ground pepper. Cover with a lid and bring to the boil, then lower the heat and allow to simmer.

3 Simmer the soup gently for approximately 10 minutes, stirring occasionally, then check that the vegetables are tender. Don't let the potatoes overcook because they will disintegrate into the soup.

4 Transfer the soup to a blender, add the wine, and blend until smooth. Stir in the cream and lemon juice, then check the seasoning and adjust to taste. Serve the soup in bowls with snipped chives to garnish.

Satisfyingly thick and tasty, leek and potato soup makes good use of your winter crops.

TRY THESE

Whatever the season, there is likely to be something in your vegetable garden that you can use to make delicious soup for a quick and healthy meal.

Onions—The useful onion finds its way into many soups, but it is outstanding in piping hot French onion soup.

Carrots—These add a wonderfully vibrant color to soup. Tangy carrot and orange soup is a popular recipe.

Parsnips—Nothing is more filling and warming on a cold winter day than a bowl of curried parsnip soup.

Broccoli—Try melting a blue cheese, such as Stilton, into creamy broccoli soup for a rich blend of flavors.

MAKING SOUPS

At-a-glance advice

In this section you will find quick-reference planners to remind you of the key timings for each crop. There is also a troubleshooting guide to pests, diseases, and nutritional deficiencies, to help you identify whatever is causing unsavoury spots on your apples, or chewing holes in your cabbages.

Fruit: crop planner

Use this table to check when to sow, plant, prune, and harvest your fruit. Timings will vary for different climates so adjust them for your own site and weather conditions. Planting times refer to bare-root plants; container-grown shrubs and trees can be planted year-round.

CROPS		J	F	M	A	M	J	J	A	S	O	N	D
APPLES	SOW												
	PLANT	■	■									■	■
	HARVEST									■	■	■	■
	PRUNE	■	■					■	■				
APRICOTS	SOW												
	PLANT	■	■									■	■
	HARVEST							■	■				
	PRUNE			■	■		■						
BLACKBERRIES & HYBRIDS	SOW												
	PLANT										■	■	
	HARVEST							■	■				
	PRUNE											■	
BLUEBERRIES	SOW												
	PLANT											■	■
	HARVEST								■	■			
	PRUNE											■	■
HAZELNUTS	SOW												
	PLANT											■	■
	HARVEST										■		
	PRUNE							■	■				
CHERRIES	SOW												
	PLANT	■	■									■	■
	HARVEST						■	■	■				
	PRUNE			■	■			■					
CURRANTS—BLACK	SOW												
	PLANT										■	■	■
	HARVEST							■					
	PRUNE											■	■
CURRANTS—RED & WHITE	SOW												
	PLANT	■	■								■	■	■
	HARVEST							■	■	■			
	PRUNE						■					■	■
FIGS	SOW												
	PLANT											■	■
	HARVEST								■	■			
	PRUNE		■	■			■	■					
GOOSEBERRIES	SOW												
	PLANT	■	■									■	■
	HARVEST					■	■						
	PRUNE	■										■	■

KEY	
▒▒▒	SOWN, PLANTED, HARVESTED UNDER COVER
▬▬▬	SOWN, PLANTED, HARVESTED OUTDOORS

Key: ● = outdoors, ○ = under cover

CROPS		J	F	M	A	M	J	J	A	S	O	N	D
GRAPES—OUTDOOR	SOW												
	PLANT	●	●	●								●	●
	HARVEST									●	●		
	PRUNE				○	○	○	○				●	●
MELONS	SOW				○	●	●						
	PLANT					●	●						
	HARVEST								●	●			
	PRUNE												
NECTARINES & PEACHES	SOW												
	PLANT	●	●									●	●
	HARVEST								●	●			
	PRUNE					●	●						
PEARS	SOW												
	PLANT	●	●									●	●
	HARVEST									●	●		
	PRUNE	●	●					●	●	●	●		
PLUMS, DAMSONS, & GAGES	SOW												
	PLANT	●	●									●	●
	HARVEST								●	●			
	PRUNE					●	●						
RASPBERRIES—SUMMER	SOW												
	PLANT	●	●								●	●	
	HARVEST							●	●				
	PRUNE		●			●				●	●	●	
RASPBERRIES—FALL	SOW												
	PLANT	●	●	●							●	●	●
	HARVEST								●	●			
	PRUNE		●										
RHUBARB	SOW												
	PLANT	●	●	●								●	●
	HARVEST			●	●	●	●						
	PRUNE												
STRAWBERRIES—JUNEBEARING	SOW												
	PLANT							●	●	●			
	HARVEST				○	●	●						
	PRUNE												
STRAWBERRIES—EVERBEARING	SOW												
	PLANT			●	●							●	
	HARVEST							●	●	●	●		○
	PRUNE												

Vegetable: crop planner

Use this table to check when to sow, plant, prune, and harvest your vegetables. Timings will vary for different climates, so adjust them for your own site and weather conditions. For continuity, replace crops harvested in spring and summer with plants sown later.

CROPS		J	F	M	A	M	J	J	A	S	O	N	D
ASPARAGUS	SOW												
	PLANT				■								
	HARVEST					■	■						
EGGPLANT	SOW			■									
	PLANT					■							
	HARVEST								■	■	■		
BEANS—BROAD	SOW	■	■									■	
	PLANT			■									
	HARVEST					■	■	■					
BEANS—SNAP	SOW					■							
	PLANT						■	■					
	HARVEST							■	■	■			
BEANS—RUNNER	SOW					■							
	PLANT						■	■					
	HARVEST							■	■	■			
BEET	SOW				■	■	■	■					
	PLANT												
	HARVEST					■	■	■	■				
BROCCOLI—PURPLE SPROUTING	SOW			■	■	■							
	PLANT						■	■	■	■	■		
	HARVEST	■	■	■									
BROCCOLI	SOW			■		■	■						
	PLANT												
	HARVEST							■	■	■	■		
BRUSSEL SPROUTS	SOW		■		■								
	PLANT					■							
	HARVEST	■											■
CABBAGE—CHINESE	SOW					■	■	■					
	PLANT												
	HARVEST								■	■	■		
CABBAGE—WINTER	SOW					■							
	PLANT							■					
	HARVEST												■
CABBAGE—SPRING	SOW							■	■				
	PLANT									■	■	■	
	HARVEST				■	■							
CABBAGE—SUMMER	SOW			■	■								
	PLANT				■	■							
	HARVEST								■	■	■	■	
CARROTS	SOW			■	■	■	■	■					
	PLANT												
	HARVEST					■	■	■	■	■	■	■	■

KEY

▒▒▒▒▒	SOWN, PLANTED, HARVESTED UNDER COVER
█████	SOWN, PLANTED, HARVESTED OUTDOORS

CROPS		J	F	M	A	M	J	J	A	S	O	N	D
CAULIFLOWER—WINTER	SOW					█							
	PLANT							█	█				
	HARVEST			█	█	█							
CAULIFLOWER—SUMMER	SOW			█	█						█		
	PLANT			█	█	█		█					
	HARVEST							█	█	█	█		
CELERIAC	SOW		▒	▒									
	PLANT					█							
	HARVEST	█	█	█							█	█	█
CELERY—SELF BLANCHING	SOW		▒	▒									
	PLANT					█							
	HARVEST								█	█	█		
CELERY	SOW			▒	▒								
	PLANT					█							
	HARVEST	█									█	█	█
RADICCHIO	SOW					█	█						
	PLANT						█	█		▒	▒		
	HARVEST	█							█	█	█	█	█
BELGIAN ENDIVE	SOW					█	█	█					
	PLANT						█	█	█				
	HARVEST	█										█	█
ZUCCHINI	SOW				▒	▒	█						
	PLANT					▒	█	█					
	HARVEST							█	█	█	█		
CUCUMBER	SOW				▒	▒							
	PLANT					▒	▒						
	HARVEST							█	█	█	█		
ENDIVE	SOW					▒	█	█	█				
	PLANT					█	█	█	▒				
	HARVEST							█	█	█	█	█	█
FLORENCE FENNEL	SOW				▒	█							
	PLANT					█							
	HARVEST						█	█	█	█			
GARLIC	SOW												
	PLANT		█	█							█	█	
	HARVEST						█	█	█				
GLOBE ARTICHOKE	SOW		▒	▒	█								
	PLANT				█								
	HARVEST	█									█	█	█
JERUSALEM ARTICHOKE	SOW												
	PLANT		█	█	█								
	HARVEST	█									█	█	█

CROPS		J	F	M	A	M	J	J	A	S	O	N	D
KALE	SOW				●	●	●	●					
	PLANT						●	●					
	HARVEST	●	●	●							●	●	●
KOHLRABI	SOW		○	●	●	●	●	●					
	PLANT					●	●	●					
	HARVEST						●	●	●	●	●	●	
LEEKS	SOW	○	○	●	●								
	PLANT					●	●						
	HARVEST	●	●	●						●	●	●	●
LETTUCE	SOW	○	○	●	●	●	●	●					
	PLANT				●	●	●						
	HARVEST				●	●	●	●	●	●	●	●	○
MUSHROOMS	SOW	○	○	○	○	○	○	○	○	○	○	○	○
	PLANT												
	HARVEST	○	○	○	○	○	○	○	○	○	○	○	○
ONION—OVERWINTERING	SOW								●				
	PLANT									●	●		
	HARVEST						●						
ONION—SUMMER	SOW	○		●	●								
	PLANT		●	●	●								
	HARVEST							●	●				
BOK CHOY	SOW						●	●					
	PLANT												
	HARVEST							●	●	●	●	●	
PARSNIPS	SOW		○	●	●								
	PLANT												
	HARVEST	●										●	●
PEAS	SOW	○	○	●	●	●	●				●		
	PLANT			●	●								
	HARVEST					●	●	●					
PEPPERS—CHILE	SOW		○										
	PLANT					○							
	HARVEST							○	●	●	●		
PEPPERS—SWEET	SOW			○									
	PLANT					○	●						
	HARVEST							○	●	●			
POTATOES—EARLY	SOW												
	PLANT			●	●								
	HARVEST						●	●	●	●	●		
POTATOES—LATE	SOW												
	PLANT				●	●							
	HARVEST									●	●		
POTATOES—MID-SEASON	SOW												
	PLANT						●						
	HARVEST									●	●	●	●
PUMPKIN	SOW				○	○	●						
	PLANT					●	○						
	HARVEST									●	●		
RADISHES—SUMMER	SOW	○											
	PLANT												
	HARVEST				●	●	●	●	●	●	●	●	●

CROPS		J	F	M	A	M	J	J	A	S	O	N	D
RADISHES—WINTER	SOW								■				
	PLANT												
	HARVEST	■	■	■							■	■	■
ARUGULA	SOW	■	■	■	■	■	■	■	■	■			
	PLANT												
	HARVEST			■	■	■	■	■	■	■	■	■	■
SALAD LEAVES	SOW	■	■	■	■	■	■	■	■	■			
	PLANT												
	HARVEST	■	■	■	■	■	■	■	■	■	■	■	■
SALISFY	SOW				■	■							
	PLANT												
	HARVEST	■	■	■								■	■
SHALLOTS—SETS	SOW												
	PLANT		■	■									
	HARVEST							■	■				
SPINACH	SOW		■	■		■	■	■	■				
	PLANT			■	■								
	HARVEST				■	■	■	■	■	■	■	■	
GREEN ONIONS	SOW			■	■	■	■	■	■	■	■		
	PLANT												
	HARVEST	■	■	■	■	■	■	■	■	■	■	■	■
SPROUTING SEEDS	SOW	■	■	■	■	■	■	■	■	■	■	■	■
	PLANT												
	HARVEST	■	■	■	■	■	■	■	■	■	■	■	■
SQUASH—SUMMER	SOW				■	■	■						
	PLANT						■						
	HARVEST							■	■	■	■		
SQUASH—WINTER	SOW					■	■						
	PLANT						■	■					
	HARVEST									■	■		
RUTABAGA	SOW					■	■						
	PLANT												
	HARVEST									■	■	■	
CORN	SOW				■	■	■						
	PLANT						■						
	HARVEST								■	■	■		
SWISS CHARD	SOW						■		■	■			
	PLANT												
	HARVEST	■	■	■	■	■	■	■	■	■	■	■	■
SPINACH	SOW		■	■			■	■	■				
	PLANT												
	HARVEST	■	■	■	■	■	■	■	■	■	■	■	■
TOMATO	SOW			■									
	PLANT					■	■						
	HARVEST							■	■	■	■		
TURNIPS	SOW				■	■	■	■					
	PLANT												
	HARVEST						■	■	■	■	■	■	

Common pests

Most plants in the kitchen garden are prone to attack by many different insect and animal pests. Healthy crops often cope well with attacks, but stay vigilant and check for pests regularly because some can multiply quickly, seriously harming plants and reducing harvests.

1 APHIDS
Small sap-suckers, clusters of these wingless insects can be found on young shoots of most plants. They distort new growth and transmit viruses. Squash them, encourage natural predators, or use pyrethrum.

2 ASPARAGUS BEETLE
Adult beetles and their larvae feed on asparagus foliage and bark in late spring and summer, causing foliage to die back. Pick off the pest, spray with pyrethrum, or burn cut stems in fly.

BIRDS (not illustrated)
Hungry birds feed on seeds, buds, fruit, and foliage. Soft fruit and brassicas are favourite targets. Cover vulnerable beds and bushes with netting, well secured at the base to prevent birds getting in and becoming trapped.

3 CABBAGE CATERPILLARS
Several butterfly and moth species lay eggs on brassicas, which then hatch into leaf-eating caterpillars. Pick off eggs and caterpillars, cover with fine netting, or spray with *Basillus thuringiensis*.

4 CABBAGE MAGGOT FLY
From spring to fall these white larvae feed on brassica roots, and do serious damage to seedlings and young plants. Place discs around the bases of young plants to prevent eggs being laid.

5 PLANT BUGS
These tiny insects suck sap from many plants, including currants and apples, causing brown-edged holes and deformed flowers. Control is usually unnecessary, but apples can be sprayed with pyrethrin after flowering.

6 CARROT RUST FLY

The thin, creamy maggots of this small fly tunnel into carrots and parsnips. Grow resistant crop varieties and cover your seedlings with row cover.

CATS (not illustrated)

Cats love digging in soft seedbeds and may also tear netting and fleece. Use chicken wire to keep them off.

7 CODLING MOTH

The larvae bore into apples and pears in summer. In late spring, hang pheromone traps. Spray trees with kaolin clay at petal fall. Cover fruitlets with paper bags.

8 COLORADO POTATO BEETLE

A serious pest, the black and yellow striped beetle, about ½in (1 cm) long, feeds on the foliage of potatoes, tomatoes, eggplant, and peppers. Mulch plant deeply with straw; spray larvae with spinosad or neem.

9 CUTWORMS

Not, in fact, worms but the caterpillars of a nocturnal moth species, cutworms chew through the stems of young plants or make holes in root vegetables. Handpick the pale brown caterpillars from the soil at night when they feed, or apply a biological control.

FLEA BEETLE (not illustrated)

These tiny black beetles pepper the leaves of brassicas with countless little holes, damaging seedlings and spoiling salad vegetables such as rocket. Grow your brassica crops under fleece or treat affected areas with pyrethrum.

10 IMPORTED CURRANTWORM

The green, black-spotted larvae of the sawfly defoliate gooseberries and redcurrants in spring and summer, and can cause severe damage. Pick them off by hand, use a biological control, or spray with pyrethrum.

11 LEEK MOTH

The young caterpillars create pale brown patches on onion and leek foliage by mining the leaves, while more mature caterpillars bore into the flesh of the vegetables. Look out for silky, pupae-containing cocoons on the leaves and crush them to control numbers.

MEALYBUGS (not illustrated)

Usually found only on greenhouse and indoor plants, these sap-sucking insects are covered in white, fluffy wax and secrete a sticky honeydew. Squash them, treat with biological controls, or use insecticidal soap.

12 CABBAGE APHIDS

A pest on all brassicas, these minute aphids have a whitish-gray, mealy coating. They suck sap on the underside of leaves, which damages new growth, and secrete sticky honeydew. Control by crushing them or using insecticidal soap.

MICE AND RATS (not illustrated)
Pea and bean seeds in the soil, ripe ears of corn, and stored fruit and vegetables are all irresistible to these destructive rodents. They are difficult to control, but you can set traps where they might be a problem.

13 ONION MAGGOT
The white fly maggots eat the roots of onion and leek seedlings in early summer and tunnel into onions in late summer, causing rotting. Destroy all affected plants and practice crop rotation. It is best to grow onions from sets, which are less vulnerable.

14 PEA AND BEAN WEEVIL
Little gray-brown beetles that nibble notches from leaf edges. The larvae feed among the roots of peas and broad beans. Large plants tolerate damage, but if heavy attacks seem likely, raise young plants in pots.

15 PEA MOTH
Adult moths fly throughout summer, laying their eggs on flowering peas. Caterpillars hatch and grow inside pods, eating the peas. Early and late sowings avoid the egg-laying adults, but summer crops should be netted.

PEAR LEAF BLISTER MITE
(not illustrated)
The small pink or yellow blisters caused by this tiny mite appear on pear leaves in spring and darken to black. This damage won't affect the fruit crop. On small trees, pick off affected leaves.

16 PEAR MIDGE
The signs of pear midge are pear fruitlets that turn black at the base, stop growing, and drop by early summer. The maggots hatch from eggs laid in blossom and feed on the fruit. Remove and destroy affected fruitlets to help control pest numbers in the future.

17 FRUIT MOTH
The pale pink, brown-headed caterpillars feed near the stones of plums, peaches, and apricots, causing significant damage. Hang up pheromone traps in June, to attract and trap adult males and disrupt mating.

ROOT-KNOT NEMATODE (not illustrated)
Many vegetable crops that turn yellow and die early may have been attacked by these nematodes. The microscopic root-feeding pests can persist in soil for 10 years. Rotate crops and grow resistant varieties.

18 RASPBERRY BEETLE
The grubs of this pest feed on the fruit of raspberries, blackberries, and hybrids. They may be found in the fruit, and they cause dry, gray-brown patches. Control raspberry beetle by spraying pyrethrum or deltamethrin as soon as the first fruits start to turn pink.

19 SPIDER MITES

Various species of spider mites can cause dull, mottled leaves on a range of plants. Keep greenhouse humidity high in hot weather and use a biological control. Try insecticidal soap sprays outdoors.

20 ROOT APHIDS

Crops including carrots, lettuces, and beans attract these white aphids to feed on their roots, affecting growth and causing wilting in hot weather. Rotate your crops annually and water well during summer.

21 SLUGS AND SNAILS

These all-too-familiar slimy pests eat holes in leaves and roots, and can destroy rows of seedlings in a remarkably short time. Limit their numbers by collecting them at night, during winter hibernation, or in traps. Biological control is effective in summer.

22 WASPS

Wasps are good early summer pollinators, but they eat ripe fruit, especially plums, grapes, and apples, as the season progresses. Distract them with honey traps or damaged ripe fruit placed away from trees.

23 WHITEFLY

White-winged, sap-feeding insects that secrete sticky honeydew, whitefly are usually at their worst on greenhouse crops such as tomatoes and cucumbers. Biological control with *Encarsia formosa*, a parasitic wasp, is effective.

24 WIREWORMS

Larvae of the click beetle, these slim, orange-brown worms live in the soil, biting through seedlings and damaging root crops such as potatoes and carrots. Remove any visible larvae and dig up root crops promptly when they are ready to be harvested.

WOOLLY APHID (not illustrated)

A sap-sucking aphid covered in fluffy white wax, the woolly aphid is found on apple trees. Control isn't practical on large trees, but with smaller trees you can brush off the insects or spray with pyrethrum or insecticidal soaps.

For general advice on organic pest control, see pages 104–105.

Common diseases

It can seem like there's an army of bacteria, fungi, and viruses out there to thwart your attempts to grow your own food. Fortunately, healthy plants can resist disease, so tend them well, keep the garden neat to reduce sources of infection, and rotate crops to prevent disease from building up.

1 AMERICAN GOOSEBERRY MILDEW
Powdery white patches on foliage, stems, and fruits of blackcurrants and gooseberries are caused by a fungus that thrives in stagnant air. Grow resistant varieties and prune to improve air flow.

2 BACTERIAL LEAF SPOT
Dead spots on leaves, surrounded by a yellow "halo," indicate bacterial infection, usually spread by splashing water. Brassicas and cucumbers are particularly prone. Remove affected leaves and water plants at the base.

BACTERIAL SOFT ROT (not illustrated)
This causes sunken, rotten areas on the roots and fruits of crops, such as brassicas, potatoes, tomatoes, and zucchini. The infection is spread by insects or dirty tools. Disinfect tools and remove affected plants.

3 BITTER PIT
Dark spots or pits appear on the skin of developing apples, and fruit may taste bitter. The problem is due to drought-induced calcium deficiency, so mulch apple trees and water well in dry weather.

BLACKCURRANT VIRUSES (not illustrated)
Viruses spread by mites can cause swollen buds and stunted growth. Remove and burn infected plants and buy certified disease-free stock.

BLOSSOM BLIGHT (not illustrated)
A fungal disease associated with brown rot (see below), blossom blight causes blossom, spurs, and small branches to die back on apples, pears, plums, and cherries. Remove affected flowers, wood, and fruit promptly to prevent spread.

4 BLOSSOM END ROT

This appears as dark patches at the base of tomatoes, peppers, and other fruit. It is due to calcium deficiency, usually caused by drought conditions. Water consistently to protect developing crops.

5 BOTRYTIS

This fungus commonly infects plants that are growing under cover, in addition to lettuce and soft fruit. It causes a fuzzy gray mold, rotting, and die-back. Remove any infected growth quickly and ventilate greenhouses well to reduce humidity.

6 BROWN ROT

A widespread fungus that infects tree fruit by entering through damaged areas, causing rotten patches and creamy pustules. Remove infected fruit promptly, along with branches affected by blossom blight (see above).

7 CANKER

Many fruit trees are affected by bacterial and fungal cankers, which cause shoots to die back, foliage holes, and sunken bark that may ooze resin. Prune back to healthy growth or treat bacterial infections with copper fungicides.

8 BEAN LEAF SPOT

Brown spots appear on foliage, stems, and pods of bean plants, which may reduce or destroy the crop. The best way to keep bean leaf spot from happening is to grow plants widely spaced and on well-drained soil.

9 CLUB ROOT

This fungal infection produces enlarged, distorted roots on brassica plants, causing wilting, purple-tinged foliage, and sometimes die-back. Grow varieties resistant to club root. Reducing the acidity of soil by liming may also help.

10 CUCUMBER MOSAIC VIRUS

The virus is carried by aphids between cucumbers and related crops, such as zucchini. Leaves pucker and yellow, and fruit becomes distorted and inedible. Remove and burn infected plants.

11 DAMPING OFF

The disease causes seedlings, especially those grown indoors, to collapse suddenly. To reduce the risk of damping off, which is caused by fungi, use clean pots and clean water. Sow plants thinly, provide good ventilation, and apply a compost tea.

12 DOWNY MILDEW

This fungus thrives in humid conditions, causing brown patches on upper leaves, with fluffy growth beneath. Brassicas, lettuces, and many other plants are affected. Destroy diseased leaves and give plants ample space.

FIREBLIGHT (not illustrated)
Apples and pears are infected by this bacterial disease through their flowers. Flowers and shoots rapidly shrivel and die and wood under the bark is stained orange-brown. Cut back and burn all infected material.

FOOT AND ROOT ROTS (not illustrated)
Common in greenhouse-grown melons, cucumbers, and tomatoes, these fungal rots set in at the base of the stem, killing the whole plant. Remove and destroy infected plants, and practice good garden hygiene to prevent further rot.

13 FUNGAL LEAF SPOT
Circular gray or brown spots on leaves, sometimes with tiny black fruiting bodies, are caused by fungi on many types of crops, from strawberries to celery. This is not usually serious, but remove affected leaves to prevent the fungus from spreading further.

HALO BLIGHT (not illustrated)
Caused by bacteria, darkening leaf spots with a yellow halo can spread to the pods of dwarf snap and runner beans. Pick off affected leaves and avoid overhead watering, which spreads the infection.

14 HONEY FUNGUS
Fruit trees and bushes can be killed by honey fungus, which causes gradual or sudden die-back. Dig up and destroy plants with white fungal growth and a mushroom smell under the bark at the base. If you find honey-colored toadstools, destroy those, too.

15 ONION NECK ROT
This fungal rot often affects onions, shallots, and garlic in storage, causing softening of the bulb and fuzzy gray mold. Check stores regularly and dispose of any infected bulbs. To prevent infection, don't grow onions, or related crops, in the same bed year after year.

16 ONION WHITE ROT
Yellowing and wilting foliage on onions, leeks, and garlic is a sign that white rot fungus may have attacked the roots and bulb. It is a serious disease that persists in soil for many years, so avoid spreading contamination through soil and plants from infected sites.

17 PARSNIP CANKER
Affected roots have orange-brown damage, particularly near the top. This can usually be cut out to leave the rest of the root still edible. The canker is caused by a fungus that enters through injured roots. To avoid infection, grow resistant varieties on well-drained soil.

18 POTATO BLACK LEG
Yellowing foliage, seen as early as June, and black areas at stem bases are signs of this bacterial disease. Remove and destroy infected plants promptly and rotate crops to prevent infection.

19 LATE BLIGHT

A problem in warm, wet summers, this fungus affects potatoes and tomatoes (see tomato blight p.244), causing foliage to rot and, later, infecting tubers too. Remove and destroy infected foliage, lift tubers early, and grow resistant varieties.

20 POTATO COMMON SCAB

Potato scab causes unsightly, raised brown, scabby patches on the skins of potatoes. This bacterial infection is worse on dry and alkaline soils, so water well and avoid liming before potatoes crop. Choose resistant varieties.

POTATO POWDERY SCAB

(not illustrated)
A fungal infection causing sunken, spore-filled scabs on potato skins, this disease is more likely to be a problem on wet soils, where it can also infect tomato roots. To avoid, make sure you have good drainage and opt for resistant varieties.

21 POWDERY MILDEW

Many edible crops, including peas, zucchini, and currants, catch this fungal disease, which causes a white dusty layer on foliage. It is worse in dry conditions, so water well, remove fallen leaves, and use approved fungicides.

22 RASPBERRY CANE BLIGHT

During summer this fungal disease causes leaves to wither and canes to die after becoming split and brittle. Prevent infection by taking care not to damage canes or to plant in infected soil. Cut back and burn affected canes.

RASPBERRY CANE SPOT

(not illustrated)
The white-centered purple spots caused by this fungus appear on canes and leaves of raspberries and hybrid berries, sometimes spreading and killing canes. Cut down and burn affected canes and treat the rest with copper oxychloride.

RASPBERRY VIRUSES (not illustrated)

Yellow mosaic patterns and downward turned edges on the leaves of cane fruits are signs of viruses, some of which are spread by aphids. Such infections reduce crops, so remove and burn all infected plants and avoid replanting cane fruit on the same site.

23 RUST

Beans, leeks, and plums are among various crops infected by fungal rusts. Signs of infection are orange pustules on leaves and stems. Remove and destroy infected material at harvest time or leaf fall, and rotate crops if possible.

24 SCAB

Apples and pears develop small, dark brown patches on their skin, which can spread to leaves and branches. The fungi responsible overwinter on fallen leaves, so neaten up detritus in the fall. Grow scab-resistant varieties to reduce the risk.

25 SCLEROTINA

This serious and persistent fungal disease affects lettuces, cucumbers, celery, tomatoes, and beans. Plants rapidly yellow and collapse with wet stem rot and fluffy white mold. Quickly remove and destroy diseased plants.

26 SCORCH

Hot sun and cold dry winds can both scorch leaves and flowers, turning them brown and crisp. Sun scorch is especially damaging if there are water droplets on the plants. Avoid watering at the hottest times of day and ensure that greenhouse plants have adequate shading.

27 SILVER LEAF

Plums, cherries, apricots, and peaches are affected by this fungal disease. Leaves develop a silvery sheen, cut wood is darkly stained, and branches die. Infectious spores are produced in fall and winter, so prune in summer.

28 STRAWBERRY VIRUSES

Strawberries are susceptible to a number of viral infections spread by insects or by pests in the soil, such as eelworms. The symptoms include yellow-blotched or crumpled leaves and poor growth. Dig up and destroy infected plants and rotate your crops.

29 TOMATO BLIGHT

Outdoor tomatoes are more susceptible to this fungal disease than those in the greenhouse. Watch for rapidly spreading wet rots on leaves and brown patches on fruit. Quickly remove and destroy infected material.

30 TOMATO GHOST SPOT

This fungal infection causes pale green or yellow rings to appear on tomatoes. There will be no further deterioration and the discoloration does not make the fruit inedible. Keep the area surrounding your plants neat to reduce sources of infection.

VIOLET ROOT ROT (not illustrated)

Root vegetables and celery are damaged by this fungus. Usually found on wet, acid soils, it produces a mass of purple threads around roots, which then rot. Lift and burn infected plants.

WHITE BLISTER (not illustrated)

This fungus produces shiny, white pustules on the undersides of brassica leaves, sometimes distorting them. Remove infected leaves or badly affected plants. To avoid further infection, rotate crops and grow resistant varieties.

Common nutrient deficiencies

Plants need a balanced intake of nutrients to remain healthy; mainly nitrogen, potassium (potash), and phosphorus, plus essential trace elements. Nutrients are often present in soil, but "locked up" if the pH is too high or low, or conditions are dry, so it pays to improve your soil.

1 BORON
Typical symptoms include splitting and discoloration of root vegetables and poorly developed ears of corn. Heavily limed or dry soils are the cause. Apply borax with horticultural sand.

2 CALCIUM
Apple bitter pit and blossom end rot of tomatoes (p.240) are the most common signs. Calcium uptake is limited in dry and acidic conditions, so water consistently and add lime to acid soils to raise the pH.

3 IRON
Leaves of affected plants turn yellow between the veins and brown at the edges. Iron is locked up in alkaline soils, so apply acidic mulches and use a chelated iron treatment.

4 MAGNESIUM
This is a common deficiency in acid soils, after heavy rains, or use of high potash fertilizers. Older leaves are the first to yellow, then they turn red, purple, or brown between the veins. Treat with Epsom salts as a foliar spray.

5 NITROGEN
Nitrogen washes out of soil easily and all plants, except peas and beans, can become deficient, showing yellow leaves and spindly growth. Dig in well-rotted compost and add high nitrogen fertilizer.

6 POTASSIUM
Leaves tinged yellow or purple, and poor flowering and fruiting, suggest deficiency, especially in potatoes and tomatoes. This is a common problem on light soils, where potassium washes away. Apply sulfate of potash or tomato food.

Useful websites

Fruit and Vegetable Nurseries

ADAMS COUNTY NURSERY
26 Nursery Road
P.O. Box 108
Aspers, PA 17304
717-677-8105
www.acnursery.com
Fruit trees

ALMOST EDEN PLANTS
1240 Smith Road
Merryville, LA 70653
337-375-2114
www.almostedenplants.com
Tropical and unusual fruits

BAKER CREEK HEIRLOOM SEED
2278 Baker Creek Road
Mansfield, MO 65704
417-924-8917
www.RareSeeds.com.com
Large selection of heirloom vegetable and herb seeds

BIG HORSE CREEK FARM
P.O. Box 70
Lansing, NC 28643
www.bighorsecreekfarm.com
Heirloom apple trees

BURNT RIDGE NURSERY & ORCHARDS
432 Burnt Ridge Road
Onalaska, WA 98570
360-985-2873
www.burntridgenursery.com
Fruit trees, vines, and bushes

CUMMINS NURSERY
1408 Trumansburg Road
Ithaca, NY 14456
607-227-6147
www.cumminsnursery.com
Fruit trees

EDIBLE LANDSCAPING ONLINE
361 Spirit Ridge Lane
Afton, VA 22920
434-361-9134
www.eat-it.com
Fruit trees, vines, and bushes

FEDCO TREES
P.O. Box 520
Waterville, ME 04903
207-873-7333
www.fedcoseeds.com/trees.htm
Fruit trees and berries

FORESTFARM
990 Tetherow Road
Williams, OR 97544
541-845-7269
www.forestfarm.com
Fruit trees and plants

HIDDEN SPRINGS NURSERY
270 Hidden Springs Lane
Cookeville, TN 38501
931-268-2592
www.hiddenspringsnursery.com
Organically grown fruit trees

JOHNNY'S SELECTED SEEDS
955 Benton Avenue
Winslow, ME 04901
877-564-6697
www.johnnyseeds.com
Vegetable and flower seeds, including heirloom varieties and organic seeds

LOGEE'S GREENHOUSES
141 North Street
Danielson, CT 06239
888-330-8038
www.logees.com
Tropical fruit trees and vines

MILLER NURSERIES
5060 West Lake Road
Canandaigua, NY 14424
800-836-8028
www.millernurseries.com
Fruit trees and vines

NOURSE FARMS
41 River Road
South Deerfield, MA 01373
413-665-2568
www.noursefarms.com
Berry bushes

ORGANICA SEED COMPANY
P.O. Box 611
Wilbraham, MA 01095
413-559-0264
www.organicaseed.com
Vegetable and herb seeds, both heirloom and open-polinated, and some fruit, coffee, and tea

PARK SEED COMPANY
1 Parkton Avenue
Greenwood, SC 29647
800-845-3366
www.parkseed.com
Vegetable, herb, and flower seeds

PENSE NURSERY
2318 Highway 71NE
Mountainburg, AR 72946
479-369-2494
www.alcasoft.com/pense
Berries and grapevines

RAINTREE NURSERY
391 Butts Road
Morton, WA 98356
360-496-6400
www.raintreenursery.com
Fruit trees and unusual fruits

SAND HILL PRESERVATION CENTER
1878 230th Street
Calamus, IA 52729
563-246-2299
www.sandhillpreservation.com
Heirloom seeds and plants

ST. LAWRENCE NURSERIES
325 State Highway
Potsdam, NY 13676
315-265-6739
www.sln.potsdam.ny.us
Fruit and nuts for northern gardens

THE STRAWBERRY STORE
107 Wellington Way
Middletown, DE 19709
302-378-3633
www.thestrawberrystore.com
Alpine and heirloom strawberries

STREAMBANK GARDENS
22481 Burton Road
Milton, DE 18868
302-258-7095
streambankgardens.com
Vegetable and herb plants

TERRITORIAL SEED COMPANY
P.O. Box 158
Cottage Grove, OR 97424
800-626-0866
www.territorial-seed.com
Unusual and heirloom fruit and vegetables seeds and plants

TREES OF ANTIQUITY
20 Wellsona Road
Paso Robles, CA 93446
805-467-9909
www.treesofantiquity.com
Heirloom fruit trees

UNDERWOOD GARDENS
1414 Zimmerman Road
Woodstock, IL 60098
888-878-5247
www.underwoodgardens.com
Wide range of heirloom, rare, and open-pollinated vegetable seeds

WHITMAN FARMS
3995 Gibson Road NW
Salem, OR 97304
503-510-0486
www.whitmanfarms.com
Berry bushes

Garden Supplies

GARDENER'S SUPPLY COMPANY BURLINGTON GARDEN CENTER
128 Intervale Road
Burlington, VT 05401
802-660-3505

WILLISTON GARDEN CENTER AND OUTLET
472 Marshall Avenue
Williston, VT 05495
802-658-2433
www.gardeners.com
Plants, garden tools, organic fertilizers and compost bins, pest control, and gardening advice

GARDENS ALIVE
WWW.GARDENSALIVE.COM
5100 Schenley place
Lawrenceburg, In 47025
513-354-1482
www.gardensalive.com
Environmentally responsible fertilizers, and weed, pest, and disease control

PEACEFUL VALLEY FARM AND GARDEN SUPPLY
125 Clydesdale Court
Grass Valley, CA 95945
888-784-1722/530-272-4769
www.groworganic.com
Fruit and nut trees, vegetable sets, garden tools, irrigation and composting systems, organic soil and other growing supplies

THE NATURAL GARDENING COMPANY
P.O. Box 750776
Petaluma CA 94975
707-766-9303
www.naturalgardening.com
Organic plants, seeds, drip irrigation, supplies

Index

Page numbers in *Italic* indicate illustrations. Page numbers in **bold** indicate featured topics.

Acknowledgments

Author's acknowledgments
Thanks to the following: Chauney Dunford, Alison Shackleton, Alison Donovan, Esther Ripley, and the team at Dorling Kindersley for your hard work and much appreciated input; Malcolm Dodds who, as ever, has patiently been my technical support and emergency photographer; and finally Judy and Paul Whittingham for their enthusiastic growing and willingness to compare notes.

Dorling Kindersley would like to thank:
Robin and Brenda Beresford-Evans, Mike Aldridge, and the growers at Cannizaro Allotments, Wimbledon, London.

Dobies/Suttons, Floranova, Marshalls/Unwins, Thompson & Morgan, and Victoriana Nursery Gardens for their kind permission to reproduce their photographs.

Commissioned photography
Peter Anderson

Index Elizabeth Wiggans

Proofreading Emma Callery

Picture credits
The publisher would like to thank the following for their kind permission to reproduce their photographs:

(Key: a-above; b-below/bottom; c-centre; f-far; l-left; r-right; t-top)

6 GAP Photos: Jo Whitworth (r). **7 GAP Photos:** Pat Tuson (c). **Harpur Garden Library:** Jerry Harpur (br). **Photolibrary:** Stephen Hamilton (t). **8 GAP Photos:** Maxine Adcock (cl); Lynn Keddie (bl). **8-9 The Garden Collection:** Nicola Stocken Tomkins, Clinton Lodge. **9 GAP Photos:** Friedrich Strauss (tc). **10 GAP Photos:** Lee Avison (tr); Geoff Kidd (cra). **Photolibrary:** Mark Winwood (tl). **11 GAP Photos:** BIOS/Gilles Le Scanff & Joëlle-Caroline Mayer (b). **Victoriana Nursery Gardens:** (c). **12 GAP Photos:** Elke Borkowski (r); Juliette Wade (l). **13 The Garden Collection:** Nicola Stocken Tomkins, Designer: Karen Maskell HCFS 2002 (br). **Photolibrary:** Mark Bolton (l). **14 GAP Photos:** Charles Hawes (bl). **Photolibrary:** Corbis (br); Jerry Pavia (tl). **16 GAP Photos:** Fiona Lea (br). **Marianne Majerus Garden Images:** Marianne Majerus (t). **18 Alamy Images:** David Chapman (bl). **Chauney Dunford:** (tl). **GAP Photos:** Friedrich Strauss (tr). **20 GAP Photos:** BBC Magazines Ltd (br); Elke Borkowski (cb); Rob Whitworth (bl). **21 Chauney Dunford:** (tr). **22-23 Garden World Images:** Lee Thomas. **24 Corbis:**

Ryman/photocuisine (cb). **Getty Images:** Michael Rosenfeld (bl). **Photolibrary:** Joff Lee (tr). **25 Getty Images:** Spencer Jones (tl). **Photolibrary:** Fleurent (ca). **31 Mike Shackleton:** (tc). **33 GAP Photos:** Michael King/Design: Deborah Bird (bl); Michael King/Design: Greenfield Primary School (br); Clive Nichols/Location: Chelsea 2001 (bc). **34 Photolibrary:** Howard Rice (cl). **35 Alamy Images:** Gary Curtis (bl). **37 Thompson & Morgan:** (tr) (crb). **38 Getty Images:** Michael Rosenfeld (tr). **39 Photolibrary:** Riou (tc). **40 Photolibrary:** Francois De Heel (tl). **41 Thompson & Morgan:** (cl). **44 Dobies of Devon:** (tl) (tc). **iStockphoto.com:** (cl). **Photolibrary:** Michael Howes (bl). **Thompson & Morgan:** (tr). **47 Corbis:** Paul Taylor (cr). **GAP Photos:** Lee Avison (cl). **50 Corbis:** Ocean (bl/tatsoi). **GAP Photos:** Jonathan Buckley, Design: Sarah Raven (c). **51 Corbis:** amanaimages (fcr); photocuisine (br). **GAP Photos:** Juliette Wade (cl). **Photolibrary:** Jo Whitworth (cr). **52 Getty Images:** James Carrier (c). **Photolibrary:** Gerard Lacz (bc). **53 Photolibrary:** Foodfolio (bc). **54 GAP Photos:** Abby Rex (tr). **55 Alamy Images:** Brian Hoffman (tl). **The Garden Collection:** Torie Chugg (tc). **Garden World Images:** MAP/Alain Guerrier (tr). **56 Dobies of Devon:** (c) (cr). **Victoriana Nursery Gardens:** (tr). **57 Marshalls Seeds:** (br). **Thompson & Morgan:** (tr).

58 Mr Fothergill's Seeds: (c). **59 Marshalls Seeds:** (tc). **Suttons Seeds:** (tr) (br). **61 Floranova Ltd.:** (tl). **Thompson & Morgan:** (tc) (bc). **69 Corbis:** Image Source (crb); Imagemore Co., Ltd. (cra); Helmut Meyer zur Capellen (br); Hein van den Heuvel (cr). **70 Garden World Images:** Juliette Spears (fcl). **Photolibrary:** Howard Rice (fcr). **71 Thompson & Morgan:** (c). **72 GAP Photos:** John Glover (cb). **Photolibrary:** Karen Thomas (ca). **73 Photolibrary:** Martin Brigdale (tr); James Guilliam (cl); Carl Pendle (crb). **74 Corbis:** Bill Barksdale/ AgStock Images (bl); Radius Images (bc). **GAP Photos:** John Glover (fbl). **Photolibrary:** Maxine Adcock (tl). **Victoriana Nursery Gardens:** (cl). **75 GAP Photos:** FhF Greenmedia (bc). **76 Dobies of Devon:** (c). **Marshalls Seeds:** (br). **Suttons Seeds:** (cr). **77 Dobies of Devon:** (br). **Victoriana Nursery Gardens:** (tr). **78 Marshalls Seeds:** (tc). **79 Dobies of Devon:** (bc). **GAP Photos:** Howard Rice (c). **Mr Fothergill's Seeds:** (tr). **Thompson & Morgan:** (br). **80 Marshalls Seeds:** (bc). **Photoshot:** (tr). **Victoriana Nursery Gardens:** (br). **87 Photolibrary:** Botanica (tr); Michael Howes (bl/slug pellets). **90 Photolibrary:** Joshua McCullough (tl). **91 Corbis:** Image Source (tr); Photolibrary (cl). **92 Getty Images:** Rosemary Calvert (tl). **93 Photolibrary:** Martin Brigdale (cr). **94 Photoshot:** (cr/salsify). **Suttons Seeds:** (bl). **96 Thompson & Morgan:** (tr) (b) (cr). **www.dtbrownseeds.co.uk:** (c). **97 GAP Photos:** Dave Bevan (bc); Geoff Kidd (c). **105 Chauney Dunford:** (crb). **FLPA:** Jef Meul/FN/Minden (cra); Martin B Withers (cr). **106 Corbis:** Klaus Hackenberg (br). **108 Photolibrary:** FoodCollection (tr); Norris (cla). **109 Photolibrary:** Sue Atkinson (cra); Tim Hill (br); David Marsden (cb). **110 Getty Images:** Michael Grimm (tr). **112 Alamy Images:** Grant Heilman Photography (tr). **GAP Photos:** Juliette Wade (c). **113 Garden World Images:** Trevor Sims (c). **Thompson & Morgan:** (tr). **Victoriana Nursery Gardens:** (tc). **114 Photolibrary:** Francesca Yorke (tl). **www.dtbrownseeds.co.uk:** (fcl) (cr). **115 Photolibrary:** Maxine Adcock (tc). **117 Thompson & Morgan:** (crb). **121 Royal Horticultural Society, Wisley:** (tr). **122 Alamy Images:** Mark Boulton.

123 FLPA: Nigel Cattlin (tr) (cr). **125 Marianne Majerus Garden Images:** Marianne Majerus/The Old Rectory, Sudborough (l). **Thompson & Morgan:** (br). **126 Corbis:** image100 (tl); Ocean (bl). **127 Thompson & Morgan:** (bc). **131 Photolibrary:** Caren Alpert (clb); Asset (tc); IPS Photo Index (cr). **132 Mr Fothergill's Seeds:** (tr). **134 Photoshot:** (tr). **Thompson & Morgan:** (br). **136 FLPA:** Nigel Cattlin (br). **naturepl. com:** Gary K. Smith (bl). **Photoshot:** (cl). **137 Blackmoor Nurseries:** (cl). **138 Photolibrary:** Photos Lamontagne (tr). **141 Garden World Images:** Rita Coates (bl). **142 Corbis:** Wally Eberhart/ Visuals Unlimited (fcr); Klaus Hackenberg (cl). **143 Corbis:** Henglein and Steets/cultura (cr). **GAP Photos:** Jonathan Buckley (tr). **Thompson & Morgan:** (c). **www.dtbrownseeds.co.uk:** (tc/sunburst). **152 GAP Photos:** Sarah Cuttle (tl). **Photolibrary:** Foodfolio (br); Sian Irvine (cb). **155 Marshalls Seeds:** (tl). **Suttons Seeds:** (ftl). **Thompson & Morgan:** (ftr). **156 FLPA:** Nigel Cattlin (tr). **159 Corbis:** AgStock Images (cl); Emma Shervington (tr). **164 Photolibrary:** Stéphanie Barçon (c). **167 Blackmoor Nurseries:** (tr/'fantasia'). **Photolibrary:** Paroli Galperti (cr). **168 Photolibrary:** Michael Howes (tr). **171 GAP Photos:** Maxine Adcock (l). **172 Photolibrary:** Joshua Mccullough (ca); Photos Lamontagne (cra). **173 Photolibrary:** Sally Reed (cr); Carol Sharp (br); Gary K Smith (crb). **174 Victoriana Nursery Gardens:** (br). **181 Suttons Seeds:** (tr). **184 Suttons Seeds:** (tc) (tr). **www.dtbrownseeds. co.uk:** (tl). **185 Photolibrary:** Gavin Kingcome (br). **186 Dobies of Devon:** (tc) (cr). **Victoriana Nursery Gardens:** (b). **187 GAP Photos:** Howard Rice (t). **188 Alamy Images:** David Chilvers (cr). **Photolibrary:** Mark Bolton (tl). **Jo Whittingham:** (cl). **189 Photolibrary:** Botanica (tr). **193 Corbis:** C.Murtin/ photocuisine (cl); John Smith (c). **Chauney Dunford:** (br). **196 Getty Images:** Miachael Paul (bl). **197 Getty Images:** Foodcollection (cl). **Photolibrary:** Cuboimages (bl); Philippe Desnerck (tc); Foodfolio (tl); Joff Lee (crb). **198 Esther Ripley:** (cl) (bl). **199 Photolibrary:** Martin Page (br). **Esther Ripley:** (c). **205 Photolibrary:** Michael Howes (bl); Craig Roberts (cl). **208 GAP Photos:** Elke Borkowski (bl);

Jonathan Buckley, Design: Sarah Raven (r). **iStockphoto.com:** John Sigler (c). **Marshalls Seeds:** (br). **Photolibrary:** Michael Davis (fbr). **Suttons Seeds:** (fbl). **209 Photolibrary:** Lynn Keddie (bl); Mark Winwood (tr). **Photoshot:** (cl/ salsify). **214 Photolibrary:** Roger Tidman/FLPA (cl). **216 Victoriana Nursery Gardens:** (bl). **217 Dobies of Devon:** (tc). **GAP Photos:** Victoria Firmston (tr). **Mike Shackleton:** (br). **220 Victoriana Nursery Gardens:** (cr). **222-223 GAP Photos:** Lee Avison (b). **223 Corbis:** Bill Barksdale/AgStock Images (bc); PictureNet (cl). **GAP Photos:** Leigh Clapp (tc). **Photolibrary:** Emma Peios (tl). **224 Corbis:** Ocean (cr/ pak choi). **Photolibrary:** Juliette Wade (br). **225 Corbis:** Kai Schwabe/ Westend61 (cr). **GAP Photos:** Nicola Browne (tr); Keith Burdett (tl). **Suttons Seeds:** (bl) (bc). **Thompson & Morgan:** (fbl). **227 Thompson & Morgan:** (crb) (br). **236 Getty Images:** Jan Tove Johansson (crb). **Royal Horticultural Society, Wisley:** (bc) (br). **237 FLPA:** Nigel Cattlin (bl). **Royal Horticultural Society, Wisley:** (clb) (br). **238 Corbis:** Jacqui Hurst (br). **Royal Horticultural Society, Wisley:** (clb) (cb). **239 Alamy Images:** Nigel Cattlin (br). **Garden World Images:** Dave Bevan (crb). **Royal Horticultural Society, Wisley:** (bc) (clb). **240 Garden World Images:** Dave Bevan (cb). **Royal Horticultural Society, Wisley:** (bc). **241 FLPA:** Nigel Cattlin (bl) (bc) (clb). **242 FLPA:** Nigel Cattlin (clb). **GAP Photos:** Dave Bevan (bl). **Garden World Images:** Dave Bevan (br). **Photolibrary:** Brian Carter (cb). **Royal Horticultural Society, Wisley:** (crb). **243 Royal Horticultural Society, Wisley:** (cb) (bc) (bl) (crb). **244 GAP Photos:** Geoff Kidd (cb). **Royal Horticultural Society, Wisley:** (crb) (br). **Science Photo Library:** Dr Jeremy Burgess (bl). **245 FLPA:** Nigel Cattlin (cb) (bc) (clb)

All other images © Dorling Kindersley
For further information see:
www.dkimages.com